Chicken *Soup*
for the *Soul*.

The Original 30th Anniversary Edition
Chicken *Soup*
for the *Soul*.

Chicken Soup for the Soul 30th Anniversary Edition
Jack Canfield, Mark Victor Hansen, Amy Newmark

Published by Chicken Soup for the Soul, LLC www.chickensoup.com
Copyright ©2023 by Chicken Soup for the Soul, LLC. All Rights Reserved.

The publisher gratefully acknowledges the many publishers and individuals who granted Chicken Soup for the Soul permission to reprint the cited material.

Front cover illustration of number 30 courtesy of iStockphoto.com (©Gugai), pattern illustration courtesy of iStockphoto.com (©ilonitta)

Cover and Interior by Daniel Zaccari

Publisher's Cataloging-in-Publication data

Names: Canfield, Jack, 1944- editor. | Hansen, Mark Victor, editor. | Newmark, Amy, editor.
Title: Chicken soup for the soul 30th anniversary edition / Jack Canfield, Mark Victor Hansen, Amy Newmark.
Description: Cos Cob, CT: Chicken Soup for the Soul, LLC, 2023.
Identifiers: LCCN: 2023933235 | ISBN: 978-1-61159-105-7 (print) | 978-1-61159-342-6 (ebook)
Subjects: LCSH Conduct of life. | Spiritual life. | Self help. | BISAC SELF HELP / Motivational and Inspirational | SELF HELP / Personal Growth / Happiness | SELF HELP / Personal Growth / General
Classification: LCC BJ1581.2 C87 2023| DDC 158/.12--dc23

Library of Congress Control Number: 2023933235

PRINTED IN THE UNITED STATES OF AMERICA
on acid∞free paper

30 29 28 27 26 25 24 23   01 02 03 04 05 06 07 08 09

Chicken Soup
for the Soul.

The Original 30th Anniversary Edition
Chicken Soup
for the Soul.
Plus 30 Bonus Stories

Jack Canfield
Mark Victor Hansen
Amy Newmark

CSS

Chicken Soup for the Soul, LLC
Cos Cob, CT

Changing the World One Story at a Time®
www.chickensoup.com

Table of Contents

❶

~On Love~

❷
~Learning to Love Yourself~

❸
~On Parenting~

❹

~On Learning~

❺

~Live Your Dream~

❻

~Overcoming Obstacles~

❼

~Eclectic Wisdom~

Introduction

We know everything we need to know to end
the needless emotional suffering that many people
currently experience. High self-esteem and personal
effectiveness are available to anyone willing
to take the time to pursue them.

t is difficult to translate the spirit of a live presentation into the written word. Stories we tell every day have had to be rewritten five times to work as well in print as they do live. When you are reading these stories, please forget everything you ever learned in your speed-reading classes. Slow down. Listen to the words in your heart as well as in your mind. Savor each story. Let it touch you. Ask yourself, what does it awaken in me? What does it suggest for my life? What feeling or action does it call forth from my inner being? Let yourself have a personal relationship with each story.

Some stories will speak louder to you than others. Some will have deeper meaning. Some will make you cry. Some will make you laugh. Some will give you a warm feeling all over. Some may hit you right between the eyes. There is no right reaction. There is only *your* reaction. Let it happen and let it be.

Don't hurry through this book. Take your time. Enjoy it. Savor it. Engage it with your whole being. It represents thousands of hours of culling the "best of the best" from our 40 years of combined experience.

We've added 30 new stories for you in this 30th Anniversary

Edition of the original *Chicken Soup for the Soul*. You'll find them at the beginning of each chapter and they are "bolded" in the Table of Contents. These stories are from some of the best thought leaders in existence today and we are pleased to have their wisdom and insights added to those found in the original collection. We're confident this new edition of *Chicken Soup for the Soul* will be just as relevant for the next 30 years as it has been for the last 30.

One last thing: Reading a book like this is a little like sitting down to eat a meal of all desserts. It may be a little too rich. It is a meal with no vegetables, salad or bread. It is all essence with very little froth.

If you find yourself moved to share a story with others, do it. When a story makes you think of another person, call the person it brings to mind and share it. Engage these stories and let them move you to do whatever comes up for you. They are meant to inspire and motivate you.

For a lot of these stories we went back to the original source and asked them to write it or tell it in their own words. Many of the stories will be in their voice, not ours. We have attributed every story we could to the original source. For all of those that are from fellow speakers and trainers, we have included a contributors section in the back of the book where we have listed their name, address and phone number so you can contact them yourself if you wish. You'll also find a separate contributor bio section for the 30 bonus stories in this volume.

We hope you will enjoy reading this book as much as we have enjoyed writing it.

How It All Began

This manuscript of yours that has just come back from
another editor is a precious package. Don't consider it
rejected. Consider that you've just addressed it "to the
editor who can appreciate my work" and it has just
come back stamped "not at this address." Just keep
looking for the right address.
~Barbara Kingsolver

have spent my whole life as a teacher—first as a high school
teacher and for the last 50 years as a speaker and trainer in the
human development field. I am often on the road two weeks out
of every month flying from city to city to conduct one-day workshops and weeklong trainings.

I learned early on that if you want a concept or principle to be
remembered, you had to illustrate it with a moving story. So I had
always collected and used a lot of stories to drive home the points I
was teaching in my seminars about the importance of operating from a
space of love, believing in yourself and your dreams, always following
your heart, trusting your intuition, setting high goals, overcoming
obstacles, and never ever giving up on your dreams.

In 1991, a strange thing happened. One day, out of the blue,
someone asked me, "Is that story you told about the Girl Scout who
sold 3,526 boxes of Girl Scout Cookies in one year in a book anywhere?
My daughter needs to read it." And the very next day someone asked,

"That story about the boy and the puppy — is that in a book anywhere? I need to read it to my son." And it continued day after day for the next month. "I need to read that story about the boy with the amputated leg who went on to become a tennis star to my staff. I need to show them that they really have no excuses not to excel in life." "Is that story you told about the boy who was burned in the motorcycle accident in a book anywhere? I want to send it to my son in college." Day after day I was asked the same question — "Is that story in a book anywhere?"

One evening I was flying back from Boston to Los Angeles, where I was living at the time, and it suddenly struck me. It was as if God were knocking on the side of my head and saying, "Wake up! You're supposed to put all of these stories you have been collecting into a book!" For the remainder of the flight I made a list of every story I had ever used in a speech or a workshop. By the time we landed in LA I had a list of 70 stories.

That night I made a commitment to myself to write up two of the stories on the list every week until I had them all completed. So every night from about ten o'clock until midnight I would work on a story, writing and rewriting it until I was satisfied with it. After nearly a year I had completed all 70 stories I had listed on that plane ride plus a few more I had picked up during the year.

It was about that time that I met my friend Mark Victor Hansen for breakfast. Early on in our conversation Mark asked me if I was working on anything exciting. I told him about the book, and he immediately said, "I would like to do that book with you."

"Mark," I said. "I'm almost completely finished with the book. Why would I do that?"

"It's easy," he replied. "First of all, I think you should have 101 stories, not 75. When I was a student ambassador in India, I learned that 101 is a number of completion. Second, some of your best stories you originally learned from me. And third, I am a really good marketer and promoter, and I think we would make an awesome team."

I told Mark if he could contribute the remaining 26 stories, and if they were really great, that I would be willing to do it. I loved Mark and I knew that he was a consummate promoter and salesman. True to his word, in less than a month Mark came up with the remaining stories we needed to get to 101. Now all we had to do was sell the book to a publisher.

About a week later Mark and I met Jeff Hermann, a literary agent, at a party in Palm Springs, California. We told Jeff about our book and he got very excited about it. He asked us what the title was. Funny thing — we were so engrossed in finishing the book, we had never even bothered to come up with one. We brainstormed a few at the party, but nothing seemed to capture the essence of the book. Since Mark and I were both meditators, we agreed to spend at least a half hour every morning for the next week in meditation seeking a title.

The first two days we both drew blanks. Nothing had come to us. And then on the third morning while I was meditating, I suddenly saw the image of a huge green chalkboard like the ones in school classrooms. Then a hand appeared — I imagined it was the hand of God — and wrote the words *Chicken Soup* on the chalkboard. I said to the hand, "What the heck does chicken soup have to do with this book?"

The hand replied, "When you were sick as a child, your grandmother gave you chicken soup."

"This book is not about sick people," I replied.

"People's spirits are sick. They are living in resignation, fear and hopelessness. This book will help them rise above it."

My mind mulled that over. *Chicken Soup for the Spirit*, I thought. Hmmm. *Chicken Soup for the Soul.* Wham! All of a sudden I was covered in goosebumps. *Chicken Soup for the Soul: Stories to Rekindle the Spirit!* Ooh, I liked that. The goosebumps grew stronger. I was excited. I immediately opened my eyes and ran to tell my wife. She got goosebumps too. Then I called Mark and he got goosebumps as well. Mark then told me that several of his friends called them "God bumps," and that it meant you were getting divine inspiration. That felt right to me.

We then called our agent, and he also got goosebumps. Armed with our book and our title we headed off to New York to meet with a series of publishers over several very cold and windy February days to see if we could sell our book.

Sadly, no one in those meetings in New York got goosebumps.

In meeting after meeting we were told that collections of short stories didn't sell, the stories were too "nicey-nice," too Pollyanna, too positive, and that the title, which had evolved into *Chicken Soup for the Soul: 101 Stories to Open the Heart and Rekindle the Spirit*, was dumb.

Obviously disappointed, we returned to our hotel and prepared to fly back to Southern California. But before we did, we headed over to St. Patrick's Cathedral on Fifth Avenue, and while neither of us is Catholic, we lit a candle and prayed that God would help us find a publisher.

A few weeks later our agent called us and told us that he had talked to several other publishers since our New York trip and they had all declined as well. He then said he was giving us back the book because he was convinced he couldn't sell it.

We asked him what a publisher would need to know in order to be willing to publish the book, and he replied, "They'd need to be absolutely convinced that they could sell 20,000 copies. This would assure them that they could recover their investment in editing, producing, printing, distributing and promoting the book. If they knew they could sell 20,000 copies, they would definitely be willing to publish it."

That gave Mark and me an idea. Because we were speaking to large groups several times a week — some as large as 1,000 people — we could print up a Pre-Order Form and ask people to put into writing their commitment to buy one or more copies when the book was eventually published.

For the next several months we put what we called "A Commitment to Buy" form on every chair in every audience we spoke to. At the end of our speech or workshop we asked people to fill out the form with their name and address and write down how many books they promised to purchase. Because we were telling many of the stories in our presentations, people knew the quality of what they would be getting, so almost everyone participated. Raymond Aaron, a success coach and trainer in Canada, even committed to buy 1,700 copies — one for each of his students — when the book was published. (Much to our delight he later followed through with that commitment.) It wasn't long before we had several Bankers Boxes full of completed forms adding up to more than 20,000 books! By that time we had also collected almost 100 rejection slips from what seemed like every major publisher in America.

By now the book had become a "divine obsession" with us. We knew from all of the positive feedback we received from the participants in our workshops that the stories were inspiring, healing, motivational and transformational, and we were committed to getting these stories out to people. No matter how many rejections we received, we were committed to never giving up.

One day a friend of ours suggested we attend the American Booksellers Association convention in Anaheim, California, which was not far from where we lived, and do something we later learned was called "walking the floor." More than 4,000 publishers would be in attendance and we could simply go up to each publisher's booth in the exhibit area and ask them if they would be interested in our book. So off we headed to the Anaheim convention center with two backpacks full of spiral-bound copies of our best 30 stories to see if we could find a publisher.

For two very long days we "walked the floor." By the end our legs were sore, our feet were hurting, and our minds were numb from repeating the same sales pitch over and over. "We know this book will sell because we already have written commitments from people to buy over 20,000 copies," we'd say, as we showed people examples of the completed commitment forms. For some reason we still weren't gaining any traction. I don't think they'd ever seen anything like us. No one had ever gone out and collected promises to buy before. Perhaps they didn't trust that we had really collected 20,000 of them.

Eventually, however, late on the second day, Peter Vegso and Gary Seidler, who ran HCI, a small publisher in Florida, agreed to take one of our sample manuscripts and read it when they got home. Much to our delight, a few weeks later the phone rang and it was Peter and Gary. They were gushing about how much they loved the book! "Your book made us laugh and it made us cry. We love it and we want to publish it." They even said they got goosebumps when they were reading it!

We asked them how many copies of the book they thought we

might sell. They said, "Maybe 25,000 copies, if we're lucky."

"That's not our vision," we said. "We want to sell 150,000 copies by Christmas and a million and a half in a year and a half."

We heard laughter on the other side of the phone line. They thought we were totally crazy.

The book was finally published in late June of 1993. All the people who had agreed to buy the book did, but then the sales seemed to stall. Mark and I visited our very wise friend Ron Scolastico and asked for his advice. He told us, "If you were to go to a tree with an axe and take five solid cuts with the axe every day, eventually even the largest tree in the forest would have to come down."

From that conversation Mark and I created what we call our "Rule of Five." We agreed to take five action steps every single day to promote or sell our book. Some days we would send out five books to book reviewers at newspapers. Other days we would call five network-marketing companies to see if they would purchase multiple copies to use to motivate their distributors. One day we even sent a whole box of books to the jury in the O.J. Simpson trial. A week later we received a nice letter from Judge Ito thanking us for our gift. Eventually that became a news story and landed us a lot of great publicity.

One day I spotted a little red book at the checkout counter of my supermarket. It was *The Celebrity Address Book* and it contained addresses and phone numbers for motion picture and television stars. I bought it and for weeks we sent out five free copies a day to celebrities in Hollywood, hoping they would like the book and promote it to their friends and fans.

One of those books ended up in the hands of the producer of the television show *Touched by an Angel*. She was so moved by the book that she required all of her writers, actors and even the crew to read the book. That story ended up in *The Hollywood Reporter* and eventually was syndicated across the country, leading to even more publicity.

As a result we ended up selling 135,000 copies by Christmas and 1.3 million in a year and a half, and eventually that first book, which had been rejected by 144 publishers, went on to sell ten million copies. Our publisher stopped laughing. He asked us to write a sequel. To his surprise we were ready. When the book was about to be printed, he had informed us that because of the way the books were formatted for printing, there were a few blank pages at the end of the book, and he had asked us if there was anything we would like to print on those pages. We submitted the following paragraph:

Share your heart with the rest of the world. If you have a story, poem or article (your own or someone else's) that you feel belongs in a future volume of *Chicken Soup for the Soul*, please send it to us.

Little did we know what we would unleash. We started getting hundreds of stories a day in the mail. It seemed that everyone had a story to tell. Not all of them were usable, but there were enough good ones to help us create the first six books in the series.

Eventually, Marci Shimoff suggested we compile a book of stories just for women. That became *Chicken Soup for the Woman's Soul*. My sister, Kimberly Kirberger, then suggested a book of stories just for teens, and the *Chicken Soup for the Teenage Soul* series was born. Dr. Marty Becker, a veterinarian, came up with the idea to compile a book of stories for pet lovers, and with his writing partner Carol Kline another line in the series was launched. The rest, as they say, is history.

Several years after the first *Chicken Soup for the Soul* book was published, we learned from Peter Vegso, our first publisher, that he, too, had been in New York City in February of 1992, and had been deeply concerned about the sharp decline in his struggling company's sales. He, too, had gone to St. Patrick's Cathedral, lit a candle, and prayed, asking God to send him an author or a book that would turn his company around. When he shared that story with us, we all got goosebumps one more time!

— Jack Canfield —

On Love

The day will come when, after harnessing space, the winds,
the tides and gravitation, we shall harness for God the energies of love.
And on that day, for the second time in the history of the world,
we shall have discovered fire.

~Teilhard de Chardin

Remembering What Has Been Forgotten

All the art of living lies in a fine mingling
of letting go and holding on.
~Havelock Ellis

Dad was strong. Ten damn years with Alzheimer's — amazing what you can get used to. The new normal was a nursing home, where Dad seemed to enjoy the aquarium and singing along to "You Are My Sunshine." His singing that song to the five of us kids in the back of the station wagon on Sunday drives was one of the few soft and joyous things I remember about my father when I was young. "You'll never know, dear, how much I love you. Please don't take my sunshine away." Somehow, I knew he meant it. He really loved us. Years later, watching the well-meaning nursing home volunteer with her guitar coax those words from my father's failing brain broke my heart.

There would be plenty more heartbreak where that came from — seeing him in a diaper and bib for the first time; watching him being hoisted from his wheelchair to his bed with a lift, dangling and helpless like a marionette. The catheter, the baby food, the drool; his blank stare... "Where are you, Dad?" I wondered each time I visited him. "Where are you?" I often wept in the elevator on the way down from his floor;

doing my best to finish crying and to wipe my face before the doors opened into the lobby.

In the quiet of endless days, my tough, frightening, crude, funny, and wickedly smart dad slipped away. Eventually, the disease won. But it also lost. Alzheimer's lost when it tried to fracture my family. We group-chatted and talked and visited with one another, in some ways closer than ever before. Alzheimer's lost when it tried to distance me from my dad, teaching me instead how much it meant just to sit in silence and hold his hand until he fell asleep. I think about shaving him in his wheelchair, feeling both heartbroken and deeply moved by the intimacy of it all — touched by his tender dependency on me in that moment. The old Yiddish proverb is true: "When a father gives to his son, both laugh; when a son gives to his father, both cry."

Grief is surprising. Not at first, when you are prepared for it to pick you up and slam you against the rocky shore, but later, in a month or two or ten. Anyone who thinks the shortest distance between two points is a straight line does not understand grief. I am fine, I am out to dinner with friends and casually take a crust of bread to soak up the last drops of sauce — wiping my plate spotlessly clean. *Hmmm, just like my dad*, I think while Betsy and our friends keep chattering. He would have loved this sauce, this bread. I am fine. I want to cry. I am fine. I want to cry. "I really miss my dad," I say to Betsy, fighting back tears. She understands. Her dad is dead too. I want to go home. Instead, I push it all down.

You could not tell by looking at me that I was in mourning. You still cannot tell by looking at me. Sometimes I wish you could. I wish people could know when I am missing my dad — like some neon sign blinking above my head that reads, "Be gentle with me. My heart is broken." But at the same time, I don't want people to know that sometimes when I am with them, I am really with my dad, far away. We who mourn fake it a lot. We wear a mask of normalcy, and sometimes you are talking to that mask, not us. We are elsewhere because of our grief. That is the truth that we want you to know and the truth we also hide.

I wish I could say that all my years as a rabbi prepared me in some way to handle my grief better than others do. But it isn't true. When it comes to missing my dad, I am entirely his son. I found that prayer helps. I was rescued so many mornings by the words of the Mourner's Prayer. Those words, that truth, must be said out loud and standing whether we feel like it or not, whether in that moment we believe it or not. I don't know how people get through grief without some ritual to remember, some vessel into which you can pour your sadness. For me, it was that prayer, but it could also be lighting a candle each day, or gazing at a picture, or reciting the Twenty-Third Psalm, or some other prayer or poem, or holding or wearing some object that belonged to your loved one. The Victorians created jewelry with hair from their deceased loved ones woven into it. Find something, anything that works as permission to remember, to be sad and then to say, "Now, I can go on, at least for today."

Reaching out helps. I was on sabbatical holed up in my sister's empty house in Palm Springs for the entire month of May trying to write the first draft of my book about loss called *The Beauty of What Remains*. For hours each day, I thought of nothing but death. I kept the house cold and dark. I wrote and paced. Most nights I walked around the golf course where I walked with my dad a thousand times over all the years I visited him and Mom at their Palm Springs condo. As I walked, I wondered again out loud, "Where are you, Dad? Where are you?" I looked up, and there on the back patio of a golf course condo I saw a sign containing the lyrics to "You Are My Sunshine." I texted my three sisters and my brother a picture of the sign. "Walking Mesquite golf course missing Dad so much and saw this sign." Sherry texted back a sketch of Dad: "I couldn't sleep last night and drew this." Greg texted back the lyrics to Dad's favorite Hank Williams song:

The silence of a falling star
Lights up a purple sky
And as I wonder where you are
I'm so lonesome I could cry

"You guys are all making me cry now," Marilyn responded. Somehow knowing they miss Dad too helped me. It means I am not alone. I am not the only one who loved him or who remembers him or who cares about him and is grateful to him and yet must accept the decree. Do not dwell alone in your grief. Reaching out really can help us heal.

Often, when a person dies, the doctor will say, "His heart has stopped." I have learned in my grief and my journey since my father's death that his heart beats within me often and in ways far more beautiful than I had ever thought possible. When I am eating something delicious or walking among the boulders of the Joshua Tree National Park, or see ripe lemons on a tree and think about pocketing one, or listen to a salesman and am certain he is full of shit, or watch my son handle tools or hear my daughter look at a big steak and say, "Papa would have loved this," or when I sit down to write and use some rhetorical device I learned in college because my dad worked hard to be able to send me there, or when I see a red flannel shirt or clunky shoes or a hot fudge sundae, or when the only expression that fits a situation perfectly is in Yiddish, or when I am afraid, or, or, or…

If I could put my ear to my own chest, I know, my father's heart still beats within. Memory is light, illuminating and reminding me of so many things about my dad; summoning each of us who mourn a love both gone and yet still present, still warm and aglow even when skies are gray. When we remember, nothing can take our sunshine away.

— Rabbi Steve Leder —

A Second Chance

We all have big changes in our lives that
are more or less a second chance.
~Harrison Ford

Maui for Christmas. Hiking the rainforest in Saint Lucia. A twilight boat ride to a candlelight dinner in Annapolis. Wedding vows in Key West on the beach at sunset with only two witnesses. Horseback riding in Barbados.

This was life in my first marriage long ago.

Serenaded by an opera singer at Victor's Café, sipping Dom Perignon at La Panetière, wearing pajamas for brunch on New Year's Day at La Terrasse. Learning to fly a Cessna 150 at Wings Field. Always on the move, looking for the latest, for glamour and flash.

And so it went for years until…

During yard work, a loud snap in his back, accompanied by excruciating pain and a limp that morphed into a stagger. He couldn't lie flat to sleep and soon his flawless speech was affected. He sounded ill, groggy. He was an announcer by trade, so obviously that wouldn't do. A consummate professional who could read copy "cold and in one take," he sounded slightly tipsy, with a speech impediment.

We went from doctor to doctor, with test after test, until finally the diagnosis, a death sentence. Cancer. A neuroendocrine tumor, something treatable today but certainly not then.

From diagnosis to death was six weeks. He dwindled from a robust

6'2" 200+ pounds to 150. He saw angels crowding his hospital room and at the very end when he slipped into a coma. I knew he heard me as I kept talking, telling stories as tears rolled down his sunken cheeks until he was gone. I'd not only lost him but me, as well.

My friends, neighbors and co-workers were wonderful but that help by its very nature only lasts so long. I put one foot in front of the other, burying myself eventually in a return to work. But the panic attacks were shocking and I was stunned by the wolves circling, "friends" and even a boss of his who tried to play me while I was still raw.

Because my dad suffered a stroke upon hearing about Dan's illness, my family did not circle the wagons but remained hours away, taking care of him. I couldn't blame them since I hadn't given them a second thought in years. So I knew I'd have to face this battle myself and try to retrieve a big part of what I was missing. The Catholic priest in my parish, Father Picard, was warm and welcoming, listening carefully and kindly to the blubbering mess disintegrating there in his office. He suggested I begin bereavement counseling to get me back on track and to ask God for help. I wish I could say it was a smooth transition, after being away from my religion for decades, but I persevered and was able to slowly and haltingly find grace.

It took a few years, but I began to feel better. I knew it was time to put together the next chapter of my life. Would it be the same, finding someone to wrap myself up with? Would it be us against the world? Or would I allow for other things, other people to share my life?

After kissing a few frogs, I found Louis, who was different, who believes in family, in sharing, in surrounding us with food and fun and life, although we didn't have to become globetrotters or spend tons of money to find what we needed. I took the initiative to reconcile and befriend my mother, who slowly responded to my overtures. We now are close, often on the phone for long chats that I never would have imagined possible.

Louis and I married before my family in an old church, Father Picard presiding, and everyone toasting us at a beautiful reception.

These days, I am undoing years of neglect both spiritually and with my family. I love the ritual of the Mass, which keeps me from feeling so alone. It is my meditation and my strength.

Although Dad died shortly after my second marriage, I started an annual tradition with the rest of my family at an Outer Banks beach house. It's not perfect. There is often drama and squabbling with all the clashing personalities, but I wouldn't want it any other way. We've been going strong now for seventeen years and I've come full circle. All I can say now is: Thank God. A second chance to do things right.

— Pat Farnack —

The Vulnerable Heart

Vulnerability is the only bridge to build connection.
~Brené Brown

When my son was in elementary school, he would bring home daily a vocabulary word we were supposed to discuss over dinner for his homework. The practice was called "Dinner Plate Words" because after we talked about the word my son would write, on a paper plate, two sentences using the word. One evening his word was "vulnerable." He read a definition out loud: "A state of weakness; open to attack." He composed the sentences quickly. I recall one said, "The mouse was vulnerable after the cat attacked it." His next sentence also mentioned an attack or some other kind of struggle.

I wanted to tell him there is another way to be vulnerable, but I wasn't sure he would understand if I tried to explain the emotional aspect of the word. Maybe I hesitated because I was and still am confused about vulnerability and have much to learn.

Around the same time I attended a writers' conference and a panel moderated by a writer whose work I had only just come to know even though his publishing career spans nearly 40 years. We had met briefly through a mutual friend a few weeks earlier so I would have called him an acquaintance. After the session ended, I waited until the usual post-talk crowd dissipated. I wanted to say hello and comment further on a question someone else had asked. When it was all clear

I approached the writer. He looked at me, then touched his fingers to his lips and held up his hand in greeting. My heart thumped hard, flipping a full somersault in my chest. I paused and checked my steps to make sure I wouldn't fall over. *What in the world was that?* I managed to compose myself and make my comments, but this question occupied me for days, even weeks.

At first I took the easy route to understanding. I thought *Oh, I have a new crush.* But to use the word "crush" — a silly one, especially at my age — would be to play around quite dishonestly with language. If "crush" were my Dinner Plate Word, I'd have to address this definition: "a temporary romantic attraction." It sounded wrong, like a childish equivocation. I was too old to not recognize that moment felt bigger than a crush — and more important.

This I knew for certain. When the elder gentleman touched that kiss my way, he had me. I don't know if he knew it, but he had me. That was it. I loved him from that moment on. I had no idea what he really thought of me. And I knew absolutely nothing about him. He could have had a reputation as a notorious flirt for all I knew but it really didn't matter because all I could speak to was the way it affected me. Why did my heart react that way?

As any flawed human would do, I sifted through useless, common notions (*maybe he reminds me of a grandfather, or I'm star-struck by his celebrity*) before I challenged myself to think higher. The piercing, needle-to-the-heart epiphany came when I finally thought of this: I had been floored by a moment of grace.

What is grace? It is love where it does not have to exist, where there is no reason for it. I see grace in acts of affection that occur without explanation — just as the grace God bestows on us every minute of every day. Grace is the love, unconditional and whole, given for no other reason than we are who we are. I think of the John Legend song lyric, "All of me loves all of you/all your curves and all your edges/all your perfect imperfections." I know the singer is thinking romantically, but I always hear grace in those words. This kind of love carries me through my days. I ride it like a river coursing through my being. It never occurred to me how it could suddenly flow out of me, undammed and free. And I think that's what happened in that moment with the writer.

I can only think my years of exploring the human spirit have brought me to this place where my heart is open, quivering, and accessible. I am open to love. And now my heart is as exposed and vulnerable as a child without a coat in the rain. My instinct, like any mother's, would be to cover up my heart, to protect it. We're supposed to love, love everyone. While this fact usually prompts a discussion of how hard it is to do that, my moment in the conference center made me realize I had come to a point where I have no choice in the matter. My heart loves. It is frightening. It is exhilarating.

This is a dangerous way to be. Even to write this is dangerous because there are so many misconceptions about love. We are quick to categorize — romantic love, filial love, platonic love. We think in terms of marriages, affairs, relationships, and friendships. But I'm only concerned with the love that commands we love one another as we love ourselves. Somehow, I think, we have led ourselves to believe such love is polite and sedentary when in reality it can dash boundaries and crush them to dust. It leaves us exposed — vulnerable.

So that small act, the touch of a kiss and not even a real kiss, set me whirling with its essence of grace. Even now I think, "How can I return it?" And not necessarily to this person — I mean can I return it, unconditionally, to everyone I meet? The answer, whether I want it to be or not, must be yes. In one moment love knocked me over with the force of an oceanic wave. I have risen, a total wreck — covered in sand and salt and seaweed. But I recognize I must get up and pursue the living water even as it retreats. I will dive into its heart. I am willing to drown.

— Sophfronia Scott —

My Soul Mate

Love must be as much a light, as it is a flame.
~Henry David Thoreau

I am more than a happily married man. I am a joyfully married man. Not everyone can say that. What my wife Crystal and I have is what I call a "Twin Flame Relationship." We seldom hear about these relationships, because they are rare, ideal, and private. They seem unreal to most people who only experience them as a dream written about in romance novels.

Twin flames positively and correctly mirror each other, are in divine and exquisite harmony constantly and without ceasing. They experience and express a delightful, divine destiny together. They desire to be, do, and have as much for their partner as they desire to be, do, and have for themselves. They think alike in many ways yet are strong where the other is weak and weak where they need the other's strength.

The twin flame relationship is one in which their individual qualities complement and complete their circle of love. It is not a relationship of competition or degradation in order to hold righteous positions against the other, but rather to affirm with kindness, compassion, absolute love, and tenderness. And just as when two candle flames merge, twin flames understand it is in this way their individual flame merges with the other and becomes not only twice as bright, but infinitely brighter.

Crystal and I find great joy in fully engaging in our relationship.

We understand that our relationship is the rock that our lives function and flow upon so naturally; it becomes paramount to business, friends, family, church, or any outside offerings.

As co-creator of the legendary *Chicken Soup for the Soul* book series, a super busy professional speaker, and a TV personality, the question I am asked most is: "How did you find such a perfect soul mate?" The more frequently unasked question is: "How can I do it, too? You two seem to be in perfect love, outrageous joy, inexplicable friendship, and live in cooperative harmony. How are you able to do this and to be together 24/7 365 days a year?"

Because this delightful question is repeated with such frequency, I choose to answer it openly and completely. It is my hope that this will serve to expand your love, thinking, being, and becoming a soul mate from the inside out. If you are looking to become a complete soul mate or looking for a soul mate, may this inspire the hope that it is fully possible to do so. The beginning insight I must clearly impart is that first you have to become exactly what you are looking for.

In our Twin Flame Relationship, we understand that we together create today, tomorrow, and our future. We do that by holding a space that is free from emotional baggage of the past. Because life and emotional triggers continue to happen, we dedicate the first hour of our morning in prayer and meditation together. We dream about how we want to share the rest of our lives together and how we will maximize our life experience and our love.

So, the question is: 'How did I get here?' I witnessed my parents having agreements and disagreements, but overridingly, they loved and cared for their children and each other. They put the family unit and their relationship above the frays and vicissitudes of our life experience. I thought that was what happened in all marriages. They worked as a partnership and ironed out their differences in kind and omni-considerate ways.

My first marriage experience was something very different. While my ex-wife was an important part of my life for many years, over time the relationship became combative, complicated, and confrontational. After 27 years of giving everything I had to give I knew I had to end the marriage. I felt I had partially lost the essence of who I was and what was left would drain away if I stayed. I filed for divorce.

Even with scores of friends and fans around me all of the time, it felt frightening and lonely to not be in a marriage anymore. I realized that being married to my soul mate had been my top priority my entire life, which is why I hung on in a dysfunctional marriage for so long. I somehow thought I could turn it around.

As I pondered where to start over, battling mild depression from what felt like a heartbreaking loss, I came back to the thought that God had painted on my heart long ago, that my soul mate was still out there somewhere, and I would find her. I started dreaming a new dream of what perfection would be like, even if it only existed in the secret places of my own mind.

In many of my books and teachings throughout the years, I taught manifestation principles: *figure out exactly what you want... write it down in detail with specificity... visualize it to realize it... etc.*

So I did just that! I sat down and wrote out 267 things I desired in my future soul mate. I shared them in confidence with only two of my mastermind partners, because they seemed to border on the impossible. I tucked my list safely away.

A short time after that, I was speaking at an aspiring author's conference in Los Angeles. From the stage I clearly saw a radiant spirit of a woman in the middle of the audience. I was so drawn to what I saw. She made a dynamic, lasting and irresistible first impression. That was the good news. The bad news was she was seated next to some guy. Later, after the lunch break, she was again before my eyes as a striking human presence, only this time she was alone. My soul rejoiced. I asked someone about her and they told me she too was divorced and single and her name was Crystal.

During the early evening VIP reception, people surrounded me from my lecture, asking endless questions. I saw Crystal across the room. To my utter delight, another attendee waived her hands wildly and inadvertently knocked over a full glass of red wine, dousing Crystal's white slacks.

I quickly dashed from the circle of fans surrounding me and

rushed to her side, immediately offering to save her just drenched slacks with club soda from a nearby kitchen in the hotel. Fortunately, I knew my way around the hotel because I had spoken there tens of times. Finally! I had gotten my moment alone with her.

After solving her stained slacks problem, I asked if she had had dinner. She had not. I kindly asked her to join me, with the proviso that we had to leave the premises because hundreds of attendees would not let us speak privately. She agreed and we were off to a phenomenal Hollywood restaurant.

When we arrived, there was a long waiting line. We went to the front of the line. The maître d' ignored me and mumbled: "Who is she?"

I replied: "You don't know her?"

"I'm not sure."

Jokingly, I said, "The Queen of Denmark."

"Seriously?"

I raised my eyebrows.

"Okay, so who are you?"

My answer would determine whether or not we got a table. So, in the spirit of creating a worthwhile memory, I said: "Who travels with the Queen?"

He thought a minute, and blurted out, "The King… you're not…"

I smiled, nodded and we proceeded to get the best private table in the place.

Happily seated, we giggled together over what had just happened! Time disappeared as we each unfolded our entire lives before the other. Our hearts and souls seemed to synchronize in a way neither of us had ever felt. It was a brand new experience for both of us. We tingled just being together. We were in bliss. Three years later, under the majestic red rocks of Sedona, Arizona, we were joyfully married.

About six months into my wedded bliss, I was cleaning my computer desktop and stumbled upon a document called "Soul Mate Goals." I was tickled because I wanted to see how close I had gotten to the characteristics, virtues, and qualities I had so deeply desired in a soul mate.

As I read through them, I was astounded. I realized God had

manifested my dreams and beyond for my perfect life partner. Crystal literally was everything I had hoped for and more. I believe that my dreams and prayers were heard and answered.

Here I share 112 of those original soul mate qualities I wrote down. I only share them with you to inspire you to achieve the same or more. If you're already married, may I recommend that you write down everything imaginable that you want in your ideal relationship and see how close you're coming to being that person you dream of. Perhaps, as both of you write out your own journey to soul matedness, later, you will feel open to sharing, comparing, and growing evermore loving towards one another. Often when people are dissatisfied in marriage it's because they're not clearly communicating their most important needs and truths.

My recommendation is that you generate your own comprehensive list. My list is for inspirational and launching purposes only. Remember, whatever you want wants you. Most importantly, you have to live up to and exceed personally all that you request of another. When I did my list, I knew with the help of my mastermind partners, that I needed to become more of the things I desired and I set to work on myself to accomplish that.

The question you always need to ask yourself when you address your own wants and needs is: "Who do I have to be to attract this woman/man? Do I and will I demonstrate these attributes myself?"

Mark's desires in his future soul mate:

1. Available
2. **Master kisser/lovingly tactile***
3. **Similar values**
4. Has great personal strength
5. User friendly
6. Elegant
7. Intelligent
8. Conservative personality
9. **Great lover**
10. Adventure

11. Lives in So. Cal or willing to move here or we agree to another place
12. Well-traveled and willing to travel
13. **Totally loves me and demonstrates it**
14. Working on self-mastery and spiritual mastery
15. **Likes my business**
16. **Beautiful and takes care of herself**
17. **We become each other's number one priority**
18. Excited and enthusiastic about life and living
19. Vitally healthy, health oriented
20. Into personal growth and self-development
21. **Happy**
22. **Slender and radiantly fit**
23. **Has a great personality**
24. **Superb conversationalist**
25. Wise
26. Witty
27. Wonderful
28. Imaginative
29. Magnanimous
30. Philanthropic before I showed up
31. **Fun to be with**
32. **A smile**
33. **Clean, neat, and smells good naturally**
34. **Inspires evermore love**
35. Cooperative
36. Financially savvy
37. **Under-spender — lives below her means**
38. **Has created some of her own means**
39. Knows herself
40. Flexible
41. Social graces and practices
42. Wants us to entertain and be entertaining
43. Playful and adventurous
44. Loves to dance

45. Thinks abundance
46. Wants to create superior memories
47. We can talk forever through the decades
48. Lives in ideas
49. Wants to make the world work
50. Is passionately on purpose
51. Sophisticated
52. We have a profound and growing soulular connection
53. We are soul mates
54. Loves to exercises, stretch and work on her strength, health, flexibility, aerobics and balance daily
55. Wants to see the world
56. **Nurturing spirit**
57. **Has deep spiritual practices**
58. **Meditates**
59. Creative
60. Non-smoker
61. Non-alcoholic
62. Non-drug user
63. Charitable
64. Has great etiquette
65. Is pro-organic foods and healthy eating
66. My friends love and enjoy her personality and are thrilled to be with her
67. Loves my family, kids and grandkids and our kids get along—if hers exist
68. Culturally, politically, financially, socially, emotionally, and spiritually aware
69. I can fully feel her love for me
70. **Has her own businesses, products, and services to create**
71. My staff loves, enjoys, respects, admires, and appreciates her
72. My career is second to her
73. She helps me know and expand my love
74. We share similar tastes in almost everything
75. Energetic and enthusiastic

76. Wholesome
77. Fresh, Spring-like
78. Young-minded and thinks forever young
79. Neat, Clean
80. Original rich mindset
81. Loves me in all my dimensions
82. Disciplines
83. Not jealous
84. Monogamous
85. Enchanting
86. Seeks out the good
87. Compellingly joyful
88. Sacred experiences
89. Bright-eyed
90. Eager to learn forever
91. Wants to serve
92. Positive mental attitude
93. Socially adept
94. Extraordinary
95. Proud to be with me and vice versa
96. Great design sense personally, professionally, for the home's interior, et al
97. Great dresser
98. Beautiful to behold
99. Lives with ease, grace, and spiritual dignity
100. Adoring
101. We give ourselves totally and completely to each other
102. Works on her own wellbeingness
103. Has mutually agreed upon boundaries
104. Truly becomes my best and closest friend
105. Loyalty
106. Trust
107. Faithfulness
108. Integrity
109. Honesty

110. Compassion
111. Passion
112. Integrated

*Bold indicates my absolute must haves

Now you've seen the clear intention I wrote about before I met Crystal. In the secret place within my mind, I knew she had to exist and be alive somewhere or I couldn't have had such a clear, purposeful vision of her. I knew she had to be alive and that with every breath I took, I was getting closer and closer.

— Mark Victor Hansen —

The Spirit of Love

Everything in the universe is within you.
Ask all from yourself.
~Rumi

In the West what we generally call love is mostly a feeling, not a power. This feeling can be delicious, even ecstatic, but there are many things love is meant to do that feelings cannot.

When love and spirit are brought together, their power can accomplish anything. Then love, power, and spirit are one.

There has never been a spiritual master — not Buddha, Krishna, Christ, or Mohammed — who wasn't a messenger of love, and the power of the message has always been awesome: it has changed the world. Perhaps the very immensity of such teachers has made the rest of us reticent. We do not accept the power love can create inside us, and therefore we turn our backs on our divine status.

Love is spirit. Spirit is the Self.

Self and spirit are the same. Asking "What is spirit?" is just a way of asking "Who am I?" There isn't spirit outside you; you are It. Why aren't you aware of it? You are, but only in a limited way, like someone who has seen a glass of water but not the ocean. Your eyes see because in spirit you are the witness to everything. You have thoughts because in spirit you know all. You feel love toward another person because in spirit you are infinite love.

Restoring the spiritual dimension to love means abandoning the notion of a limited self with its limited ability to love and regaining the Self with its unbounded ability to love. The "I" that is truly you is made of pure awareness, pure creativity, pure spirit. Its version of love is free from all memories or images from the past. Beyond all illusion is the source of love, a field of pure potential.

That potential is you.

What is the Path?

The most valuable thing you can bring into any relationship is your spiritual potential. This is what you have to offer when you begin to live your love story at the deepest level. Like the seed needed to start the life of a tree, your spiritual potential is the seed for your growth in love. Nothing is more precious. Seeing yourself with the eyes of love makes it natural to see others that way too. You will be able to say of your beloved, as the poet Rumi does:

You are the secret of God's secret.
You are the mirror of divine beauty.

The path to love is something you consciously choose to follow, and everyone who has ever fallen in love is shown the first step on that path. The unfolding of spiritual potential has been the chief concern of all the great seers, saints, prophets, masters, and sages in human history. Theirs was a carefully charted quest for the Self, a far cry from our notion of love as a messy, emotional affair.

In India, the spiritual path is called Sadhana, and although a tiny minority of people give up normal life to wander the world as seekers of enlightenment (these are monks, or sadhus), everyone, from those in the most ancient civilization of Vedic India until today, considers their life to be Sadhana, a path to the Self. Although the Self seems separated from us, it is actually intertwined in everything a person thinks, feels, or does. The fact that you do not intimately know your

Self is amazing, if you come to think about it. Looking for your Self, the Vedic sages declared, is like a thirsty fish looking for water. But as long as the Self has yet to be found, sadhana exists.

The goal of the path is to transform your awareness from separation to unity. In unity we perceive only love, express only love, are only love.

While the inner transformation is taking place, every path must have some outer form to sustain it. In India a person's nature leads him to the style of path appropriate to reaching fulfillment. Some people are naturally intellectual and are therefore suited to the path of knowledge, or Gyana. Some are more devotional and are suited to the path of worship, or Bhakti. Some are more outwardly motivated and are suited to the path of action, or Karma.

The three are not mutually exclusive; ideally, one would include in one's lifestyle daily periods of study, worship, and service. All three approaches would then be integrated into a single path. It is, however, entirely possible to be so taken with a single approach that your whole existence may be centered on reading the scriptures, contemplation, and scholarly debate — the life of Gyana. Or you may spend your time meditating, chanting, and participating in temple rituals — the life of bhakti. Or you could do social work, apply yourself to mental and physical purification, and do God's bidding in daily activity — the life of karma. Even in the most traditional sectors of India today, these paths have broken down, giving way to modern lifestyles in which study and work have little or nothing to do with spiritual aspirations.

What does this mean for a Westerner who has never been exposed to sadhana? I propose that being on the spiritual path is such a natural and powerful urge that everyone's life, regardless of culture, obeys it. A path is just a way to open yourself to spirit, to God, to love. These are aims we all may cherish, but our culture has given us no established, organized way to reach them. Indeed, never in history has a seeker been confronted with such a disorganized and chaotic spiritual scene.

What we are left with is relationships. The desire to love and be loved is too powerful ever to be extinguished, and fortunately a spiritual path exists based upon this unquenchable longing. The expression path to love is not simply a metaphor; it reappears throughout spiritual history in many guises. The most ancient version is the bhakti or devotional tradition from Vedic India, in which all forms of love ultimately serve the search for God. The Sufis of Islam have their own devotional lineage. Rumi, who I quote so often, was more than a poet; he was a great teacher of this path. To him God was the sweetest, most desirable lover, whose touch he could feel against the skin:

When it's cold and raining,
You are more beautiful.

And the snow brings me
even closer to Your Lips.

The Inner Secret, that which was never born,
You are that freshness, and I am with You now.

Christ initiated another version of the path in his supreme teaching, "Love thy neighbor as thyself." Jesus always spoke of God as a loving father. The Christian version of the path is therefore a relationship not so much between lovers as between parent and child or a shepherd and his flock (we shouldn't forget, though, the image of Christ as bridegroom and the worshiper's soul as the bride).

So it isn't the tradition that is lacking. One might more fairly say that in most religions the teaching of love, as originally presented, seems to have faded, to become more an ideal than a practical reality. But amidst all the confusion and breakdown of traditional teaching, there is still the spark of love that brings two people together, and out of that a path can be made.

Like the tiny spark of fire that consumes a forest, the spark of love is all you need to experience love in its full power and glory, in all its aspects, earthly and divine. Love is spirit, and all experiences of love, however insignificant they seem, are actually invitations to the cosmic dance. Within every love story hides the wooing of the gods and goddesses.

In a different age the most fleeting of infatuations had spiritual meaning; the nearness of God in the beloved was taken seriously. Since the advent of Freud, however, psychologists have assured us that falling in love is illusory; the sense of ecstasy that is part of falling in love is illusory; the sense of ecstasy that is part of falling in love isn't realistic. We must learn to accept the temporary nature of romance and disregard the "projected fantasy" that we might be as immortal and invulnerable as passionate lovers feel. We would therefore have to be skeptical of Walt Whitman when he rapturously declares,

I am the mate and companion of people, all just as immortal and fathomless as myself, (They do not know how immortal, but I know.)

—Deepak Chopra, MD—

Love: The One Creative Force

*Spread love everywhere you go: first of all in your
own house. Give love to your children, to your wife or
husband, to a next door neighbor... Let no one ever
come to you without leaving better and happier. Be the
living expression of God's kindness; kindness in your
face, kindness in your eyes, kindness in your smile,
kindness in your warm greeting.*

~Mother Teresa

A college professor had his sociology class go into the Baltimore slums to get case histories of 200 young boys. They were asked to write an evaluation of each boy's future. In every case the students wrote, "He hasn't got a chance." Twenty-five years later another sociology professor came across the earlier study. He had his students follow up on the project to see what had happened to these boys. With the exception of 20 boys who had moved away or died, the students learned that 176 of the remaining 180 had achieved more than ordinary success as lawyers, doctors and businessmen.

The professor was astounded and decided to pursue the matter further. Fortunately, all the men were in the area and he was able to ask each one, "How do you account for your success?" In each case the reply came with feeling, "There was a teacher."

The teacher was still alive, so he sought her out and asked the old but still alert lady what magic formula she had used to pull these boys out of the slums into successful achievement.

The teacher's eyes sparkled and her lips broke into a gentle smile. "It's really very simple," she said. "I loved those boys."

— Eric Butterworth —

All I Remember

There is a comfort in the strength of love;
'Twill make a thing endurable, which else
Would overset the brain, or break the heart.
~William Wordsworth

When my father spoke to me, he always began the conversation with "Have I told you yet today how much I adore you?" The expression of love was reciprocated and, in his later years, as his life began to visibly ebb, we grew even closer... if that were possible.

At 82 he was ready to die, and I was ready to let him go so that his suffering would end. We laughed and cried and held hands and told each other of our love and agreed that it was time. I said, "Dad, after you've gone I want a sign from you that you're fine." He laughed at the absurdity of that; Dad didn't believe in reincarnation. I wasn't positive I did either, but I had had many experiences that convinced me I could get some signal "from the other side."

My father and I were so deeply connected I felt his heart attack in my chest at the moment he died. Later I mourned that the hospital staff, in their sterile wisdom, had not let me hold his hand as he had slipped away.

Day after day I prayed to hear from him, but nothing happened. Night after night I asked for a dream before I fell asleep. And yet four long months passed and I heard and felt nothing but grief at his loss.

Mother had died five years before of Alzheimer's, and, though I had grown daughters of my own, I felt like a lost child.

One day, while I was lying on a massage table in a dark quiet room waiting for my appointment, a wave of longing for my father swept over me. I began to wonder if I had been too demanding in asking for a sign from him. I noticed that my mind was in a hyper acute state. I experienced an unfamiliar clarity in which I could have added long columns of figures in my head. I checked to make sure I was awake and not dreaming, and I saw that I was as far removed from a dreamy state as one could possibly be. Each thought I had was like a drop of water disturbing a still pond, and I marveled at the peacefulness of each passing moment. Then I thought, "I've been trying to control the messages from the other side; I will stop that now."

Suddenly my mother's face appeared — my mother, as she had been before Alzheimer's disease had stripped her of her mind, her humanity and 50 pounds. Her magnificent silver hair crowned her sweet face. She was so real and so close I felt I could reach out and touch her. She looked as she had a dozen years ago, before the wasting away had begun. I even smelled the fragrance of Joy, her favorite perfume. She seemed to be waiting and did not speak. I wondered how it could happen that I was thinking of my father and my mother appeared, and I felt a little guilty that I had not asked for her as well.

I said, "Oh, Mother, I'm so sorry that you had to suffer with that horrible disease."

She tipped her head slightly to one side, as though to acknowledge what I had said about her suffering. Then she smiled — a beautiful smile — and said very distinctly, "But all I remember is love." And she disappeared.

I began to shiver in a room suddenly gone cold, and I knew in my bones that the love we give and receive is all that matters and all that is remembered. Suffering disappears; love remains.

Her words are the most important I have ever heard, and that moment is forever engraved on my heart.

I have not yet seen or heard from my father, but I have no doubt that someday, when I least expect it, he will appear and say, "Have I told you yet today that I love you?"

— Bobbie Probstein —

Heart Song

*To a father growing old nothing
is dearer than a daughter.*
~Euripides

Once upon a time there was a great man who married the woman of his dreams. With their love, they created a little girl. She was a bright and cheerful little girl and the great man loved her very much.

When she was very little, he would pick her up, hum a tune and dance with her around the room, and he would tell her, "I love you, little girl."

When the little girl was growing up, the great man would hug her and tell her, "I love you, little girl." The little girl would pout and say, "I'm not a little girl anymore." Then the man would laugh and say, "But to me, you'll always be my little girl."

The little girl who-was-not-little-anymore left her home and went into the world. As she learned more about herself, she learned more about the man. She saw that he truly was great and strong, for now she recognized his strengths. One of his strengths was his ability to express his love to his family. It didn't matter where she went in the world, the man would call her and say, "I love you, little girl."

The day came when the little girl who-was-not-little-anymore received a phone call. The great man was damaged. He had had a stroke. He was aphasic, they explained to the girl. He couldn't talk anymore and they weren't sure that he could understand the words spoken to him. He could no longer smile, laugh, walk, hug, dance or tell the little girl who-was-not-little-anymore that he loved her.

And so she went to the side of the great man. When she walked into the room and saw him, he looked small and not strong at all. He looked at her and tried to speak, but he could not.

The little girl did the only thing she could do. She climbed up on the bed next to the great man. Tears ran from both of their eyes and she drew her arms around the useless shoulders of her father.

Her head on his chest, she thought of many things. She remembered the wonderful times together and how she had always felt protected and cherished by the great man. She felt grief for the loss she was to endure, the words of love that had comforted her.

And then she heard from within the man, the beat of his heart. The heart where the music and the words had always lived. The heart beat on, steadily unconcerned about the damage to the rest of the body. And while she rested there, the magic happened. She heard what she needed to hear.

His heart beat out the words that his mouth could no longer say…

I love you I love you I love you Little girl Little girl Little girl.

And she was comforted.

— Patty Hansen —

True Love

Beauty without grace is a hook without a bait.
~Ninon de l'Enclos

Moses Mendelssohn, the grandfather of the well-known German composer, was far from handsome. Along with a rather short stature, he had a grotesque hunchback.

One day he visited a merchant in Hamburg who had a lovely daughter named Frumtje. Moses fell hopelessly in love with her. But Frumtje was repulsed by his misshapen appearance.

When it was time for him to leave, Moses gathered his courage and climbed the stairs to her room to take one last opportunity to speak with her. She was a vision of heavenly beauty, but caused him deep sadness by her refusal to look at him. After several attempts at conversation, Moses shyly asked, "Do you believe marriages are made in heaven?"

"Yes," she answered, still looking at the floor. "And do you?"

"Yes I do," he replied. "You see, in heaven at the birth of each boy, the Lord announces which girl he will marry. When I was born, my future bride was pointed out to me. Then the Lord added, 'But your wife will be humpbacked.'

"Right then and there I called out, 'Oh Lord, a humpbacked woman would be a tragedy. Please, Lord, give me the hump and let her be beautiful.'"

Then Frumtje looked up into his eyes and was stirred by some deep memory. She reached out and gave Mendelssohn her hand and later became his devoted wife.

— Barry and Joyce Vissell —

The Hugging Judge

Don't bug me! Hug me!
~Bumper Sticker

L ee Shapiro is a retired judge. He is also one of the most genuinely loving people we know. At one point in his career, Lee realized that love is the greatest power there is. As a result, Lee became a hugger. He began offering everybody a hug. His colleagues dubbed him "the hugging judge" (as opposed to the hanging judge, we suppose). The bumper sticker on his car reads, "Don't bug me! Hug me!"

About six years ago Lee created what he calls his Hugger Kit. On the outside it reads "A heart for a hug." The inside contains 30 little red embroidered hearts with stickums on the back. Lee will take out his Hugger Kit, go around to people and offer them a little red heart in exchange for a hug.

Lee has become so well known for this that he is often invited to keynote conferences and conventions, where he shares his message of unconditional love. At a conference in San Francisco, the local news media challenged him by saying, "It is easy to give out hugs here in the conference to people who self-selected to be here. But this would never work in the real world."

They challenged Lee to give away some hugs on the streets of San Francisco. Followed by a television crew from the local news station, Lee went out onto the street. First he approached a woman walking by. "Hi, I'm Lee Shapiro, the hugging judge. I'm giving out these hearts in exchange for a hug." "Sure," she replied. "Too easy," challenged the local commentator. Lee looked around. He saw a meter maid who was being given a hard time by the owner of a BMW to whom she was giving a ticket. He marched up to her, camera crew in tow, and said, "You look like you could use a hug. I'm the hugging judge and I'm offering you one." She accepted.

The television commentator threw down one final challenge. "Look, here comes a bus. San Francisco bus drivers are the toughest people in the whole town. Let's see you get him to hug you." Lee took the challenge.

As the bus pulled up to the curb, Lee said, "Hi, I'm Lee Shapiro, the hugging judge. This has got to be one of the most stressful jobs in the whole world. I'm offering hugs to people today to lighten the load a little. Would you like one?" The six-foot-two, 230-pound bus driver got out of his seat, stepped down and said, "Why not?"

Lee hugged him, gave him a heart and waved goodbye as the bus pulled out. The TV crew was speechless. Finally, the commentator said, "I have to admit, I'm very impressed."

One day, Lee's friend Nancy Johnston showed up on his doorstep. Nancy is a professional clown and she was wearing her clown costume, make-up and all. "Lee, grab a bunch of your Hugger Kits and let's go out to the home for the disabled."

When they arrived at the home, they started giving out balloon hats, hearts and hugs to the patients. Lee was uncomfortable. He had never before hugged people who were terminally ill, severely retarded or quadriplegic. It was definitely a stretch. But after a while it became easier, with Nancy and Lee acquiring an entourage of doctors, nurses and orderlies who followed them from ward to ward.

After several hours they entered the last ward. These were 34 of the worst cases Lee had seen in his life. The feeling was so grim it took his heart away. But because of their commitment to share their love and to make a difference, Nancy and Lee started working their way around the room followed by the entourage of medical staff, all of whom by now had hearts on their collars and balloon hats on their heads.

Finally, Lee came to the last person, Leonard. Leonard was wearing a big white bib, which he was drooling on. Lee looked at Leonard dribbling onto his bib and said, "Let's go, Nancy. There's no way we can get through to this person." Nancy replied, "C'mon, Lee. He's a fellow human being, too, isn't he?" Then she placed a funny balloon hat on his head. Lee took one of his little red hearts and placed it on Leonard's bib. He took a deep breath, leaned down and gave Leonard a hug.

All of a sudden Leonard began to squeal, "Eeeeehh! Eeeeeehh!" Some of the other patients in the room began to clang things together. Lee turned to the staff for some sort of explanation only to find that every doctor, nurse and orderly was crying. Lee asked the head nurse, "What's going on?"

Lee will never forget what she said: "This is the first time in 23 years we've seen Leonard smile."

How simple it is to make a difference in the lives of others.

—Jack Canfield and Mark Victor Hansen—

It Can't Happen Here?

We need 4 hugs a day for survival.
We need 8 hugs a day for maintenance.
We need 12 hugs a day for growth.
~Virginia Satir

We always teach people to hug each other in our workshops and seminars. Most people respond by saying, "You could never hug people where I work." Are you sure?

Here is a letter from a graduate of one of our seminars.

Dear Jack,

I started out this day in rather a bleak mood. My friend Rosalind stopped over and asked me if I was giving hugs today. I just grumbled something but then I began to think about hugs and everything during the week. I would look at the sheet you gave us on "How to Keep the Seminar Alive" and I would cringe when I got to the part about giving and getting hugs because I couldn't imagine giving hugs to the people at work.

Well, I decided to make it "hugs day" and I started giving hugs to the customers who came to my counter. It was great to see how people just brightened up. An MBA student jumped up on top of the counter and did a dance. Some people actually came back and asked for more. These two Xerox repair guys, who were kind of just walking along not really talking to each other, were so surprised, they just woke up and suddenly were talking and laughing down the hall.

It feels like I hugged everybody in the Wharton Business School, plus whatever was wrong with me this morning, which included some physical pain, is all gone. I'm sorry that this letter is so long but I'm just really excited. The neatest thing was, at one point there were about 10 people all hugging each other out in front of my counter. I couldn't believe this was happening.

Love,
Pamela Rogers

P.S. On the way home I hugged a policeman on 37th Street. He said, "Wow! Policemen never get hugs. Are you sure you don't want to throw something at me?"

Another seminar graduate, Charles Faraone, sent us the following piece on hugging:

Hugging Is

Hugging is healthy. It helps the immune system, cures depression, reduces stress and induces sleep. It's invigorating, rejuvenating and has no unpleasant side effects. Hugging is nothing less than a miracle drug.

Hugging is all natural. It is organic, naturally sweet, no artificial ingredients, nonpolluting, environmentally friendly and 100 percent wholesome.

Hugging is the ideal gift. Great for any occasion, fun to give and receive, shows you care, comes with its own wrapping and, of course, fully returnable.

Hugging is practically perfect. No batteries to wear out, inflation-proof, nonfattening, no monthly payments, theft-proof and nontaxable.

Hugging is an underutilized resource with magical powers. When we open our hearts and arms, we encourage others to do the same.

Think of the people in your life. Are there any words you'd like to say? Are there any hugs you want to share? Are you waiting and hoping someone else will ask first? Please don't wait! Initiate!

— Jack Canfield —

Who You Are Makes a Difference

*Most of us, swimming against the tides of trouble the
world knows nothing about, need only a bit of praise or
encouragement — and we will make the goal.*
~Jerome Fleishman

A teacher in New York decided to honor her seniors in high
school by telling them the difference they each made. Using
a process developed by Helice Bridges of Del Mar, California,
she called each student to the front of the class, one at a time.
First she told them they made a difference to her and the class. Then
she presented each of them with a blue ribbon imprinted with gold
letters that read, "Who I Am Makes a Difference."

Afterwards the teacher decided to do a class project to see what
kind of impact recognition would have on a community. She gave each
of the students three more ribbons and instructed them to go out and
spread this acknowledgment ceremony. Then they were to follow up
on the results, see who honored whom and report back to the class
in about a week.

One of the boys in the class went to a junior executive in a nearby
company and honored him for helping him with his career planning.
He gave him a blue ribbon and put it on his shirt. Then he gave him

two extra ribbons, and said, "We're doing a class project on recognition, and we'd like you to go out, find somebody to honor, give them a blue ribbon, then give them the extra blue ribbon so they can acknowledge a third person to keep this acknowledgment ceremony going. Then please report back to me and tell me what happened."

Later that day the junior executive went in to see his boss, who had been noted, by the way, as being kind of a grouchy fellow. He sat his boss down and he told him that he deeply admired him for being a creative genius. The boss seemed very surprised. The junior executive asked him if he would accept the gift of the blue ribbon and give him permission to put it on him. His surprised boss said, "Well, sure."

The junior executive took the blue ribbon and placed it right on his boss's jacket above his heart. As he gave him the last extra ribbon, he said, "Would you do me a favor? Would you take this extra ribbon and pass it on by honoring somebody else? The young boy who first gave me the ribbons is doing a project in school and we want to keep this recognition ceremony going and find out how it affects people."

That night the boss went home to his 14-year-old son and sat him down. He said, "The most incredible thing happened to me today. I was in my office and one of the junior executives came in and told me he admired me and gave me a blue ribbon for being a creative genius. Imagine. He thinks I'm a creative genius. Then he put this blue ribbon that says 'Who I Am Makes a Difference' on my jacket above my heart. He gave me an extra ribbon and asked me to find somebody else to honor. As I was driving home tonight, I started thinking about whom I would honor with this ribbon and I thought about you. I want to honor you.

"My days are really hectic and when I come home I don't pay a lot of attention to you. Sometimes I scream at you for not getting good enough grades in school and for your bedroom being a mess, but somehow tonight, I just wanted to sit here and, well, just let you know that you do make a difference to me. Besides your mother, you are the most important person in my life. You're a great kid and I love you!"

The startled boy started to sob and sob, and he couldn't stop crying. His whole body shook. He looked up at his father and said through his tears, "I was planning on committing suicide tomorrow, Dad, because I didn't think you loved me. Now I don't need to."

— Helice Bridges —

One at a Time

*We ourselves feel that what we are doing is just
a drop in the ocean. But the ocean would be less
because of that missing drop.*
~Mother Teresa

friend of ours was walking down a deserted Mexican beach at sunset. As he walked along, he began to see another man in the distance. As he grew nearer, he noticed that the man kept leaning down, picking something up and throwing it out into the water. Time and again he kept hurling things out into the ocean.

As our friend approached even closer, he noticed that the man was picking up starfish that had been washed up on the beach and, one at a time, he was throwing them back into the water.

Our friend was puzzled. He approached the man and said, "Good evening, friend. I was wondering what you are doing."

"I'm throwing these starfish back into the ocean. You see, it's low tide right now and all of these starfish have been washed up onto the shore. If I don't throw them back into the sea, they'll die up here from lack of oxygen."

"I understand," my friend replied, "but there must be thousands of starfish on this beach. You can't possibly get to all of them. There are simply too many. And don't you realize this is probably happening on hundreds of beaches all up and down this coast? Can't you see that you can't possibly make a difference?"

The man smiled, bent down, and picked up yet another starfish, and as he threw it back into the sea, he replied, "Made a difference to that one!"

—Jack Canfield and Mark Victor Hansen—

The Gift

How beautiful a day can be
When kindness touches it!
~George Elliston

Bennett Cerf relates this touching story about a bus that was bumping along a back road in the South.

In one seat a wispy old man sat holding a bunch of fresh flowers. Across the aisle was a young girl whose eyes came back again and again to the man's flowers. The time came for the old man to get off. Impulsively he thrust the flowers into the girl's lap.

"I can see you love the flowers," he explained, "and I think my wife would like for you to have them. I'll tell her I gave them to you." The girl accepted the flowers, then watched the old man get off the bus and walk through the gate of a small cemetery.

— As told by Bennett Cerf —

A Brother Like That

Sometimes being a brother is even better
than being a superhero.
~Marc Brown

A friend of mine named Paul received an automobile from his brother as a Christmas present. On Christmas Eve when Paul came out of his office, a kid was walking around the shiny new car, admiring it. "Is this your car, Mister?" he asked.

Paul nodded. "My brother gave it to me for Christmas." The boy was astounded. "You mean your brother gave it to you and it didn't cost you nothing? Boy, I wish…" He hesitated.

Of course Paul knew what he was going to wish for. He was going to wish he had a brother like that. But what the lad said jarred Paul all the way down to his heels.

"I wish," the boy went on, "that I could be a brother like that."

Paul looked at the boy in astonishment, then impulsively he added, "Would you like to take a ride in my automobile?"

"Oh yes, I'd love that."

After a short ride, the boy turned and with his eyes aglow, said, "Mister, would you mind driving in front of my house?"

Paul smiled a little. He thought he knew what the lad wanted. He wanted to show his neighbors that he could ride home in a big automobile. But Paul was wrong again. "Will you stop where those two steps are?" the boy asked.

He ran up the steps. Then in a little while Paul heard him coming back, but he was not coming fast. He was carrying his little crippled brother. He sat him down on the bottom step, then sort of squeezed up against him and pointed to the car.

"There she is, Buddy, just like I told you upstairs. His brother gave it to him for Christmas and it didn't cost him a cent. And some day I'm gonna give you one just like it... then you can see for yourself all the pretty things in the Christmas windows that I've been trying to tell you about."

Paul got out and lifted the lad to the front seat of his car. The shining-eyed older brother climbed in beside him and the three of them began a memorable holiday ride.

That Christmas Eve, Paul learned what Jesus meant when he said: *"It is more blessed to give..."*

— Dan Clark —

On Courage

A brother is a friend given by Nature.
~Jean Baptiste Legouvé

"So you think I'm courageous?" she asked.

"Yes, I do."

"Perhaps I am. But that's because I've had some inspiring teachers. I'll tell you about one of them. Many years ago, when I worked as a volunteer at Stanford Hospital, I got to know a little girl named Liza who was suffering from a rare and serious disease. Her only chance of recovery appeared to be a blood transfusion from her five-year-old brother, who had miraculously survived the same disease and had developed the antibodies needed to combat the illness. The doctor explained the situation to her little brother, and asked the boy if he would be willing to give his blood to his sister. I saw him hesitate for only a moment before taking a deep breath and saying, 'Yes, I'll do it if it will save Liza.'

"As the transfusion progressed, he lay in a bed next to his sister and smiled, as we all did, seeing the color returning to her cheeks. Then his face grew pale and his smile faded. He looked up at the doctor and asked with a trembling voice, 'Will I start to die right away?'

"Being young, the boy had misunderstood the doctor; he thought he was going to have to give her *all* his blood.

"Yes, I've learned courage," she added, "because I've had inspiring teachers."

— Dan Millman —

Big Ed

*Wisdom is the reward you get for a lifetime of listening
when you'd have preferred to talk.*
~Doug Larson

When I arrived in the city to present a seminar on Tough-Minded Management, a small group of people took me to dinner to brief me on the people I would talk to the next day.

The obvious leader of the group was Big Ed, a large burly man with a deep rumbling voice. At dinner he informed me that he was a troubleshooter for a huge international organization. His job was to go into certain divisions or subsidiaries to terminate the employment of the executive in charge.

"Joe," he said, "I'm really looking forward to tomorrow because all of the guys need to listen to a tough guy like you. They're gonna find out that my style is the right one." He grinned and winked.

I smiled. I knew the next day was going to be different from what he was anticipating.

The next day he sat impassively all through the seminar and left at the end without saying anything to me.

Three years later I returned to that city to present another management seminar to approximately the same group. Big Ed was there again. At about ten o'clock he suddenly stood up and asked loudly, "Joe, can I say something to these people?"

I grinned and said, "Sure. When anybody is as big as you are, Ed, he can say anything he wants."

Big Ed went on to say, "All of you guys know me and some of you know what's happened to me. I want to share it, however, with all of you. Joe, I think you'll appreciate it by the time I've finished.

"When I heard you suggest that each of us, in order to become really tough-minded, needed to learn to tell those closest to us that we really loved them, I thought it was a bunch of sentimental garbage. I wondered what in the world that had to do with being tough. You had said toughness is like leather, and hardness is like granite, that the tough mind is open, resilient, disciplined and tenacious. But I couldn't see what love had to do with it.

"That night, as I sat across the living room from my wife, your words were still bugging me. What kind of courage would it take to tell my wife I loved her? Couldn't anybody do it? You had also said this should be in the daylight and not in the bedroom. I found myself clearing my throat and starting and then stopping. My wife looked up and asked me what I had said, and I answered, 'Oh nothing.' Then suddenly, I got up, walked across the room, nervously pushed her newspaper aside and said, 'Alice, I love you.' For a minute she looked startled. Then the tears came to her eyes and she said softly, 'Ed, I love you, too, but this is the first time in 25 years you've said it like that.'

"We talked a while about how love, if there's enough of it, can dissolve all kinds of tensions, and suddenly I decided on the spur of the moment to call my older son in New York. We have never really communicated well. When I got him on the phone, I blurted out, 'Son, you're liable to think I'm drunk, but I'm not. I just thought I'd call you and tell you I love you.'

"There was a pause at his end and then I heard him say quietly, 'Dad, I guess I've known that, but it's sure good to hear. I want you to know I love you, too.' We had a good chat and then I called my younger son in San Francisco. We had been closer. I told him the same thing and this, too, led to a real fine talk like we'd never really had.

"As I lay in bed that night thinking, I realized that all the things you'd talked about that day — real management nuts and bolts — took on extra meaning, and I could get a handle on how to apply them if I really understood and practiced tough-minded love.

"I began to read books on the subject. Sure enough, Joe, a lot of great people had a lot to say, and I began to realize the enormous practicality of applied love in my life, both at home and at work.

"As some of you guys here know, I really changed the way I work with people. I began to listen more and to really hear. I learned what it was like to try to get to know people's strengths rather than dwelling on their weaknesses. I began to discover the real pleasure of helping build their confidence. Maybe the most important thing of all was that I really began to understand that an excellent way to show love and respect for people was to expect them to use their strengths to meet objectives we had worked out together.

"Joe, this is my way of saying thanks. Incidentally, talk about practical! I'm now executive vice-president of the company and they call me a pivotal leader. Okay, you guys, now listen to this guy!"

—Joe Batten—

Love and the Cabbie

You can't live a perfect day without doing something
for someone who will never be able to repay you.
~John Wooden

I was in New York the other day and rode with a friend in a taxi. When we got out, my friend said to the driver, "Thank you for the ride. You did a superb job of driving."

The taxi driver was stunned for a second. Then he said, "Are you a wise guy or something?"

"No, my dear man, and I'm not putting you on. I admire the way you keep cool in heavy traffic."

"Yeah," the driver said and drove off.

"What was that all about?" I asked.

"I am trying to bring love back to New York," he said. "I believe it's the only thing that can save the city."

"How can one man save New York?"

"It's not one man. I believe I have made that taxi driver's day. Suppose he has 20 fares. He's going to be nice to those 20 fares because someone was nice to him. Those fares in turn will be kinder to their employees or shopkeepers or waiters or even their own families. Eventually the goodwill could spread to at least 1,000 people. Now that isn't bad, is it?"

"But you're depending on that taxi driver to pass your goodwill to others."

"I'm not depending on it," my friend said. "I'm aware that the system isn't foolproof so I might deal with 10 different people today. If out of 10 I can make three happy, then eventually I can indirectly influence the attitudes of 3,000 more."

"It sounds good on paper," I admitted, "but I'm not sure it works in practice."

"Nothing is lost if it doesn't. It didn't take any of my time to tell that man he was doing a good job. He neither received a larger tip nor a smaller tip. If it fell on deaf ears, so what? Tomorrow there will be another taxi driver I can try to make happy."

"You're some kind of a nut," I said.

"That shows how cynical you have become. I have made a study of this. The thing that seems to be lacking, besides money of course, for our postal employees, is that no one tells people who work for the post office what a good job they're doing."

"But they're not doing a good job."

"They're not doing a good job because they feel no one cares if they do or not. Why shouldn't someone say a kind word to them?"

We were walking past a structure in the process of being built and passed five workmen eating their lunch. My friend stopped. "That's a magnificent job you men have done. It must be difficult and dangerous work."

The workmen eyed my friend suspiciously.

"When will it be finished?"

"June," a man grunted.

"Ah. That really is impressive. You must all be very proud."

We walked away. I said to him, "I haven't seen anyone like you since *Man of La Mancha.*"

"When those men digest my words, they will feel better for it. Somehow the city will benefit from their happiness."

"But you can't do this all alone!" I protested. "You're just one man."

"The most important thing is not to get discouraged. Making people in the city become kind again is not an easy job, but if I can enlist other people in my campaign..."

"You just winked at a very plain-looking woman," I said.

"Yes, I know," he replied. "And if she's a schoolteacher, her class will be in for a fantastic day."

—Art Buchwald—

A Simple Gesture

Everybody can be great... because anybody can serve.
You don't have to have a college degree to serve. You
don't have to make your subject and verb agree to
serve. You only need a heart full of grace.
A soul generated by love.
~Martin Luther King, Jr.

Mark was walking home from school one day when he noticed the boy ahead of him had tripped and dropped all of the books he was carrying, along with two sweaters, a baseball bat, a glove and a small tape recorder. Mark knelt down and helped the boy pick up the scattered articles. Since they were going the same way, he helped to carry part of the burden. As they walked Mark discovered the boy's name was Bill, that he loved video games, baseball and history, that he was having a lot of trouble with his other subjects and that he had just broken up with his girlfriend.

They arrived at Bill's home first and Mark was invited in for a Coke and to watch some television. The afternoon passed pleasantly with a few laughs and some shared small talk, then Mark went home. They continued to see each other around school, had lunch together once or twice, then both graduated from junior high school. They ended up in the same high school where they had brief contacts over the years. Finally the long awaited senior year came, and three weeks before graduation, Bill asked Mark if they could talk.

Bill reminded him of the day years ago when they had first met. "Do you ever wonder why I was carrying so many things home that day?" asked Bill. "You see, I cleaned out my locker because I didn't want to leave a mess for anyone else. I had stored away some of my mother's sleeping pills and I was going home to commit suicide. But after we spent some time together talking and laughing, I realized that if I had killed myself, I would have missed that time and so many others that might follow. So you see, Mark, when you picked up my books that day, you did a lot more. You saved my life."

—John W. Schlatter—

The Smile

Smile at each other, smile at your wife, smile at
your husband, smile at your children, smile at each
other — it doesn't matter who it is — and that will
help you to grow up in greater love for each other.
~Mother Teresa

Many Americans are familiar with *The Little Prince*, a wonderful book by Antoine de Saint-Exupéry. This is a whimsical and fabulous book and works as a children's story as well as a thought-provoking adult fable. Far fewer are aware of Saint-Exupéry's other writings, novels and short stories.

Saint-Exupéry was a fighter pilot who fought against the Nazis and was killed in action. Before World War II, he fought in the Spanish Civil War against the fascists. He wrote a fascinating story based on that experience entitled *The Smile (Le Sourire)*. It isn't clear whether or not he meant this to be autobiographical or fiction. I choose to believe it is the former.

He said that he was captured by the enemy and thrown into a jail cell. He was sure from the contemptuous looks and rough treatment he received from his jailers that he would be executed the next day. From here, I'll tell the story as I remember it in my own words.

"I was sure that I was to be killed. I became terribly nervous and distraught. I fumbled in my pockets to see if there were any cigarettes that had escaped their search. I found one and because of my shaking hands, I could barely get it to my lips. But I had no matches; they had taken those.

"I looked through the bars at my jailer. He did not make eye contact with me. After all, one does not make eye contact with a thing, a corpse. I called out to him 'Have you got a light, *por favor*?' He looked at me, shrugged and came over to light my cigarette.

"As he came close and lit the match, his eyes inadvertently locked with mine. At that moment, I smiled. I don't know why I did that. Perhaps it was nervousness, perhaps it was because, when you get very close, one to another, it is very hard not to smile. In any case, I smiled. In that instant, it was as though a spark jumped across the gap between our two hearts, our two human souls. I know he didn't want to, but my smile leaped through the bars and generated a smile on his lips, too. He lit my cigarette but stayed near, looking at me directly in the eyes and continuing to smile.

"I kept smiling at him, now aware of him as a person and not just a jailer. And his looking at me seemed to have a new dimension, too. 'Do you have kids?' he asked.

"'Yes, here, here.' I took out my wallet and nervously fumbled for the pictures of my family. He, too, took out the pictures of his *niños* and began to talk about his plans and hopes for them. My eyes filled with tears. I said that I feared that I'd never see my family again, never have the chance to see them grow up. Tears came to his eyes, too.

"Suddenly, without another word, he unlocked my cell and silently led me out. Out of the jail, quietly and by back routes, out of the town. There, at the edge of town, he released me. And without another word, he turned back toward the town.

"My life was saved by a smile."

Yes, the smile — the unaffected, unplanned, natural connection between people. I tell this story in my work because I'd like people to consider that underneath all the layers we construct to protect ourselves, our dignity, our titles, our degrees, our status and our need to be seen in certain ways — underneath all that, remains the authentic, essential self. I'm not afraid to call it the soul. I really believe that if that part of you and that part of me could recognize each other, we wouldn't be enemies. We couldn't have hate or envy or fear. I sadly conclude that all those other layers, which we so carefully construct through our lives, distance and insulate us from truly contacting others. Saint-Exupéry's story speaks of that magic moment when two souls recognize each other.

I've had just a few moments like that. Falling in love is one example. And looking at a baby. Why do we smile when we see a baby? Perhaps it's because we see someone without all the defensive layers, someone whose smile for us we know to be fully genuine and without guile. And that baby-soul inside us smiles wistfully in recognition.

— Hanoch McCarty —

Amy Graham

*The most important thing in illness
is never to lose heart.*
~Nikolai Lenin

After flying all night from Washington, D.C., I was tired as I arrived at the Mile High Church in Denver to conduct three services and hold a workshop on prosperity consciousness. As I entered the church, Dr. Fred Vogt asked me, "Do you know about the Make-A-Wish Foundation?"

"Yes," I replied.

"Well, Amy Graham has been diagnosed as having terminal leukemia. They gave her three days. Her dying wish was to attend your services."

I was shocked. I felt a combination of elation, awe and doubt. I couldn't believe it. I thought kids who were dying would want to go see Disneyland, meet Sylvester Stallone, Mr. "T" or Arnold Schwarzenegger. Surely they wouldn't want to spend their final days listening to Mark Victor Hansen. Why would a kid with only a few days to live want to come hear a motivational speaker? Suddenly my thoughts were interrupted...

"Here's Amy," Vogt said as he put her frail hand in mine. Before me stood a 17-year-old girl wearing a bright red and orange turban to cover her head, which was bald from all of the chemotherapy treatments. Her frail body was bent and weak. She said, "My two goals were to graduate from high school and to attend your sermon. My doctors didn't believe I could do either. They didn't think I'd have enough energy. I got discharged into my parents' care… This is my mom and dad."

Tears welled in my eyes; I was choked up. My equilibrium was being shaken. I was totally moved. I cleared my throat, smiled and said, "You and your folks are our guests. Thanks for wanting to come." We hugged, dabbed our eyes and separated.

I've attended many healing seminars in the United States, Canada, Malaysia, New Zealand and Australia. I've watched the best healers at work and I've studied, researched, listened, pondered and questioned what worked, why and how.

That Sunday afternoon I held a seminar that Amy and her parents attended. The audience was packed to overflowing with over a thousand attendees eager to learn, grow and become more fully human.

I humbly asked the audience if they wanted to learn a healing process that might serve them for life. From the stage it appeared that everyone's hand was raised high in the air. They unanimously wanted to learn.

I taught the audience how to vigorously rub their hands together, separate them by two inches and feel the healing energy. Then I paired them off with a partner to feel the healing energy emanating from themselves to another. I said, "If you need a healing, accept one here and now."

The audience was in alignment and it was an ecstatic feeling. I explained that everyone has healing energy and healing potential. Five percent of us have it so dramatically pouring forth from our hands that we could make it our profession. I said, "This morning I was introduced to Amy Graham, a 17-year-old, whose final wish was to be at this seminar. I want to bring her up here and let you all send healing life force energy toward her. Perhaps we can help. She did not request it. I am just doing this spontaneously because it feels right."

The audience chanted, "Yes! Yes! Yes! Yes!"

Amy's dad led her up onto the stage. She looked frail from all of the chemotherapy, too much bed rest and an absolute lack of exercise. (The doctors hadn't let her walk for the two weeks prior to this seminar.)

I had the group warm up their hands and send her healing energy, after which they gave her a tearful standing ovation.

Two weeks later she called to say that her doctor had discharged her after a total remission. Two years later she called to say she was married.

I have learned never to underestimate the healing power we all have. It is always there to be used for the highest good. We just have to remember to use it.

— Mark Victor Hansen —

A Story for Valentine's Day

We often take for granted the very things
that most deserve our gratitude.
~Cynthia Ozick

Larry and Jo Ann were an ordinary couple. They lived in an ordinary house on an ordinary street. Like any other ordinary couple, they struggled to make ends meet and to do the right things for their children.

They were ordinary in yet another way — they had their squabbles. Much of their conversation concerned what was wrong in their marriage and who was to blame.

Until one day when a most extraordinary event took place.

"You know, Jo Ann, I've got a magic chest of drawers. Every time I open them, they're full of socks and underwear," Larry said. "I want to thank you for filling them all these years."

Jo Ann stared at her husband over the top of her glasses. "What do you want, Larry?"

"Nothing. I just want you to know I appreciate those magic drawers."

This wasn't the first time Larry had done something odd, so Jo Ann pushed the incident out of her mind until a few days later.

"Jo Ann, thank you for recording so many correct check numbers in the ledger this month. You put down the right numbers 15 out of 16 times. That's a record."

Disbelieving what she had heard, Jo Ann looked up from her

mending. "Larry, you're always complaining about my recording the wrong check numbers. Why stop now?"

"No reason. I just wanted you to know I appreciate the effort you're making."

Jo Ann shook her head and went back to her mending. "What's got into him?" she mumbled to herself.

Nevertheless, the next day when Jo Ann wrote a check at the grocery store, she glanced at her checkbook to confirm that she had put down the right check number. "Why do I suddenly care about those dumb check numbers?" she asked herself.

She tried to disregard the incident, but Larry's strange behavior intensified.

"Jo Ann, that was a great dinner," he said one evening. "I appreciate all your effort. Why, in the past 15 years I'll bet you've fixed over 14,000 meals for me and the kids."

Then "Gee, Jo Ann, the house looks spiffy. You've really worked hard to get it looking so good." And even "Thanks, Jo Ann, for just being you. I really enjoy your company."

Jo Ann was growing worried. "Where's the sarcasm, the criticism?" she wondered.

Her fears that something peculiar was happening to her husband were confirmed by 16-year-old Shelly, who complained, "Dad's gone bonkers, Mom. He just told me I looked nice. With all this make-up and these sloppy clothes, he still said it. That's not Dad, Mom. What's wrong with him?"

Whatever was wrong, Larry didn't get over it. Day in and day out he continued focusing on the positive.

Over the weeks, Jo Ann grew more accustomed to her mate's unusual behavior and occasionally even gave him a grudging "Thank you." She prided herself on taking it all in stride, until one day something so peculiar happened, she became completely discombobulated:

"I want you to take a break," Larry said. "I am going to do the dishes. So please take your hands off that frying pan and leave the kitchen."

(Long, long pause.) "Thank you, Larry. Thank you very much!"

Jo Ann's step was now a little lighter, her self-confidence higher and once in a while she hummed. She didn't seem to have as many blue moods anymore. "I rather like Larry's new behavior," she thought.

That would be the end of the story except one day another most extraordinary event took place. This time it was Jo Ann who spoke.

"Larry," she said, "I want to thank you for going to work and providing for us all these years. I don't think I've ever told you how much I appreciate it."

Larry has never revealed the reason for his dramatic change of behavior no matter how hard Jo Ann has pushed for an answer, and so it will likely remain one of life's mysteries. But it's one I'm thankful to live with.

You see, I am Jo Ann.

—Jo Ann Larsen—
Deseret News

Carpe Diem!

Why not go out on a limb? Isn't that where the fruit is?
~Frank Scully

One who stands as a shining example of courageous expression is John Keating, the transformative teacher portrayed by Robin Williams in *Dead Poets Society*. In this masterful motion picture, Keating takes a group of regimented, uptight and spiritually impotent students at a rigid boarding school and inspires them to make their lives extraordinary.

These young men, as Keating points out to them, have lost sight of their dreams and ambitions. They are automatically living out their parents' programs and expectations for them. They plan to become doctors, lawyers and bankers because that is what their parents have told them they are going to do. But these dry fellows have given hardly any thought to what their hearts are calling them to express.

An early scene in the movie shows Mr. Keating taking the boys down to the school lobby where a trophy case displays photos of earlier graduating classes. "Look at these pictures, boys," Keating tells the students. "The young men you behold had the same fire in their eyes that you do. They planned to take the world by storm and make something magnificent of their lives. That was 70 years ago. Now they are all pushing up daisies. How many of them really lived out their dreams? Did they do what they set out to accomplish?" Then Mr. Keating leans into the cluster of preppies and whispers audibly,

"Carpe diem! Seize the day!"

At first the students do not know what to make of this strange teacher. But soon they ponder the importance of his words. They come to respect and revere Mr. Keating, who has given them a new vision — or returned them to their original ones.

All of us are walking around with some kind of birthday card we would like to give — some personal expression of joy, creativity or aliveness that we are hiding under our shirt.

One character in the movie, Knox Overstreet, has a terminal crush on a gorgeous girl. The only problem is that she is the girlfriend of a famous jock. Knox is infatuated with this lovely creature down to a cellular level but he lacks the confidence to approach her. Then he remembers Mr. Keating's advice: *Seize the day!* Knox realizes he cannot just go on dreaming — if he wants her, he is going to have to do something about it. And so he does. Boldly and poetically he declares to her his most sensitive feelings. In the process he gets turned away by her, punched in the nose by her boyfriend and faces embarrassing setbacks. But Knox is unwilling to forsake his dream, so he pursues his heart's desire. Ultimately she feels the genuineness of his caring and opens her heart to him. Although Knox is not especially good-looking or popular, the girl is won over by the power of his sincere intention. He has made his life extraordinary.

I had a chance to practice seizing the day myself. I developed a crush on a cute girl I met in a pet store. She was younger than I, she led a very different lifestyle and we did not have a great deal to talk about. But somehow none of this seemed to matter. I enjoyed being with her and I felt a sparkle in her presence. And it seemed to me she enjoyed my company as well.

When I learned her birthday was coming up, I decided to ask her out. On the threshold of calling her, I sat and looked at the phone for about half an hour. Then I dialed and hung up before it rang. I felt like a high school boy, bouncing between excited anticipation and fear of rejection. A voice kept telling me that she would not like me and that

I had a lot of nerve asking her out. But I felt too enthusiastic about being with her to let those fears stop me. Finally I got up the nerve to ask her. She thanked me for asking and told me she already had plans.

I felt shot down. The same voice that told me not to call advised me to give up before I was further embarrassed. But I was intent on seeing what this attraction was about. There was more inside me that wanted to come to life. I had feelings for this woman, and I had to express them.

I went to the mall and got her a pretty birthday card on which I wrote a poetic note. I walked around the corner to the pet shop where I knew she was working. As I approached the door, that same disturbing voice cautioned me, "What if she doesn't like you? What if she rejects you?" Feeling vulnerable, I stuffed the card under my shirt. I decided that if she showed me signs of affection, I would give it to her; if she was cool to me, I would leave the card hidden. This way I would not be at risk and would avoid rejection or embarrassment.

We talked for a while and I did not get any signs one way or the other from her. Feeling ill at ease, I began to make my exit.

As I approached the door, however, another voice spoke to me. It came in a whisper, not unlike that of Mr. Keating. It prompted me, "Remember Knox Overstreet. *Carpe diem!*" Here I was confronted with my aspiration to fully express my heart and my resistance to face the insecurity of emotional nakedness. How can I go around telling other people to live their vision, I asked myself, when I am not living my own? Besides, what's the worst thing that could happen? Any woman would be delighted to receive a poetic birthday card. I decided to seize the day. As I made that choice I felt a surge of courage course through my veins. There was indeed power in intention.

I felt more satisfied and at peace with myself than I had in a long time… I needed to learn to open my heart and give love without requiring anything in return.

I took the card out from under my shirt, turned around, walked up to the counter and gave it to her. As I handed it to her I felt an incredible aliveness and excitement — plus fear. (Fritz Perls said that fear is "excitement without breath.") But I did it.

And do you know what? She was not particularly impressed. She said "Thanks" and put the card aside without even opening it. My heart sank. I felt disappointed and rejected. Getting no response seemed even worse than a direct brush-off.

I offered a polite goodbye and walked out of the store. Then something amazing happened. I began to feel exhilarated. A huge rush of internal satisfaction welled up within me and surged through my whole being. I had expressed my heart and that felt fantastic! I had stretched beyond fear and gone out on the dance floor. Yes, I had been a little clumsy, but I did it. (Emmet Fox said, "Do it trembling if you must, but do it!") I had put my heart on the line without demanding a guarantee of the results. I did not give in order to get something back. I opened my feelings to her without an attachment to a particular response.

The dynamics that are required to make any relationship work: Just keep putting your love out there.

My exhilaration deepened to a warm bliss. I felt more satisfied and at peace with myself than I had in a long time. I realized the purpose of the whole experience: I needed to learn to open my heart and give love without requiring anything in return. This experience was not about creating a relationship with this woman. It was about deepening my relationship with myself. And I did it. Mr. Keating would have been proud. But most of all, I was proud.

I have not seen the girl much since then, but that experience changed my life. Through that simple interaction I clearly saw the dynamics that are required to make any relationship and perhaps the whole world work: *Just keep putting your love out there.*

We believe that we are hurt when we don't receive love. But that is not what hurts us. Our pain comes when we do not *give* love. We were born to love. You might say that we are divinely created love machines. We function most powerfully when we are giving love. The world has led us to believe that our wellbeing is dependent on other people loving us. But this is the kind of upside-down thinking that has caused so many of our problems. The truth is that our wellbeing is dependent on our *giving* love. It is not about what comes back; it is about *what goes out!*

—Alan Cohen—

The Gentlest Need

I pet her and she pays me back in purrs.
~Terri Guillemets

At least once a day our old black cat comes to one of us in a way that we've all come to see as a special request. It does not mean he wants to be fed or to be let out or anything of that sort. His need is for something very different.

If you have a lap handy, he'll jump into it; if you don't, he's likely to stand there looking wistful until you make him one. Once in it, he begins to vibrate almost before you stroke his back, scratch his chin and tell him over and over what a good kitty he is. Then his motor really revs up; he squirms to get comfortable; he "makes big hands." Every once in a while one of his purrs gets out of control and turns into a snort. He looks at you with wide-open eyes of adoration, and he gives you the cat's long slow blink of ultimate trust.

After a while, little by little, he quiets down. If he senses that it's all right, he may stay in your lap for a cozy nap. But he is just as likely to hop down and stroll away about his business. Either way, he's all right.

Our daughter puts it simply: "Blackie needs to be purred."

In our household he isn't the only one who has that need: I share it and so does my wife. We know the need isn't exclusive to any one age group. Still, because I am a schoolman as well as a parent, I associate it especially with youngsters, with their quick, impulsive need for a hug, a warm lap, a hand held out, a coverlet tucked in, not because

On Love | 93

anything's wrong, not because anything needs doing, just because that's the way they are.

There are a lot of things I'd like to do for all children. If I could do just one, it would be this: to guarantee every child, everywhere, at least one good purring every day.

Kids, like cats, need time to purr.

— Fred T. Wilhelms —

Bopsy

I can think of no more stirring symbol of man's
humanity to man than a fire engine.
~Kurt Vonnegut

The 26-year-old mother stared down at her son who was dying of leukemia. Although her heart was filled with sadness, she also had a strong feeling of determination. Like any parent she wanted her son to grow up and fulfill all his dreams. Now that was no longer possible. The leukemia would see to that. But she still wanted her son's dreams to come true.

She took her son's hand and asked, "Bopsy, did you ever think about what you wanted to be when you grew up? Did you ever dream and wish about what you would do with your life?"

"Mommy, I always wanted to be a firefighter when I grew up."

Mom smiled back and said, "Let's see if we can make your wish come true." Later that day she went to her local fire department in Phoenix, Arizona, where she met Fireman Bob, who had a heart as big as Phoenix. She explained her son's final wish and asked if it might be possible to give her six-year-old son a ride around the block on a fire engine.

Fireman Bob said, "Look, we can do better than that. If you'll have your son ready at seven o'clock Wednesday morning, we'll make him an honorary firefighter for the whole day. He can come down to the fire station, eat with us, go out on all the fire calls, the whole nine yards! And, if you'll give us his sizes, we'll get a real fire uniform made for him, with a real fire hat — not a toy one — with the emblem of the Phoenix Fire Department on it, a yellow slicker like we wear and rubber boots. They're all manufactured right here in Phoenix, so we can get them fast."

Three days later Fireman Bob picked up Bopsy, dressed him in his fire uniform and escorted him from his hospital bed to the waiting hook and ladder truck. Bopsy got to sit up on the back of the truck and help steer it back to the fire station. He was in heaven.

There were three fire calls in Phoenix that day and Bopsy got to go out on all three calls. He rode in the different fire engines, the paramedics' van and even the fire chief's car. He was also videotaped for the local news program.

Having his dream come true, with all the love and attention that was lavished upon him, so deeply touched Bopsy that he lived three months longer than any doctor thought possible.

One night all of his vital signs began to drop dramatically and the head nurse, who believed in the Hospice concept that no one should die alone, began to call the family members to the hospital. Then she remembered the day Bopsy had spent as a firefighter, so she called the fire chief and asked if it would be possible to send a firefighter in uniform to the hospital to be with Bopsy as he made his transition. The chief replied, "We can do better than that. We'll be there in five minutes. Will you please do me a favor? When you hear the sirens screaming and see the lights flashing, will you announce over the PA system that there is not a fire? It's just the fire department coming to see one of its finest members one more time. And will you open the window to his room? Thanks."

About five minutes later a hook and ladder truck arrived at the hospital, extended its ladder up to Bopsy's third floor open window and 16 firefighters climbed up the ladder into Bopsy's room. With his mother's permission, they hugged him and held him and told him how much they loved him.

With his dying breath, Bopsy looked up at the fire chief and said, "Chief, am I really a firefighter now?"

"Bopsy, you are," the chief said.

With those words, Bopsy smiled and closed his eyes for the last time.

—Jack Canfield and Mark Victor Hansen—

Puppies for Sale

Judgments prevent us from seeing the good
that lies beyond appearances.
~Wayne Dyer

A storeowner was tacking a sign above his door that read "Puppies For Sale." Signs like that have a way of attracting small children, and sure enough, a little boy appeared under the storeowner's sign. "How much are you going to sell the puppies for?" he asked.

The storeowner replied, "Anywhere from $30 to $50."

The little boy reached in his pocket and pulled out some change. "I have $2.37," he said. "Can I please look at them?"

The storeowner smiled and whistled and out of the kennel came Lady, who ran down the aisle of his store followed by five teeny, tiny balls of fur. One puppy was lagging considerably behind. Immediately the little boy singled out the lagging, limping puppy and said, "What's wrong with that little dog?"

The storeowner explained that the veterinarian had examined the little puppy and had discovered it didn't have a hip socket. It would always limp. It would always be lame. The little boy became excited. "That is the little puppy that I want to buy."

The storeowner said, "No, you don't want to buy that little dog. If you really want him, I'll just give him to you."

The little boy got quite upset. He looked straight into the storeowner's eyes, pointing his finger, and said, "I don't want you to give him to me. That little dog is worth every bit as much as all the other dogs and I'll pay full price. In fact, I'll give you $2.37 now, and 50 cents a month until I have paid for him."

The storeowner countered, "You really don't want to buy this little dog. He is never going to be able to run and jump and play with you like the other puppies."

To this, the little boy reached down and rolled up his pant leg to reveal a badly twisted left leg supported by a big metal brace. He looked up at the storeowner and softly replied, "Well, I don't run so well myself, and the little puppy will need someone who understands!"

— Dan Clark —

Chicken Soup for the Soul

Learning to Love Yourself

*Oliver Wendell Holmes once attended a meeting in which he was
the shortest man present.*

*"Dr. Holmes," quipped a friend, "I should think you'd feel
rather small among us big fellows."*

"I do," retorted Holmes. "I feel like a dime among a lot of pennies."

The Lifesaving Power of Kindness to Strangers

One day you will tell your story of how you
overcame what you went through and
it will be someone else's survival guide.
~Brené Brown

December 30, 2016. Seat 22H. Non-stop, San Francisco to Reykjavik.

Despite a delay of more than a dozen hours, the excitement was contagious as the passengers boarded the plane. The flight attendants greeted everyone with a smile and didn't look like they were being paid to give it. I overheard the phrases "Blue Lagoon," "northern lights," and "dog sledding" repeatedly as they exchanged pleasantries with the travelers.

We were all going to the same destination, but I felt worlds away from everyone else on board. My wishes for this trip were much different than my fellow passengers, who were looking forward to making memories on a once-in-a-lifetime vacation. In my case, I hoped that a change of scenery would fix what had become not just toxic, but scary.

I turned to look at the tall, extremely good-looking man next to me and admonished myself for even thinking of those words about him. I flashed back to our first several months together, marked by intense physical and emotional chemistry like I had never felt before. He had easily earned the approval of my friends and family. It had felt like a dream, but it turned into a nightmare.

It didn't happen all at once, but gradually. The man who made me feel like I could accomplish anything began to make me doubt myself. He stopped telling me I was beautiful and started to compare me to other women. When I asked him what had changed, he turned the tables on me and said that I was to blame for his behavior. When I got defensive and said I was doing nothing differently, he took me by the hand and calmly explained that the point of a partnership is to make each other better. He claimed that if I listened to his suggestions, our relationship would bounce back to when things were good.

Unfortunately, the abuse only worsened over time. My self-esteem was at an all-time low and I felt like I needed to look to him for direction. When he said that going to Iceland might improve our relationship, I immediately booked the trip as a Christmas gift.

Just before take-off, I leaned in to take a selfie of us to commemorate the start of the trip, but he grabbed my phone to stop me. "I don't want people to know I'm here with you, okay?"

On that long flight, cut off from the world, there was no audience of friends to perform for. We could be our true selves, which for my boyfriend meant being cruel and vindictive. Among his litany of insults was that no one else would want to date me and that no one, not even my family, could love me as I was. Tears streamed down my face for the entire flight, and as I thought about what those around me must be thinking of me, it was hard not to believe him.

Midway through the flight, he stood to go to the bathroom. He looked down at me, my face red as I continued to sob. "You look ugly," he whispered before he walked away.

I was thirty-six thousand feet in the air with hundreds of strangers, but I had never felt so low and alone. I was an ocean away from anyone who cared about me.

I was lost in my thoughts when a note on a cocktail napkin slipped through the space between the two seats in front of me. At first, I didn't want to open it because I was certain it was about my in-flight breakdown, which would only make me feel worse, but curiosity got the better of me. I read it quickly and put it away, terrified he would see it when he returned from the lavatory.

> *Dear girlfriend,*
>
> *I know the Lord had me overhear your conversation to let you know you are a very beautiful young woman, that should have a man that makes you cry with wonderful laughter, not bullying. You are being abused and he will never love you like you deserve. I'm very concerned about you and I'm praying for you.*
> *Run from him. Get help and protection.*
> *He doesn't care what you think or say or do. He is a very sick man and will make you sick if you stay with him.*
> *Please take this to heart and get help fast.*

It was a punch in the gut being told he didn't care about me. It was a wake-up call he was abusive. It was a warning that my life was in danger. It was justification for his comments causing the emotions I displayed. It made me believe I deserved more. It was a reminder that there are good people in the world.

In the end, just over a hundred words written on a cocktail napkin by a complete stranger outweighed the countless acts of physical, verbal, and emotional abuse I experienced with my ex-boyfriend.

She left her contact information and one of the first things I did after the breakup was reach out to her. She told me she almost didn't write the note, and that after she passed it to me, she second-guessed her decision. She said she often wondered what had happened to me. And I got to thank her for saving my life.

It took time to comprehend what had happened, and keeping it a secret only made it weigh more heavily on me. Long after the breakup, as I edited an old photo of myself in a bikini poolside for Throwback Thursday, I realized that I couldn't remember what year it was taken or where. It felt disingenuous to be presenting overly filtered, long-forgotten days to the world as if they were the most significant, when in reality the day I remember most is December 30, 2016, when a stranger slipped me a handwritten note on a cocktail napkin on a non-stop flight to Iceland.

Judging by my newsfeed, my friends couldn't empathize with difficult times, so I devoured self-help books. Nothing impacted me more than a quote from my favorite author, Brené Brown, who said, "When we have the courage to walk into our story and own it, we get to write the ending."

I realized that if I wrote about how a random act of kindness saved my life, it could serve as a reminder to look out for each other. I shared a photo of the note and received dozens of messages from other domestic violence survivors who said that my post gave them the courage to write their own endings. Countless others said it was a reminder to be a Good Samaritan. Owning my story ended up being the best decision I ever made.

If you ever find yourself sitting in a chair like that woman, I hope you'll have the same courage she did, even if it's uncomfortable.

You might feel like you're crazy, and it might be way out of your comfort zone.

But maybe, just maybe, you'll help that person see the light at the end of the tunnel.

Maybe you'll end up being the stranger they never knew they needed.

— Laura Owens —

My Inner Physician

We have all a better guide in ourselves, if we would
attend to it, than any other person can be.
~Jane Austen

My wake-up call came on February 14, 2003. "Happy Valentine's Day, you have canSer"—spelled wrong to take my power back. At the time I was a thirty-one-year-old actress and photographer living in New York City, trying to get my life together and make something of myself. Sometimes I thrived; other times I could barely put the fast food on the table.

On my personal D-Day, I found myself lying on a cold exam table while a nurse named Mildred passed an ultrasound scanner across my belly. Piercing abdominal cramps and shortness of breath had forced me back to my primary care doctor. It was the same pain I had felt for three years, only magnified.

The nurse's distressed look forced me to ask her what she saw. "I can't tell you that," she sternly replied. "You'll have to speak with the doctor." Okay, I could wait a few more minutes. In walked the doctor. "The surface of your liver is covered with about a dozen lesions," he said. I had no idea what that meant. I thought lesions meant cuts and I wondered how I'd cut my liver. Yes, I regularly enjoyed a few cocktails and other recreational substances, but wasn't this an extreme result of a few indiscretions?

Then he clarified things for me. The lesions were tumors, a

twelve-pack of terror that made the ultrasound images of my liver look like Swiss cheese. But that wasn't all; about ten more tumors were in my lungs. And get this, the cancer (a rare sarcoma) was completely inoperable, no surgery, radiation, chemotherapy, and — here's the knockout punch — no known cure. Pass the Chardonnay!

In an instant I went from being a young woman with her whole life ahead of her, to being a young sick woman who didn't know how long she had to live or if her life would ever be normal again.

Second and third opinions, along with endless hours at the University of Google, followed. I quickly learned that illness was a business, and if I wanted to successfully navigate Hurricane Cancer, I needed to learn how to step up to the plate and advocate for myself. Goodbye Broadway. Hello CEO of Save My Ass Technologies, Inc.! I was suddenly the CEO of my health, and the doctors worked for me.

There were a few qualified applicants, as well as a bunch of duds. The doctor who suggested a triple organ transplant was rejected immediately. I mean, how rude! The one who gave me ten years to live didn't get the job either. Though my disease was advanced, it generally presents in three different ways: aggressive from the start, slow growing (I prayed for that version) and slow growing that becomes aggressive over time. Because I didn't know which version I had, pulling out organs, blasting my body with chemicals, or dying seemed a bit premature.

I traveled everywhere searching for my second in command and finally found him. Honestly, if it weren't for my oncologist, I might not be here today. And guess what he confirmed? The cancer was slow moving, so in essence I had the one thing all cancer patients long for — time. This great news allowed me to choose a radical course of treatment: Do nothing. My oncologist agreed. "We'll take a watch-and-wait approach," he said. "Let cancer make the first move."

Great! But how about a watch-and-LIVE approach? And what if I made the first move? If I couldn't be cured, could I still be healthy? Could I redefine wellness to include someone like me? Perhaps instead of calling it cancer, I would call it an imbalance. And what if I could find the source of the imbalance? Maybe, just maybe, I could help my body by participating in health rather than contributing to disease.

Clearly, I had a lot to learn, but I started to breathe again. The joy came back, and curiosity started bubbling.

This wouldn't be my battle: It would be the greatest adventure of my life.

Through deep exploration and experimentation, I met my Inner Physician. She's very smart and highly intuitive (just like yours). The prescription she offered was quite simple. "Gently renovate your life, kiddo. Learn to take self-care seriously. You're worth it. It's time to rest, replenish and renew. You have the power to create a life beyond your wildest dreams — even with cancer. Trust me, let's go." God I love her! Don't you?

Whole Foods literally became my new pharmacy. Did I know what I was doing when I first started? No way! I would race around the store frantically filling shopping carts with books, videos, supplements, powders, potions, and every piece of organic produce I could get my hands on. Kale? Okay! It was dark green and leafy, so it must be good for me. Yet in the back of my mind I wondered what the heck I'd do with this scary looking weed. If the cancer didn't kill me, this plant certainly might.

Over time I got the hang of it and fell in love with the kitchen. Like many people, I had no idea that this anti-inflammatory way of eating — filled with endless vitamins, minerals, phytochemicals, antioxidants and more — could be so very delicious. Caring for myself became a spiritual pursuit, rather than a pesky drag. Practices like meditation helped me deal with the wild animals in my head. Regular exercise became my stress release valve. And sleep transformed into a holy, non-negotiable, practice.

Did I mention that I quit my acting career? The new me craved something greater. I had spent too many years pretending to be someone I wasn't, getting endless rejection and beating myself up for not being good enough. When I learned to value my health, I realized that I had outgrown my career. It just wasn't right for my rhythm. Something better would come if I got out of the way and did the soul work.

Ten years later, I've been blessed to be able to reach thousands of health seekers through my books, film and website. Helping people all over the world has filled my life with both meaning and gratitude — the best medicine. While I still have cancer, it continues to be stable. That may change one day, but I don't focus on "one day." Today is what matters and today I feel better than ever before. Best of all, I'm happy.

We all have something in our lives that we wish we could change. And we each get to decide whether or not we will allow that something to hold us down. Let your obstacle become your mentor. Let your pain become your opportunity. Some form of suffering is inevitable. It's how we deal with the suffering that matters. Will you let it devour you or will you ride it straight into the brightness?

No one will give you permission to live. Change now. Love now. Live like you really mean it right now. That permission is your birthright, hot stuff; grab it!

— Kris Carr —

There Is Nothing Wrong with You

No one remains quite what he was
when he recognizes himself.
~Thomas Mann

The following story describes one of the most poignant and tender moments of my life.

I met Peter at a summer camp for the Royal National Institute of Blind People in Hampshire, England. Peter was in my class. I was teaching a day on self-esteem to 50 teenagers. They were like any large group of teenagers in school — creative, unruly, funny, boisterous, challenging, and very energetic. They were normal… and blind.

Peter was one of the few quiet ones. He sat at the back of the class. He was half-Chinese, half-English, about 15 years old, tall, and slender. There were many jokes flying around, most of them at my expense. Peter laughed heartily, but he never spoke. At the end of the class, he stayed behind.

"Mr. Holden," he said.

"Call me Robert," I said.

"Can we talk?" he asked.

"Certainly."

Peter looked troubled. He was pensive and painfully shy. We

talked small talk for a while as we walked around a large green sports field out behind the main college building.

"I feel I can trust you Robert, even though we've only just met," he said.

"That's a real compliment," I said.

"I need to ask you a question that I have been putting off my whole life," Peter said.

I was in no way prepared for Peter's question when it finally came.

"I need to know," he said, "is there anything wrong with me?"

"What do you mean?" I asked.

"I was born blind, and I have never seen myself. I need to know from someone I trust if I am beautiful or not," Peter said.

With all my heart, I told Peter that he was handsome, perfect, and beautiful.

"You really mean it?" he asked.

"Yes — totally."

Peter flung his arms around me.

"There's nothing wrong with me?"

"No!"

"Not even a little bit wrong?"

"Not one bit."

"What about my breath? I had pizza for lunch," he laughed.

"I love garlic," I countered.

We both laughed and cried. Rarely have I felt so moved. Peter's relief was such a joy to watch.

For six years I trained in a profession that focuses on finding things wrong with people. We take in "ugly ducklings" and merrily pluck away for disorders, dysfunctions, neuroses, psychoses, syndromes, and schemas. Psychology is obsessed with diagnosis. Every day we invent new labels, new diseases, and new courses of treatment for the "ugly ducklings." We never see them as swans.

The fear that something is wrong with you is your greatest block to joy. In truth, there is no other block. For as long as you feel there is something wrong, bad, lacking, or not good enough about you, your life will reflect this belief. On the face of it, it will look as though others reject you, the world blocks you, fate is unkind, life is against you, and the Heavens are punishing you. But in fact, it is you who are condemning yourself and sabotaging all that is good. Hence everything is a struggle, successes are hard-fought, happiness is short-lived, love always goes wrong, and there is no peace.

There is nothing wrong with you. Certainly, your perception can be sick. And your thinking can be off. And you can make poor choices. For instance, you can choose to see flaws in yourself that no one else sees. You can invent a story of how bad you are. You can try to convince the world how unlovable you are. Give these strange ideas all of your power, if you want, but who you are — your Unconditioned Self — remains whole, worthy, and well.

True psychotherapy is a process of changing your mind about yourself. Shift happens whenever you practice unconditional self-acceptance. Shift happens whenever you give yourself a break. Shift happens whenever you choose kindness instead of judgment, forgiveness instead of self-attack, and laughter instead of condemnation. Life always gets better when you treat yourself better.

The final (and only) act of healing is to accept that there is nothing wrong with you.

— Robert Holden —

From *Shift Happens: How to Live an Inspired Life… Starting Right Now!* Copyright 2011 by Robert Holden. Published by Hay House; available at www.hayhouse.com.

The Wise Monk

Respect yourself and others will respect you.
~Confucius

In my own life, I think one of the best examples of transparency and not taking myself too seriously came from an experience I had at a Buddhist temple here in Los Angeles. Back when I was first seeking on the personal growth and spiritual path, I was soaking up all kinds of different modalities and ways to calm my mind and get clear. For a period of time, I was really into Buddhist meditation, both Vipassana (I once went on a 10-day retreat and left after five 'cuz it was so intense) and chanting Nam Myoho Renge Kyo.

Well before I discovered these two different types of meditation, I came across a Buddhist temple in downtown Los Angeles. I found it through Yelp or Google, and decided to attend one of their dharma talks and meditations. I went, and the main monk gave a talk about dharma and the idea of being unattached to things, as well as many other Buddhist principles. I was totally engaged in the conversation and soaking up the wisdom from this man, who seemed to be a living sage. After the talk, we did a 20- or 30-minute closed eye meditation, which I thoroughly enjoyed. After the meditation, the session was over and the 30 or so people who were there started to disperse.

But being the seeker that I am, I decided to go up and talk with the monk and his other monks and I started asking all kinds of questions. Before I knew it, the morning was gone and it was lunchtime.

So, the robed and shaven-headed monks extended an invitation to me to come to lunch. I JUMPED at the idea because now I was REALLY going to get the inside scoop on all the sage wisdom these guys could offer me. I am a SPONGE for wisdom, so anytime I get around people who have something wise to share, I am all ears!

So I went out to my car and followed a small car packed with four REALLY Buddhist monks. I was so psyched because I felt like I was about to discover some amazing vegan or vegetarian dive restaurant in downtown L.A. And as we kept driving, my excitement grew and grew and grew. Where were these guys going? It was probably going to be awesome. So as we were driving, I saw their car pull into a parking lot. But I couldn't believe my eyes. Why in the world would four Buddhist monks pull into a Sizzler?

That's right — I was led to Sizzler by four shaven-headed, robe wearing, dharma talking, Buddhist monks. I couldn't believe it. I thought it must have been because their salad bar was so cheap. I mean after all, if you are a monk, you are not making six figures, so maybe we weren't going to eat at an amazing dive bar. Maybe we were just going to have a modest vegetarian salad from the Sizzler salad bar. I was cool with this. I didn't really care; I just wanted the wisdom.

So as we made our way into Sizzler, and I made it over to the salad bar first. Now I'm not a vegan or a vegetarian. I do my best to get non-factory-farmed meat and eat as consciously as possible. But in this moment, in front of the monks, I became an instant vegan. I was careful about my choices from the salad bar. No cheese. No dressings with dairy. No chicken or tuna from the salad bar. Just some lettuce, tomatoes, mushrooms, bell peppers, nuts and vinaigrette for me! It seemed like such a small meal, but so what — I was there for the wisdom. I thought I'd just get a big Diet Coke to fill me up for the rest of the meal while the monks and I got down to some serious dharma talking!

So as I came back to the seat; I saw the monks ordering food. And to my SHOCK, the wisest of the monks, the man who gave the dharma talk, ordered a STEAK! And another one ordered steak and the other two ordered chicken!

I was now in total shock.

Here I was the meat eater, pretending to be a vegan in the presence of the monks, and they were about to go to TOWN on some meat! And not meat from a local provider — SIZZLER steak and chicken! I just didn't get it.

So the meal went along and I was dying to ask them about why they were eating meat, but I just couldn't do it. We talked. Finally the meal came, boom — two steaks and two chickens! And I was stuck with my puny excuse for a salad. They even asked me if I was hungry 'cuz I had so little to eat.

So as the monks dove into their food, which included dead animals, I finally couldn't take it anymore! I popped! I stopped the conversation and said, "Okay, okay! Hold on you guys! What's up with the meat? You guys are Buddhist monks. Aren't you committed to Metta, which is unconditional love for all sentient beings?"

And without a twitch, the wise old monk looked up from his steak and looked at me and said, "We have a phrase around the Ashram…"

And then he paused. One of those dramatic wisdom pauses like something EPIC was about to come out of his mouth.

He said, "And that phrase is… Not Buddha YET!"

And with that they went about their meals.

I couldn't believe it! Are you freakin' kidding me! Not Buddha yet! In the moment it felt like a copout, but as I began to reflect on this phrase later in life, I saw the wisdom in it. Now I know what some of you must be thinking: "What a copout. So that means he can kill people, too? Because he's NOT BUDDHA YET?" This obviously shouldn't be used to justify bad behavior. That being said, I think it was one of the most honest things I've ever heard a "spiritual" person say to me.

The idea of not being Buddha yet is huge. We can let ourselves off the hook for not being spiritually "perfect" and instead take the journey into our ever so precious imperfection. We end up shriveling up our life when we do not allow ourselves to be human.

— Mastin Kipp —

My Sister, My Friend

A sister is a gift to the heart, a friend to the spirit, a
golden thread to the meaning of life.
~Isadora James

Tara looked so happy in her cheerleading uniform, like all the other girls who were a year ahead of me. And she knew every cheer well enough to teach me, even though I wasn't on the squad.

Sitting on the sidelines, with my chubby cheeks propped on my hands, I watched how she radiated confidence and poise, and thought, "Wow. I want to be like that."

Five years later, she came home from middle school with tales of lockers and crushes. She wore jeans that would never fit me and seemed to already be popular, which didn't surprise me at all.

As I sat there restricted in my scoliosis back brace, I watched her giggling on the phone with a friend, and thought, "Wow. I want to be like that."

One year later, she bounced up to the stage, ready to sing her heart out at a theater audition. As I watched from the back row, running my tongue along my braces, I considered finding a place to hide so I wouldn't have to sing next.

When she belted out the lyrics, with her head high and her arms spread wide, I stared in awe and admiration, and thought, "Wow. I want to be like that."

The years went on, and like trees planted too close together, we slowly grew apart.

When I left home at 22 after years of hurting and hiding, I wondered if she'd miss me at all.

I never knew how she felt about anything, and she never knew me right back.

She didn't know why I didn't love myself. She didn't know that I didn't believe in myself. She didn't know that I wanted to help myself, but couldn't seem to figure out how.

After years of moving, stumbling, and growing, I started finding my way. And I decided to do my best to help others who might feel a little lost.

Though I hoped I did that through my writing, I also reached out to my sister, who was going through a tough time and needed support.

Whether it was advice or an opinion or simply an ear, I wanted to give it all.

Five Christmases ago she gave something back, the best gift I'd ever received. Amid the boxes and bags and stockings and cards, there was a paper addressed to me.

It read:

There is a girl who inspires us all
She's blonde and stands around 5 feet tall
She's seen exotic locales and far away places
But she's grounded in life with the issues she faces

She's affected so many, especially me
Her story is one of great victory
Let's examine the journey that has been her life
It's had many highs, but also some strife

Academically talented at a very young age
Even early on, she made her way to the stage!
She traveled quite often and lived on her own
It's wonderful to see just how much she's grown

She is a success in the true sense of the word
To call her anything less would just be absurd!
I look up to her despite my being older
She's always been there for me, and offered her shoulder

I can't say enough on how much good she has done
When it comes to compassion, she is second to none.
What lies ahead for her you ask?
Her future is bright; she is up for the task

I love her so much and she makes me so proud
I hope she realizes, it is I she has wowed!

Tara has given me more than she may realize. After all those years of looking up to her as my sister, I'm grateful she's by my side as my friend.

—Lori Deschene—

The Golden Buddha

And now here is my secret, a very simple secret;
it is only with the heart that one can see rightly,
what is essential is invisible to the eye.
~Antoine de Saint-Exupéry

In the fall of 1988 my wife Georgia and I were invited to give a presentation on self-esteem and peak performance at a conference in Hong Kong. Since we had never been to the Far East before, we decided to extend our trip and visit Thailand.

When we arrived in Bangkok, we decided to take a tour of the city's most famous Buddhist temples. Along with our interpreter and driver, Georgia and I visited numerous Buddhist temples that day, but after a while they all began to blur in our memories.

However, there was one temple that left an indelible impression in our hearts and minds. It is called the Temple of the Golden Buddha. The temple itself is very small, probably no larger than thirty feet by thirty feet. But as we entered, we were stunned by the presence of a ten-and-a-half-foot tall, solid-gold Buddha. It weighs over two-and-a-half tons and is valued at approximately 196 million dollars! It was quite an awesome sight — the kindly gentle yet imposing solid-gold Buddha smiling down at us.

As we immersed ourselves in the normal sightseeing tasks (taking pictures while oohing and aahing over the statue), I walked over to a glass case that contained a large piece of clay about eight inches thick and twelve inches wide. Next to the glass case was a typewritten page describing the history of this magnificent piece of art.

Back in 1957 a group of monks from a monastery had to relocate a clay Buddha from their temple to a new location. The monastery was to be relocated to make room for the development of a highway through Bangkok. When the crane began to lift the giant idol, the weight of it was so tremendous that it began to crack. What's more, rain began to fall. The head monk, who was concerned about damage to the sacred Buddha, decided to lower the statue back to the ground and cover it with a large canvas tarp to protect it from the rain.

Later that evening the head monk went to check on the Buddha. He shined his flashlight under the tarp to see if the Buddha was staying dry. As the light reached the crack, he noticed a little gleam shining back and thought it strange. As he took a closer look at this gleam of light, he wondered if there might be something underneath the clay. He went to fetch a chisel and hammer from the monastery and began to chip away at the clay. As he knocked off shards of clay, the little gleam grew brighter and bigger. Many hours of labor went by before the monk stood face to face with the extraordinary solid-gold Buddha.

Historians believe that several hundred years before the head monk's discovery, the Burmese army was about to invade Thailand (then called Siam). The Siamese monks, realizing that their country would soon be attacked, covered their precious golden Buddha with an outer covering of clay in order to keep their treasure from being looted by the Burmese. Unfortunately, it appears that the Burmese slaughtered all the Siamese monks, and the well-kept secret of the golden Buddha remained intact until that fateful day in 1957.

As we flew home on Cathay Pacific Airlines I began to think to myself, "We are all like the clay Buddha, covered with a shell of hardness created out of fear, and yet underneath each of us is a 'golden Buddha,' a 'golden Christ' or a 'golden essence,' which is our real self. Somewhere along the way, between the ages of two and nine, we begin to cover up our 'golden essence,' our natural self. Much like the monk with the hammer and the chisel, our task now is to discover our true essence once again."

— Jack Canfield —

Start with Yourself

Attitude is a little thing that makes a big difference.
~Winston Churchill

The following words were written on the tomb of an Anglican Bishop in the Crypts of Westminster Abbey:

When I was young and free and my imagination had no limits, I dreamed of changing the world. As I grew older and wiser, I discovered the world would not change, so I shortened my sights somewhat and decided to change only my country.

But it, too, seemed immovable.

As I grew into my twilight years, in one last desperate attempt, I settled for changing only my family, those closest to me, but alas, they would have none of it.

And now as I lie on my deathbed, I suddenly realize: *If I had only changed my self first,* then by example I would have changed my family.

From their inspiration and encouragement, I would then have been able to better my country and, who knows, I may have even changed the world.

— Anonymous —

Nothing But the Truth!

The truth brings with it a great measure
of absolution, always.
~R.D. Laing

D avid Casstevens of the *Dallas Morning News* tells a story about Frank Szymanski, a Notre Dame center in the 1940s, who had been called as a witness in a civil suit at South Bend.

"Are you on the Notre Dame football team this year?" the judge asked.

"Yes, Your Honor."

"What position?"

"Center, Your Honor."

"How good a center?"

Szymanski squirmed in his seat, but said firmly: "Sir, I'm the best center Notre Dame has ever had."

Coach Frank Leahy, who was in the courtroom, was surprised. Szymanski always had been modest and unassuming. So when the proceedings were over, he took Szymanski aside and asked why he had made such a statement. Szymanski blushed.

"I hated to do it, Coach," he said. "But, after all, I *was* under oath."

— *Dallas Morning News* —

Covering All the Bases

Shoot for the moon. Even if you miss,
you'll land among the stars.
~Les Brown

A little boy was overheard talking to himself as he strode through his back yard, baseball cap in place and toting ball and bat. "I'm the greatest baseball player in the world," he said proudly. Then he tossed the ball in the air, swung and missed. Undaunted, he picked up the ball, threw it into the air and said to himself, "I'm the greatest player ever!" He swung at the ball again, and again he missed.

He paused a moment to examine bat and ball carefully. Then once again he threw the ball into the air and said, "I'm the greatest baseball player who ever lived." He swung the bat hard and again missed the ball.

"Wow!" he exclaimed. "What a pitcher!"

~Source Unknown

After church one Sunday morning, my five-year-old granddaughter was intently drawing on a piece of paper. When asked what she was drawing, she replied that she was drawing God.

"But no one knows what God looks like," I said.

"They will when I finish this picture!" she answered.

—Jacque Hall—

My Declaration of Self-Esteem

What I am is good enough if I would only be it openly.
~Carl Rogers

The following was written in answer to a 15-year-old girl's question, "How can I prepare myself for a fulfilling life?"

I am me.

In all the world, there is no one else exactly like me.

There are people who have some parts like me but no one adds up exactly like me. Therefore, everything that comes out of me is authentically mine because I alone choose it.

I own everything about me — my body, including everything it does; my mind, including all my thoughts and ideas; my eyes, including the images of all they behold; my feelings, whatever they might be — anger, joy, frustration, love, disappointment, excitement; my mouth and all the words that come out of it — polite, sweet and rough, correct or incorrect; my voice, loud and soft; all my actions, whether they be to others or myself.

I own my fantasies, my dreams, my hopes, my fears.

I own all my triumphs and successes, all my failures and mistakes.

Because I own all of me, I can become intimately acquainted with me. By so doing, I can love me and be friendly with me in all my parts. I can then make it possible for all of me to work in my best interests.

I know there are aspects about myself that puzzle me, and other aspects that I do not know. But as long as I am friendly and loving to myself, I can courageously and hopefully look for the solutions to the puzzles and for ways to find out more about me.

However I look and sound, whatever I say and do, and whatever I think and feel at a given moment in time is me. This is authentic and represents where I am at that moment in time.

When I review later how I looked and sounded, what I said and did, and how I thought and felt, some parts may turn out to be unfitting. I can discard that which is unfitting and keep that which proved fitting, and invent something new for that which I discarded.

I can see, hear, feel, think, say and do. I have the tools to survive, to be close to others, to be productive, to make sense and order out of the world of people and things outside of me.

I own me and therefore I can engineer me.

I am me and I am okay.

— Virginia Satir —

Response/Ability

*The willingness to accept responsibility for one's own life
is the source from which self-respect springs.*
~Joan Didion

the game we play
is let's pretend
and pretend
we're not
pretending

we choose to
forget
who we are
and then forget
that we've
forgotten

who are we really?

the center
that watches
and runs the show
that can choose

which way
it will go

the I AM
consciousness
that powerful
loving perfect
reflection
of the cosmos

but in our attempt
to cope with
early situations
we chose or were
hypnotized into
a passive position

to avoid
punishment
or the loss of love
we chose to deny
our
response/ability
pretending that
things just
happened
or that we were
being controlled
taken over
we put ourselves
down
and have become
used to this
masochistic

posture
this weakness
this indecisiveness

but we are
in reality
free
a center
of cosmic energy
your will
is your power

don't pretend
you don't have it

or you won't

— Bernard Gunther —

The Rules for Being Human

Every human being is a problem
in search of a solution.
~Ashley Montagu

1. **You will receive a body.**
   You may like it or hate it, but it will be yours for the entire period of this time around.

2. **You will learn lessons.**
   You are enrolled in a full-time informal school called Life. Each day in this school you will have the opportunity to learn lessons. You may like the lessons or think them irrelevant and stupid.

3. **There are no mistakes, only lessons.**
   Growth is a process of trial and error: Experimentation. The "failed" experiments are as much a part of the process as the experiment that ultimately "works."

4. **A lesson is repeated until learned.**
   A lesson will be presented to you in various forms until you have learned it. When you have learned it, you can then go on to the next lesson.

5. **Learning lessons does not end.**
   There is no part of life that does not contain its lessons. If you are alive, there are lessons to be learned.

6. **"There" is no better than "here."**
   When your "there" has become a "here," you will simply obtain

another "there" that will again look better than "here."

7. **Others are merely mirrors of you.**

   You cannot love or hate something about another person unless it reflects something you love or hate about yourself.

8. **What you make of your life is up to you.**

   You have all the tools and resources you need. What you do with them is up to you. The choice is yours.

9. **Your answers lie inside you.**

   The answers to Life's questions lie inside you. All you need to do is look, listen and trust.

10. **You will forget all this.**

   — Chérie Carter-Scott —

Chapter 3

On Parenting

Perhaps the greatest social service that can be rendered by anybody to the country and to mankind is to bring up a family.

~George Bernard Shaw

Training Camp

Sports is human life in microcosm.
~Howard Cosell

M y childhood sucked. Thank God.

My parents divorced when I was 18 months old. My dad took me because, frankly, my mother didn't want me. In fact, when the doctor first told my mother she was pregnant with me, her response was anger and disappointment. After I was born she was generally just disinterested in me and simply handed me over to my father. She was a woman who never really wanted to be a mother and thankfully for me she admitted that to herself and gave me up to my dad. He really didn't know what to do with me either, but was willing to "do what had to be done" (one of his favorite mantras).

My dad was only 23 years old when I was born, and back then, men didn't raise kids on their own. He had just moved from the San Francisco Bay Area to what must've seemed like the middle of nowhere (Albuquerque, New Mexico, where I was born) to be an overworked and grossly underpaid football coach for the university there. He was alone, lonely and wounded from the divorce, with no idea how to raise a son.

So he parented the only way he knew how — like he coached. That meant, no whining, no crying, no excuses, and lots of yelling. My dad was infamous on the gridiron for one of his coaching philosophies: no matter how hard a player was hit on the field and how hurt they got, they were not allowed to come out of the game. One time a linebacker got really smashed in the middle of the field, wobbled to the sideline and begged my dad to be taken out of the game. My dad grabbed him by the facemask and screamed, "Not unless you are showing bone." The player pulled his shoulder pad back and his collarbone was sticking out of his neck skin like a Thanksgiving turkey. Thus came the line I heard hundreds of times: "No, you cannot stay home from school sick, unless you are 'showing bone.'"

Get rejected, fail at something, fall down, scrape your knee? The only sympathy I heard was "Hey, No Pain, No Gain." He actually had that painted in big block letters on our garage where he would relentlessly slam around his Olympic size weight set starting at 5 every morning, without fail. Miss free throws at the basketball game? Do 1,000 free throw practice shots before you come home. Trouble dribbling with your left hand? Tie the right one around your back and dribble for eight hours. Get a 'C' in math, it's workbooks and math school all summer. No relenting. You didn't get love or attention in my house unless you achieved.

It is because of this "dysfunctional" childhood that I have become the highly functioning achiever I am today.

- Having to get over issues of abandonment caused me to become vigorously self-reliant.
- Growing up with a tough university football coach father developed my drive and self-motivation.
- Not being doted on taught me to be independent and self-reliant.
- Having to achieve for attention taught me to be goal-oriented and results-minded.

People often see their childhood or difficulties of their past as wounds they need to heal from. Instead I discovered that adversities are your advantage. It's like how you grow a muscle. You put it under intense stress and challenge it repeatedly. What you are actually doing is tearing the muscle fibers and breaking it down. Then it grows back bigger and stronger than before. You now have the muscles (mental, emotional and psychological) to achieve extraordinary things ordinary people cannot.

Somehow, in his own way, my dad was the best parent a future achiever could ever have. He was strong, disciplined and consistent. He parented/coached me to be the same. I'm incredibly grateful for my childhood training camp. In the end, it seems, my childhood was awesome!

— Darren Hardy —

See the Miracle

There are only two ways to live your life. One is as
though nothing is a miracle. The other is as though
everything is a miracle.
~Albert Einstein

It happened in an instant.

One small instant held everything—my life, her life, my family—in its clenched fists.

Beads broke in a rush of terror across my forehead as I bolted around the deck and down the stairs. My legs were moving but I couldn't feel them, couldn't register anything, or feel anything except for the fear closing in. All I wanted to know in that moment was that my daughter Jolie was alive.

It was one of those events that happened in a split-second and yet it held the potential to shift everything in my life. How I would wake up in the morning. How I would fall asleep at night. How I would kiss my two daughters as I tucked them in and watched them turn their heads to sleep.

My family and I were vacationing on a small private island in Fiji this past summer. When I say small, I mean so small that there is no way to get on or off the island unless it is pre-arranged. We were staying with friends in a beautiful house with a wrap-around balcony. The house was so high up that the drop below the balcony was nearly twenty feet.

The island has this amazing energy that I find hard to put into words. It's occupied by the indigenous people of Fiji, most of them whom have never left the island. Fiji is their home and they're very connected to the earth, the community, and each other.

There were seven or eight local Fijians who worked at the house we stayed in as caretakers and helpers. It was easy to connect with them. They were warm and engaging and had an instinct for getting to know the hearts of people. At one point, the women stopped and told us, "Your youngest daughter Jolie, she's special. There's something about her. She's an old soul and she's really here for a special purpose."

One night after dinner, our older daughter, Jemma, rushed in from the balcony after dinner screaming, "JOLIE FELL OFF THE DECK! JOLIE FELL OFF THE DECK!" I could see the terror in her eyes.

We rushed toward the screams to find our Jolie on the ground twenty feet below. She wasn't moving. My thoughts ran wild: *She's dead. She's dead. She's dead. Please God, don't let her be dead.*

In the seconds that followed I could not run fast enough, could not get there soon enough to scoop my daughter into my arms and hold her tight. The fears stacked on one another: *How will we get her off the island? How will we get her to a hospital? What will happen to my Jolie?*

I was trying to hold it together but inside I felt like I was going to pass out. There was blood coming from her head but we couldn't tell exactly how bad the injuries might be. All I knew was that she started moving and crying. Thankfully, she was alive and with us.

People gathered around her. Others started inspecting her body for injuries. Since there was no doctors or hospital on the island, one nurse that lived there got to us within twenty minutes. Everyone came together for little Jolie and my family in a remarkable way.

Racked and sucked dry from a fear I'd never known before, I still felt a strange sense of peace drop upon me. I suddenly knew things would be okay.

As we carried Jolie inside to the bedroom, the Fijian women asked if they could pray. They gathered around us holding hands. The nurse started praying in English and then, in a rhythm like a song, the Fijian women started chanting at the top of their lungs in their native tongue.

Each chanted her own prayer but the voices all flowed together in a surreal harmony. Tears stained their cheeks. Tears stained my cheeks. The room felt like it was trembling, like a power was sweeping over it and all I could do was cry and be thankful that my daughter was alive.

Hand in hand with relief came this overwhelming angst and worry that was all-consuming. I became obsessed with fear in the days ahead. The feelings were paralyzing. I could not stop analyzing the situation and asking myself: *What went wrong? How could we have prevented the accident?*

One afternoon, I called my dear friend and teacher, Guru Singh, and began bawling my eyes out as I retold him the story. He stopped me and said, "Eric, you're focusing on what didn't happen. What didn't happen is an illusion. Stop focusing on that."

"Start focusing on what *did* happen," he continued. "What did happen is a miracle. Just meditate on that and constantly put yourself in that space. You witnessed a miracle. You experienced a miracle. Your daughter lived through a miracle. Your daughter is a miracle."

His words shifted me into a new space of thinking. He was absolutely right. My daughter lived by the grace of a miracle and my only response from that point forward needed to be gratitude and appreciation for the sacred seconds that make up every moment we share together.

My daughter had only gone to get a glass of water and sixty seconds later she was on the ground, holding with her all of my heart and every dream I had for her. She was inches away from death but by such sacred grace she dropped twenty feet and walked away with barely a scratch.

Today my daughter Jolie is like any other three-year-old. She plays, goes to school, giggles with her sister and snuggles into our arms as if nothing ever happened. But it did and I will never forget it.

Not a day goes by that I don't look at her and am reminded by the miracle of life she represents. I know now, more than ever before, how precious every second of life is. I know with every breath I take how blessed each soul, young and old, is to have these moments.

Just as the Fijians said, I am convinced that my Jolie is here for such a special reason. *We all are.* And in embracing the miracle moments of our lives, we find more meaning, more purpose and appreciation, more conscious cosmic calling, gratitude and joy in all we do.

Life is so very fragile and yet we are here and I'm not taking one second for granted. My Jolie taught me that with her angelic spirit. She is my pure joy.

— Eric Handler —

Children Learn What They Live

It's not only children who grow. Parents do too.
As much as we watch to see what our children do with
their lives, they are watching us to see what we do with
ours. I can't tell my children to reach for the sun.
All I can do is reach for it, myself.
~Joyce Maynard

If children live with criticism,
   they learn to condemn.
If children live with hostility,
   they learn to fight.
If children live with fear,
   they learn to be apprehensive.
If children live with pity,
   they learn to feel sorry for themselves.
If children live with ridicule,
   they learn to be shy.
If children live with jealousy,
   they learn what envy is.
If children live with shame,
   they learn to feel guilty.

If children live with tolerance,
  they learn to be patient.
If children live with encouragement,
  they learn to be confident.
If children live with praise,
  they learn to appreciate.
If children live with approval,
  they learn to like themselves.
If children live with acceptance,
  they learn to find love in the world.
If children live with recognition,
  they learn to have a goal.
If children live with sharing,
  they learn to be generous.
If children live with honesty and fairness,
  they learn what truth and justice are.
If children live with security,
  they learn to have faith in themselves and in those around them.
If children live with friendliness,
  they learn that the world is a nice place in which to live.
If children live with serenity,
  they learn to have peace of mind.
With what are your children living?

— Dorothy L. Nolte —

Why I Chose My Father to Be My Dad

You can kiss your family and friends goodbye and put
miles between you, but at the same time you carry
them with you in your heart, your mind,
your stomach, because you do not just live
in a world but a world lives in you.
~Frederick Buechner

I grew up on a beautiful sprawling farm in Iowa, raised by parents who are often described as the "salt of the earth and the backbone of the community." They were all the things we know good parents to be: loving, committed to the task of raising their children with high expectations and a positive sense of self-regard. They expected us to do morning and evening chores, get to school on time, get decent grades and be good people.

There are six children. *Six* children! It was never my idea that there should be so many of us, but then no one consulted me. To make matters worse, fate dropped me off in the middle of the American heartland in a most harsh and cold climate. Like all children, I thought that there had been a great universal mistake and I had been placed in the wrong family — most definitely in the wrong state. I disliked coping with the elements. The winters in Iowa are so freezing cold that you have to make rounds in the middle of the night to see that livestock aren't stranded in a place where they would freeze to death. Newborn animals had to be taken in the barn and sometimes warmed up in order to be kept alive. Winters are *that* cold in Iowa!

My dad, an incredibly handsome, strong, charismatic and energetic man was always in motion. My brothers and sisters and I were in awe of him. We honored him and held him in the highest esteem. Now I understand why. There were no inconsistencies in his life. He was an honorable man, highly principled. Farming, his chosen work, was his passion; he was the best. He was at home raising and caring for animals. He felt at one with the earth and took great pride in planting and harvesting the crops. He refused to hunt out of season, even though deer, pheasants, quail and other game roamed our farmlands in abundance. He refused to use soil additives or feed the animals anything other than natural grains. He taught us why he did this and why we must embrace the same ideals. Today I can see how conscientious he was because this was in the mid-1950s before there was an attempt at universal commitment to earth-wide environmental preservation.

Dad was also a very impatient man, but not in the middle of the night when he was checking his animals during these late night rounds. The relationship we developed from these times together was simply unforgettable. It made a compelling difference in my life. I learned so much about him. I often hear men and women say they spent so little time with their fathers. Indeed the heart of today's men's groups is about groping for a father they never really knew. I knew mine.

Back then I felt as if I was secretly his favorite child, although it's quite possible that each of us six children felt that way. Now that was both good news and bad. The bad news was that I was the one selected by Dad to go with him for these midnight and early morning barnyard checks, and I absolutely detested getting up and leaving a warm bed to go out into the frosty air. But my dad was at his best and most lovable during those times. He was most understanding, patient, gentle and was a good listener. His voice was gentle and his smile made me understand my mother's passion for him.

It was during these times when he was a model teacher — always focusing on the whys, the reasons for doing. He talked endlessly for the hour or hour-and-a-half that it took to make the rounds. He talked about his war experiences, the whys of the war he served in and about the region, its people, the effects of war and its aftermath. Again and again he told his story. In school I found history all the more exciting and familiar.

He talked about what he gained from his travels and why seeing the world was so important. He instilled a need and love of traveling. I had worked in or visited some 30 countries by the time I was 30 years old.

He talked about the need and love of learning and why a formal education is important, and he talked about the difference between intelligence and wisdom. He wanted so much for me to go beyond my high school degree. "You can do it," he'd say over and over. "You're a Burres. You are bright, you have a good mind and, remember, you're a Burres." There was no way I was going to let him down. I had more than enough confidence to tackle any course of study. Eventually I completed a Ph.D. and later earned a second doctorate. Though the first doctorate was for Dad and the second for me, there was definitely a sense of curiosity and quest that made both easy to attain.

He talked about standards and values, developing character and what it meant in the course of one's life. I write and teach on a similar theme. He talked about how to make and evaluate decisions, when to cut your losses and walk away and when to stick it out, even in the face of adversity. He talked about the concept of *being and becoming* and not just *having and getting*. I still use that phrase. "Never sell out on your heart," he said. He talked about gut instincts and how to distinguish between those and emotional sells, and how to avoid being fooled by others. He said, "Always listen to your instincts and know that all the answers you'll ever need are within you. Take quiet time alone. Be still enough to find the answers within and then listen to them. Find something you love to do, then live a life that shows it. Your goals should stem from your values, and then your work will radiate your heart's desire. This will divert you from all silly distractions that will only serve to waste your time — your very life is about time — how much you can grow in whatever years you are given. Care about people," he said, "and always respect mother earth. Wherever you shall live, be sure you have full view of the trees, sky and land."

My father. When I reflect on how he loved and valued his children, I'm genuinely sorry for the youth who will never know their fathers in this way or will never feel the power of character, ethics, drive and sensitivity all in one person — as I do in mine. My dad modeled what he talked. And I always knew he was serious about me. I knew he felt me worthy, and he wanted me to see that worth.

Dad's message made sense to me because I never saw any conflict in the way he lived his life. He had thought about his life and he lived it daily. He bought and paid for several farms over time (he's as active today as he was then). He married and has loved the same woman for a lifetime. My mother and he, now married for nearly 50 years, are still inseparable sweethearts. They are the greatest lovers I've known. And he loved his family so much. I thought he was overly possessive and protective of his children, but now that I'm a parent I can understand those needs and see them for what they are. Though he thought he could save us from the measles and almost did, he vehemently refused to lose us to destructive vices. I also see how determined he was that we be caring and responsible adults.

To this day five of his children live within a few miles of him, and they have chosen a version of his lifestyle. They are devoted spouses and parents, and agriculture is their chosen work. They are without a doubt the backbone of their community. There is a twist to all this, and I suspect it's because of his taking me on those midnight rounds. I took a different direction than did the other five children. I began a career as an educator, counselor and university professor, eventually writing several books for parents and children to share what I had learned about the importance of developing self-esteem in the childhood years. My messages to my daughter, while altered a bit, are the values that I learned from my father, tempered with my life experiences, of course. They continue to be passed on.

I should tell you a bit about my daughter. She's a tomboy, a beautiful 5 foot 9 athlete who letters in three sports each year, frets over the difference between an A- and a B, and was just named a finalist in the Miss Teen California contest. But it's not her outward gifts and accomplishments that remind me of my parents. People always tell me that my daughter possesses a great kindness, a spirituality, a special fire deep inside that radiates outward. The essence of my parents is personified in their granddaughter.

The rewards of their children and being dedicated parents have had a most nourishing effect on the lives of my parents as well. As of this writing, my father is at the Mayo Clinic in Rochester, Minnesota, for a battery of tests, scheduled to take from six to eight days. It is December. Because of the harsh winter, he took a hotel room near the clinic (as an outpatient). Because of obligations at home, my mother was only able to stay with him for the first few days. So on Christmas Eve, they were apart.

That night I first called my dad in Rochester to say Merry Christmas. He sounded down and despondent. Then, I called my mother in Iowa. She was sad and morose. "This is the first time your father and I have ever spent the holidays apart," she lamented. "It's just not Christmas without him."

I had 14 dinner guests arriving, all ready for a festive evening. I returned to cooking, but not being able to get my parents' dilemma fully off my mind, I called my older sister. She called my brothers. We conferenced by phone. It was settled. Determined that our parents should not be without each other on Christmas Eve, my younger brother would drive the two hours to Rochester to pick up my father and bring him home without telling my mother. I called my father to tell him of the plans. "Oh, no," he said, "it's far too dangerous to come out on a night like this." My brother arrived in Rochester and knocked at my father's hotel door. He called me from Dad's room to tell me he wouldn't go. "You have to tell him, Bobbie. You're the only one he'll listen to."

"Go, Dad," I said gently.

He did. Tim and my dad started for Iowa. We kids kept track of their progress, the journey and the weather by talking with them on my brother's car phone. By now, all my guests had arrived and all were a part of this undertaking. Whenever the phone rang, we put it on the speakerphone so we could hear the latest! It was just past 9:00 when the phone rang and it was Dad on the car phone, "Bobbie, how can I possibly go home without a gift for your mom? It would be the first time in nearly 50 years I didn't get her perfume for Christmas!" By now my entire dinner party was engineering this plan. We called my sister to get the names of nearby open shopping centers so they could stop for the only gift my dad would consider giving Mom — the same brand of perfume he has given her every year at Christmas.

At 9:52 that evening, my brother and my dad left a little shopping mall in Minnesota for the trip home. At 11:50 they drove into the farmstead. My father, acting like a giggling schoolboy, stepped around the corner of the house and stood out of sight.

"Mom, I visited Dad today and he said to bring you his laundry," my brother said as he handed my mom the suitcases.

"Oh," she said softly and sadly, "I miss him so much, I might as well do these now."

Said my father coming out from hiding, "You won't have time to do them tonight."

After my brother called me to relay this touching scene between our parents — these two friends and lovers — I phoned my mother. "Merry Christmas, Mother!"

"Oh, you kids…" she said in a cracking voice, choking back tears. She was unable to continue. My guests cheered. Though I was 2,000 miles away from them, it was one of the most special Christmases I've shared with my parents. And, of course, to date my parents have not been apart on Christmas Eve. That's the strength of children who love and honor their parents and, of course, the committed and marvelous marriage my parents share.

"Good parents," Jonas Salk once told me, "give their children roots and wings. Roots to know where home is, wings to fly away and exercise what's been taught them." If gaining the skills to lead one's life purposefully and having a safe nest and being welcomed back to it is the legacy of parents, then I believe I chose my parents well. It was this past Christmas that I most fully understood why it was necessary that these two people be my parents. Though wings have taken me around the globe, eventually to nest in lovely California, the roots my parents gave me will be an indelible foundation forever.

— Bettie B. Youngs —

The Animal School

You don't get harmony when everybody
sings the same note.
~Doug Floyd

O nce upon a time, the animals decided they must do something heroic to meet the problems of "a new world." So they organized a school.

They adopted an activity curriculum consisting of running, climbing, swimming and flying. To make it easier to administer the curriculum, all the animals took all the subjects.

The duck was excellent in swimming, in fact better than his instructor, but he made only passing grades in flying and was very poor in running. Since he was slow in running, he had to stay after school and also drop swimming in order to practice running. This was kept up until his webbed feet were badly worn and he was only average in swimming. But average was acceptable in school, so nobody worried about that except the duck.

The rabbit started at the top of the class in running, but had a nervous breakdown because of so much makeup work in swimming.

The squirrel was excellent in climbing until he developed frustration in the flying class where his teacher made him start from the ground up instead of from the treetop down. He also developed a "charley horse" from overexertion and then got a C in climbing and a D in running.

The eagle was a problem child and was disciplined severely. In the climbing class he beat all the others to the top of the tree, but insisted on using his own way to get there.

At the end of the year, an abnormal eel that could swim exceedingly well, and also run, climb and fly a little, had the highest average and was valedictorian.

The prairie dogs stayed out of school and fought the tax levy because the administration would not add digging and burrowing to the curriculum. They apprenticed their children to a badger and later joined the groundhogs and gophers to start a successful private school.

Does this fable have a moral?

— George H. Reavis —

Touched

A father is always making his baby into a little woman.
And when she is a woman he turns her back again.
~Enid Bagnold

She is my daughter and is immersed in the turbulence of her 16th year. Following a recent bout with illness, she learned her best friend would soon be moving away. School was not going as well as she had hoped, nor as well as her mother and I had hoped. She exuded sadness through a muffle of blankets as she huddled in bed, searching for comfort. I wanted to reach out to her and wrench away all the miseries that had taken root in her young spirit. Yet, even aware of how much I cared for her and wanted to remove her unhappiness, I knew the importance of proceeding with caution.

As a family therapist I've been well educated about inappropriate expressions of intimacy between fathers and daughters, primarily by clients whose lives have been torn apart by sexual abuse. I'm also aware of how easily care and closeness can be sexualized, especially by men who find the emotional field foreign territory and who mistake any expression of affection for sexual invitation. How much easier it was to hold and comfort her when she was two or three or even seven. But now her body, our society and my manhood all seemed to conspire against my comforting my daughter. How could I console her while still respecting the necessary boundaries between a father and a teenage daughter? I settled for offering her a back rub. She consented.

I gently massaged her bony back and knotted shoulders as I apologized for my recent absence. I explained that I had just returned from the international back-rubbing finals, where I had placed fourth. I assured her that it's hard to beat the back rub of a concerned father, especially if he's a world-class back-rubbing concerned father. I told her all about the contest and the other contestants as my hands and fingers sought to loosen tightened muscles and unlock the tensions in her young life.

I told her about the shrunken antique Asian man who had placed third in the contest. After studying acupuncture and acupressure his entire life, he could focus all his energy into his fingers, elevating back rubbing to an art. "He poked and prodded with prestidigitatious precision," I explained, showing my daughter a sample of what I'd learned from the old man. She groaned, though I wasn't sure whether in response to my alliteration or my touch. Then I told her about the woman who had placed second. She was from Turkey and since her childhood had practiced the art of belly dancing, so she could make muscles move and ripple in fluid motion. With her back rub, her fingers awakened in tired muscles and weary bodies an urge to vibrate and quiver and dance. "She let her fingers do the walking and the muscles tagged along," I said, demonstrating.

"That's weird," emanated faintly from a face muffled by a pillow. Was it my one-liner or my touch?

Then I just rubbed my daughter's back and we settled into silence. After a time she asked, "So who got first place?"

"You'd never believe it!" I said. "It was a baby!" And I explained how the soft, trusting touches of an infant exploring a world of skin and smells and tastes was like no other touch in the world. Softer than soft. Unpredictable, gentle, searching. Tiny hands saying more than words could ever express. About belonging. About trust. About innocent love. And then I gently and softly touched her as I had learned from the infant. I recalled vividly her own infancy—holding her, rocking her, watching her grope and grow into her world. I realized that she, in fact, was the infant who had taught me about the touch of the infant.

After another period of gentle back rubbing and silence, I said I was glad to have learned so much from the world's expert back rubbers. I explained how I had become an even better back rubber for a 16-year-old daughter painfully stretching herself into adult shape. I offered a silent prayer of thanks that such life had been placed in my hands and that I was blessed with the miracle of touching even a part of it.

—Victor Nelson—

I Love You, Son

Kids spell love T-I-M-E.
~John Crudele

Thoughts while driving my son to school: Morning, Kid. You look pretty sharp in your Cub Scout gear, not as fat as your old man when he was a Cub. I don't think my hair was ever as long until I went away to college, but I think I'd recognize you anyway by what you are: a little shaggy around the ears, scuffed around the toes, wrinkled in the knees. We get used to one another.

Now that you're eight I notice I don't see a whole lot of you anymore. On Columbus Day you left at nine in the morning. I saw you for 42 seconds at lunch and you reappeared for supper at five. I miss you, but I know you've got serious business to take care of. Certainly as serious as, if not more important than, the things the other commuters on the road are doing.

You've got to grow up and out and that's more important than clipping coupons, arranging stock options or selling people short. You've got to learn what you are able to do and what you aren't — and you've got to learn how to deal with that. You've got to learn about people and how they behave when they don't feel good about themselves — like the bullies who hang out at the bike rack and hassle the smaller kids. Yeah, you'll even have to learn how to pretend that name-calling doesn't hurt. It'll always hurt, but you'll have to put up a front or they'll call you worse names next time. I only hope you remember how it feels — in case you ever decide to rank a kid who's smaller than you.

When was the last time I told you I was proud of you? I guess if I can't remember, I've got work to do. I remember the last time I yelled at you — told you we'd be late if you didn't hurry — but, on balance, as Nixon used to say, I haven't given you as many pats as yells. For the record, in case you read this, I am proud of you. I especially like your independence, the way you take care of yourself even when it frightens me just a little bit. You've never been much of a whiner and that makes you a superior kid in my book.

Why is it that fathers are so slow to realize that eight-year-olds need as many hugs as four-year-olds? If I don't watch out, pretty soon I'll be punching you on the arm and saying, "Whaddaya say, kid?!" instead of hugging you and telling you I love you. Life is too short to hide affection. Why is it that eight-year-olds are so slow to realize that 36-year-olds need as many hugs as four-year-olds?

Did I forget to tell you that I'm proud you went back to a box lunch after one week's worth of that indigestible hot lunch? I'm glad you value your body.

I wish the drive weren't so short. I want to talk about last night when your younger brother was asleep and we let you stay up and watch the Yankees game. Those times are so special. There's no way you can plan them. Every time we try to plan something together, it's not as good or rich or warm. For a few all-too-short minutes it was as if you'd already grown up and we sat and talked without any words about "How are you doing in school, son?" I'd already checked your math homework the only way I could — with a calculator.

You're better with numbers than I'll ever be. So, we talked about the game and you knew more about the players than I did and I learned from you. And we were both happy when the Yankees won.

Well, there's the crossing guard. He'll probably outlive all of us. I wish you didn't have to go to school today. There are so many things I want to say.

Your exit from my car is so quick. I want to savor the moment

and you've already spotted a couple of your friends.
I just wanted to say "I love you, son."

—Victor B. Miller—

What You Are Is as Important as What You Do

To bring up a child in the way he should go,
travel that way yourself once in a while.
~Josh Billings

t was a sunny Saturday afternoon in Oklahoma City. My friend and proud father Bobby Lewis was taking his two little boys to play miniature golf. He walked up to the fellow at the ticket counter and said, "How much is it to get in?"

The young man replied, "$3.00 for you and $3.00 for any kid who is older than six. We let them in free if they are six or younger. How old are they?"

Bobby replied, "The lawyer's three and the doctor is seven, so I guess I owe you $6.00."

The man at the ticket counter said, "Hey, Mister, did you just win the lottery or something? You could have saved yourself three bucks. You could have told me that the older one was six; I wouldn't have known the difference."

Bobby replied, "Yes, that may be true, but the kids would have known the difference."

As Ralph Waldo Emerson said, "Who you are speaks so loudly I can't hear what you're saying." In challenging times when ethics are more important than ever before, make sure you set a good example for everyone you work and live with.

— Patricia Fripp —

The Perfect American Family

One of the virtues of being very young is that you don't
let the facts get in the way of your imagination.
~Sam Levenson

t is 10:30 on a perfect Saturday morning and we are, for the moment, the perfect American family. My wife has taken our six-year-old to his first piano lesson. Our 14-year-old has not yet roused from his slumber. The four-year-old watches tiny, anthropomorphic beings hurl one another from cliffs in the other room. I sit at the kitchen table reading the newspaper.

Aaron Malachi, the four-year-old, apparently bored by the cartoon carnage and the considerable personal power obtained by holding the television's remote control, enters my space.

"I'm hungry," he says.

"Want some more cereal?"

"No."

"Want some yogurt?"

"No."

"Want some eggs?"

"No. Can I have some ice cream?"

"No."

For all I know, ice cream may be far more nourishing than processed cereal or antibiotic-laden eggs but, according to my cultural values, it is wrong to have ice cream at 10:45 on a Saturday morning.

Silence. About four seconds. "Daddy, we have very much of life left, don't we?"

"Yes, we have lots of life left, Aaron."

"Me and you and Mommy?"

"That's right."

"And Isaac?"

"Yes."

"And Ben?"

"Yes. You and me and Mommy and Isaac and Ben."

"We have very much of life left. Until all the people die."

"What do you mean?"

"Until all the people die and the dinosaurs come back."

Aaron sits down on the table, cross-legged like a Buddha, in the center of my newspaper.

"What do you mean, Aaron, 'until all the people die'?"

"You said everybody dies. When everybody dies, then the dinosaurs will come back. The cavemen lived in caves, dinosaur caves. Then the dinosaurs came back and squished 'em."

I realize that already for Aaron life is a limited economy, a resource with a beginning and an end. He envisions himself and us somewhere along that trajectory, a trajectory that ends in uncertainty and loss.

I am faced with an ethical decision. What should I do now? Should I attempt to give him God, salvation, eternity? Should I toss him some spiel like, "Your body is just a shell and after you die, we will all be together in spirit forever"?

Or should I leave him with his uncertainty and his anxiety because I think it's real? Should I try to make him an anxious existentialist or should I try to make him feel better?

I don't know. I stare at the newspaper. The Celtics are consistently losing on Friday nights. Larry Bird is angry at somebody, but I can't see who, because Aaron's foot is in the way. I don't know but my neurotic, addictive, middle-class sensibility is telling me that this is a very important moment, a moment when Aaron's ways of constructing his world are being formed. Or maybe my neurotic, addictive, middle-class sensibility is just making me think that. If life and death are an illusion, then why should I trifle with how someone else understands them?

On the table Aaron plays with an "army guy," raising his arms and balancing him on his shaky legs. It was Kevin McHale that Larry Bird was angry at. No, not Kevin McHale, it was Jerry Sichting. But Jerry Sichting is no longer with the Celtics. Whatever happened to Jerry Sichting? Everything dies; everything comes to an end. Jerry Sichting is playing for Sacramento or Orlando or he has disappeared.

I should not trifle with how Aaron understands life and death because I want him to have a solid sense of structure, a sense of the permanence of things. It's obvious what a good job the nuns and priests did with me. It was agony or bliss. Heaven and hell were not connected by long distance service. You were on God's team or you were in the soup, and the soup was hot. I don't want Aaron to get burned, but I want him to have a strong frame. The neurotic but unavoidable anxiety can come later.

Is that possible? It is possible to have a sense that God, spirit, karma, Y*H*W*H, something — is transcendent, without traumatizing the presentness of a person, without beating it into them? Can we have our cake and eat it too, ontologically speaking? Or is their fragile sensibility, their "there-ness," sundered by such an act?

Sensing a slight increase in agitation on the table, I know that Aaron is becoming bored with his guy. With an attitude of drama benefiting the moment, I clear my throat and begin with a professional tone.

"Aaron, death is something that some people believe…."

"Dad," Aaron interrupts, "could we play a video game? It's not a very violent game," he explains, hands gesticulating. "It's not like a killing game. The guys just kind of flop over."

"Yes," I say with some relief, "let's play video games. But first there's something else we have to do."

"What?" Aaron stops and turns from where he has run, already halfway to the arcade.

"First, let's have some ice cream."

Another perfect Saturday for a perfect family. For now.

— Michael Murphy —

Just Say It!

*If you were going to die soon and had only one phone
call you could make, who would you call and what
would you say? And why are you waiting?*
~Stephen Levine

One night, after reading one of the hundreds of parenting books I've read, I was feeling a little guilty because the book had described some parenting strategies I hadn't used in a while. The main strategy was to talk with your child and use those three magic words: "I love you." It had stressed over and over that children need to know unconditionally and unequivocally that you really love them.

I went upstairs to my son's bedroom and knocked on the door. As I knocked, all I could hear were his drums. I knew he was there but he wasn't answering. So I opened the door and, sure enough, there he was sitting with his earphones on, listening to a tape and playing his drums. After I leaned over to get his attention, I said to him, "Tim, have you got a second?"

He said, "Oh sure, Dad. I'm always good for one." We proceeded to sit down and after about 15 minutes and a lot of small talk and stuttering, I just looked at him and said,

"Tim, I really love the way you play drums."

He said, "Oh, thanks, Dad, I appreciate it."

I walked out the door and said, "See you later!" As I was walking downstairs, it dawned on me that I went up there with a certain message and had not delivered it. I felt it was really important to get back up there and have another chance to say those three magic words.

Again I climbed the stairs, knocked on the door and opened it. "You got a second, Tim?"

"Sure, Dad. I'm always good for a second or two. What do you need?"

"Son, the first time I came up here to share a message with you, something else came out. It really wasn't what I wanted to share with you. Tim, do you remember when you were learning how to drive, it caused me a lot of problems? I wrote three words and slipped them under your pillow in hopes that would take care of it. I'd done my part as a parent and expressed my love to my son." Finally after a little small talk, I looked at Tim and said, "What I want you to know is that we love you."

He looked at me and said, "Oh, thanks, Dad. That's you and Mom?"

I said, "Yeah, that's both of us, we just don't express it enough."

He said, "Thanks, that means a lot. I know you do."

I turned around and walked out the door. As I was walking downstairs, I started thinking, "I can't believe this. I've already been up there twice — I know what the message is and yet something else comes out of my mouth."

I decided I'm going back there now and let Tim know exactly how I feel. He's going to hear it directly from me. I don't care if he is six feet tall! So back I go, knock on the door and he yells "Wait a minute. Don't tell me who it is. Could that be you, Dad?"

I said, "How'd you know that?" and he responded, "I've known you ever since you were a parent, Dad."

Then I said "Son, have you got just one more second?"

"You know I'm good for one, so come on in. I suppose you didn't tell me what you wanted to tell me?"

I said, "How'd you know that?"

"I've known you ever since I was in diapers."

I said, "Well, here it is, Tim, what I've been holding back on. I just want to express to you how special you are to our family. It's not what you do, and it's not what you've done, like all the things you're doing with the junior high kids in town. It's who you are as a person. I love you and I just wanted you to know I love you, and I don't know why I hold back on something so important."

He looked at me and he said, "Hey, Dad, I know you do and it's really special hearing you say it to me. Thanks so much for your thoughts, as well as the intent." As I was walking out the door, he said, "Oh, hey, Dad. Have you got another second?"

I started thinking, "Oh no. What's he going to say to me?" I said, "Oh sure. I'm always good for one."

I don't know where kids get this — I'm sure it couldn't be from their parents, but he said, "Dad, I just want to ask you one question."

I said, "What's that?"

He looked at me and said, "Dad, have you been to a workshop or something like that?"

I'm thinking, "Oh no, like any other 18-year-old, he's got my number," and I said,

"No, I was reading a book, and it said how important it is to tell your kids how you really feel about them."

"Hey, thanks for taking the time. Talk to you later, Dad."

I think what Tim taught me, more than anything else that night, is that the only way you can understand the real meaning and purpose of love is to be willing to pay the price. You have to go out there and risk sharing it.

— Gene Bedley —

A Legacy of Love

Always kiss your children goodnight
— even if they're already asleep.
~H. Jackson Brown, Jr.

As a young man, Al was a skilled artist, a potter. He had a wife and two fine sons. One night, his older son developed a severe stomachache. Thinking it was only some common intestinal disorder, neither Al nor his wife took the condition very seriously. But the malady was actually acute appendicitis, and the boy died that night.

Knowing the death could have been prevented if he had only realized the seriousness of the situation, Al's emotional health deteriorated under the enormous burden of his guilt. To make matters worse his wife left him a short time later, leaving him alone with his six-year-old younger son. The hurt and pain of the two situations were more than Al could handle, and he turned to alcohol to help him cope. In time Al became an alcoholic.

As the alcoholism progressed, Al began to lose everything he possessed — his home, his land, his art objects, everything. Eventually Al died alone in a San Francisco motel room.

When I heard of Al's death, I reacted with the same disdain the world shows for one who ends his life with nothing material to show for it. "What a complete failure!" I thought. "What a totally wasted life!"

As time went by, I began to re-evaluate my earlier harsh judgment.

You see, I knew Al's now adult son, Ernie. He is one of the kindest, most caring, most loving men I have ever known. I watched Ernie with his children and saw the free flow of love between them. I knew that kindness and caring had to come from somewhere.

I hadn't heard Ernie talk much about his father. It is so hard to defend an alcoholic. One day I worked up my courage to ask him. "I'm really puzzled by something," I said. "I know your father was basically the only one to raise you. What on earth did he do that you became such a special person?"

Ernie sat quietly and reflected for a few moments. Then he said, "From my earliest memories as a child until I left home at 18, Al came into my room every night, gave me a kiss and said, 'I love you, son.'"

Tears came to my eyes as I realized what a fool I had been to judge Al as a failure. He had not left any material possessions behind. But he had been a kind loving father, and he left behind one of the finest, most giving men I have ever known.

— Bobbie Gee —
Winning the Image Game

Chicken Soup
for the Soul

On Learning

Learning is finding out what you already know.
Doing is demonstrating that you know it.
Teaching is reminding others that they know it just as well as you.
You are all learners, doers, teachers.

~Richard Bach

The Best Seat in the House

The question is not what you look at, but what you see.
~Henry David Thoreau

"You can have them," my friend offered.

"No, that's OK," I replied.

"I'm serious," he said. "They're yours."

"We'll be fine," I said. "We already have tickets."

"But these are twenty rows behind home plate. They're perfect."

"I know, but like I said, we already have tickets."

"Did you hear what I said?" my friend asked. "Twenty. Rows. Behind. Home. Plate. It doesn't get better."

And so the conversation went the day I decided to take my volunteer Little Brother to his first-ever professional baseball game.

It was a perfect night. The peanuts were fresh, the grass was recently mowed, the hot dog buns were soft (not too soft — not mushy — just right). Ryan (not his real name) was ten years old; I was almost thirty. Without a doubt, going to the game was a big deal. Why? I wasn't sure — I wasn't even that big a baseball fan myself. But surely every kid should have a chance to go to a real baseball game.

To commemorate the event, we even went to the local sporting goods store earlier in the week to try on some baseball mitts. I tossed Ryan one of the smaller-sized gloves, then continued rummaging through the aisle, looking for a baseball.

"How's it fit?" I asked.

He didn't answer.

And by the time I turned around, I understood why. Instead of putting the glove on his catching hand, he had put it on his throwing hand. The wrong hand. I couldn't believe it. Ten years old and he'd never, ever worn a baseball glove. So now it's the night of the game. The sun is about to set at Camden Yards, the home of Maryland's beloved Baltimore Orioles, and I'm ready to show Ryan how real baseball is enjoyed. I buy a hot dog, grab a program and even pick up a bag of peanuts. Sure, I want to give him the full experience, but I also don't want to spoil him — which is why I cringe when Ryan asks me the all-important question: "Where are our seats?"

It's a simple question. Where are we sitting? Are we in the outfield? Along the first base line? Back in the upper decks? In many ways, where you sit affects your whole view of the game. Indeed, I thought the same thing myself when my friend offered me his season tickets a few days earlier. It was an incredibly thoughtful offer; Chuck's seats were twenty rows behind home plate. As he said, they don't get much better. But as I prepared for our visit to the ballpark, all I kept thinking was: "If I take Ryan to those incredible seats, won't I be sending him the wrong message? Won't I be spoiling him, potentially ruining all of his subsequent ballpark visits?" Sure, I obviously was overthinking it, but I made my decision: It's better to take him to seats in the bleachers, then slowly — after a few games — work our way to the good seats up front. Teach him to appreciate the world. That's the better life lesson.

So there we are, walking up to our seats in far left field. In truth, they are bad seats. We can barely see home plate, much less the infield. The only thing we are close to is the scoreboard, and even then, it's on our far left. But as we find our aisle and make our way over to our seats, Ryan studies the view and takes it all in. He looks at the bright-green grass — the glare of the lights — and all the people surrounding us. And then, this ten-year-old boy who never has been to a ballpark in his entire life turns to me and says, "These are the best seats in the whole place."

I almost fall over right there. A wide smile takes his face. And mine.

As I said, it was a perfect night. But somehow, it just got better.

—Brad Meltzer—

I Am Happiness

*Most folks are about as happy as they
make up their minds to be.*
~Abraham Lincoln

I once witnessed a most delightful conversation between a mother and her young daughter. The whole conversation lasted barely a minute, and yet I have never forgotten it. It happened while I was sitting in a busy terminal at the New Delhi international airport, in India, waiting for my flight to be announced. The mother and her daughter, who was named Angela, were sitting opposite me. Angela, who was about three years old, was talking and drawing, talking and eating, talking and reading. Meanwhile, her mother was busy sorting out plane tickets and passports.

Although I could hear Angela talking, I wasn't really listening to what she was saying until she suddenly announced, "I am happiness, Mummy." The words caught my ear. And I found myself smiling. *What a great thought,* I thought to myself. After that, Angela leaned over and tugged on her mother's T-shirt so as to get her full attention.

"I am happiness, Mummy," said Angela.

"What, darling?" her mother asked.

"I am happiness, Mummy," repeated Angela.

"No, darling. What you mean to say is, 'I am happy,'" explained her mother.

"No, Mummy," explained Angela. "I am happiness."

By now, I noticed that several other passengers were listening in on the conversation. Angela's mother noticed also. She was a little embarrassed, but we all realized just how sweet and funny the moment was.

"I — am — happy," said Angela's mother in a slow and deliberate voice.

"I — am — happiness," replied Angela in a slow and deliberate voice.

Her mother smiled. "Okay, Angela, you are happiness."

"Yes, Mummy, I am happiness," said Angela, nodding her head.

And that was it. A short and sweet conversation finished as suddenly as it had started. But it really got me thinking.

How would you live your life if you knew you were already happy? Imagine how you would be. Imagine how good you would feel if you knew that your original nature is already happy. Imagine exactly how you would greet each new day knowing that *you are what you seek.* Imagine how much love and healing you would experience if you changed the purpose of your relationships from *finding happiness* to *sharing happiness.* Imagine how fantastic and successful you'd be if you followed your joy and you let your happiness shine through you. Imagine how you would be.

Imagine if, just for one moment, you surrendered completely to the original joy of your true nature. What a baptism that would be! Imagine how freeing it would be if you no longer needed the world to *make you happy.* What a blessing for all! Imagine how rich you would feel knowing your happiness is not separate from you and hidden away inside some external thing. Imagine how your attitude toward money would change. Imagine how much you would let yourself relax and *enjoy each moment* if you knew your joy is always with you and not someplace else. Imagine how your attitude to time would change. Imagine how you would be.

Imagine if every day you were to let the original joy of your *being* bless you and refresh you. Imagine if you made the purpose of your life not to *get happiness* but to *spread happiness.* Imagine how much you would enjoy yourself. Imagine how generous you would be. Imagine how kind you would be. Imagine what a great friend you would be. If you lived your life in the knowledge that your *being* is already happy, you would be free to be the person you "came to be." Being already happy, you would not be afraid to love. In fact, you would probably become the most loving person you could possibly imagine.

Imagine how that would be.

— Robert Holden —

From *Be Happy: Release the Power of Happiness in You*. Copyright 2009 by Robert Holden. Published by Hay House; available at www.hayhouse.com.

A Light in the Darkness

*Sadness flies on the wings of the morning and out of
the heart of darkness comes the light.*
~Jean Giraudoux

On December 14, 2012, to the collective shock of the world, twenty young children and six adults were killed in the Newtown, Connecticut school shooting. When I first heard about the event, I felt the same feelings we all feel when such tragedy happens, grief, sadness, anger, doubt about this world — but this time, with this shooting in particular, something was different.

Because I live in Newtown, Connecticut.

We've all heard the phrase "a little too close for comfort" or "too close to home" and in this case, it finally came true for me. No longer could I just watch on the news and say, "How sad…" as something happened yet again, in another town, another country, somewhere else. This time, it hit home, literally, and I could no longer allow myself to ignore the fact that at the deepest level, something had to change and I had to do whatever I could to play my part in that change.

Whether by coincidence or some sort of grand design, I've spent the last ten years studying, documenting and sharing a technique called "EFT," or simply, "Tapping." A combination of Ancient Chinese Acupressure and modern psychology, tapping has proven to be extraordinarily effective in dealing with trauma, PTSD, stress and many of the accompanying conditions from events such as this shooting. So on that fateful day, I said to myself, "As terrible as all of this is, there's an opening here for real change." After countless hours of consultations with experts around the world, in tapping, disaster relief, PTSD and more, a plan was in place.

Dr. Lori Leyden, a bright light in the world who has spent years working with genocide survivors in Rwanda, helping them heal their deepest wounds, landed just days after the tragedy. A team of over forty volunteers came together within the week to get trained in the technique, and help work with the population. And sure enough, within days, we started meeting with parents who had lost their precious children, teachers from the school, kids from the school, first-responders and more.

Our focus with each one of them was using this powerful technique to heal the trauma they had experienced, release the stress, and allow them to actually experience the grief they needed to feel. Unfortunately, all too often, when trauma is active in the mind and body, one doesn't have an opportunity to truly experience grief, a deep, necessary and often beautiful emotion.

The work continues and I'm sure it will be that way for years to come, but I'm happy to report that within the midst of such horrible tragedy, the miracles and love that I've seen have been truly remarkable.

A mother who used to hit her children, finally acknowledging she needs to change, healing her deepest old wounds, and finding a new approach to parenting.

A first-responder, initially haunted by the memories of that day, healing, letting the memories go, and rededicating his life to a message of love and compassion.

A mother who lost her child that day, connecting with her other child and committing to healing that relationship on every level.

The community, supporting each other, embracing a message of love, of healing, and forgiveness.

I know nobody here in the community will ever forget that fateful day, but it's my hope, my expectation, that each person here, and around the world, can take that tragedy and use it to remember to love more, to forgive, to heal. It's only with that approach and that intention that we can create a world where this never happens again.

— Nick Ortner —

A Visit with Grandfather

What we speak becomes the house we live in.
~Hafiz

I was born into an ancient wisdom tradition known as Toltec. My grandfather was an old *nagual* (shaman), and I worked hard all my youth to earn his respect.

As a teenager, I wanted to impress him with my opinions about everything I was learning in school. I told him my point of view about all the injustice in the world, about the violence and the conflict between good and evil. Grandfather listened patiently, which encouraged me to speak even more. Then I noticed a little smile on his face as he said, "Miguel, those are very good theories that you've learned, but everything you've told me is just a story. It doesn't mean that it's true."

Of course I felt bad and tried to defend my point of view, but then grandfather started to talk. "Most people believe there's a great conflict in the universe — a conflict between good and evil. Well, the conflict only exists in the human mind. It's not true for the rest of nature. And the real conflict in our mind is between the truth and lies. Good and evil are the *result* of that conflict.

"Believing in the truth creates goodness, love, happiness. Believing in lies and defending those lies creates what you call *evil*. It creates all the injustice and violence, all the drama and suffering, not only in society, but also in the individual."

Hmm… what grandfather said was logical, but I didn't believe him. How could all the conflict and suffering in the world be the result of something so simple? Surely it must be more complicated than that.

"Miguel, all the drama in your personal life is the result of believing in lies. And the first lie you believe is *I'm not good enough, I'm not perfect.* Everyone is born perfect and will die perfect because only perfection exists. But if you believe you aren't good enough, *thy will be done* because that is the power and magic of your faith. With that lie you begin to search for an *image of perfection* that you can never become. You search for love, for justice, for everything you believe you don't have, not knowing that everything you are searching for is already inside you. Humanity is the way it is because collectively we believe in lies that come from thousands of years ago. We react to those lies with anger and violence, but they're only lies."

I was wondering how to know the truth when my grandfather said, "We can perceive truth with our feelings, but as soon as we try to describe it with words, we distort it, and it's no longer truth. It's our story.

"Imagine that Pablo Picasso painted a portrait of you. You say, 'I don't look like that,' and Picasso says, 'Of course you do. This is how I see you.' For Picasso, it's true; he is expressing what he perceives. Well, everyone is an artist — a storyteller with a unique point of view. We use words to make a portrait of everything we witness. We make up stories, and just like Picasso we distort the truth; but for us, it *is* the truth. When we understand this, we no longer try to impose our story on others or defend what we believe. As artists, we respect the right of all artists to create their own art."

In that moment, my grandfather gave me the opportunity to become aware of all the lies we believe. Every time we judge ourselves, find ourselves guilty, and punish ourselves, it's because we believe in lies. Every time we have a conflict with our parents, our children, or our beloved, it's because we believe in lies, and they believe in them, too.

How many lies do you hear in your head? Who is judging, who is talking, who is the one with all the opinions? If you don't enjoy your life, it's because the voice in your head won't allow you to enjoy it. I call it *the voice of knowledge* because it's telling you everything you *know*, and that knowledge is contaminated with lies.

Well, if you follow two rules, the lies won't survive your skepticism and will simply disappear. First, listen to your story, but *don't believe yourself* because now you know your story is mostly fiction. Second, listen to others tell their story, but *don't believe them*. Truth survives our skepticism, but lies only survive if we *believe* them.

Just being aware of the lies that exist makes us aware that truth also exists. And by cleaning up the lies we believe about ourselves, the lies we believe about everybody else will change. Only the truth will lead us back to love, and this is a big step toward healing the human mind.

— don Miguel Ruiz —

I Like Myself Now

Once you see a child's self-image begin to improve,
you will see significant gains in achievement areas,
but even more important, you will see a child who is
beginning to enjoy life more.
~Wayne Dyer

had a great feeling of relief when I began to understand that a youngster needs more than just subject matter. I know mathematics well, and I teach it well. I used to think that was all I needed to do.

Now I teach children, not math. I accept the fact that I can only succeed partially with some of them.

When I don't have to know all the answers, I seem to have more answers than when I tried to be the expert. The youngster who really made me understand this was Eddie. I asked him one day why he thought he was doing so much better than last year. He gave meaning to my whole new orientation: "It's because I like myself now when I'm with you," he said.

—A teacher quoted by Everett Shostrum—
in *Man, The Manipulator*

All the Good Things

A kind word is like a spring day.
~Russian Proverb

He was in the third-grade class I taught at Saint Mary's School in Morris, Minnesota. All 34 of my students were dear to me, but Mark Eklund was one in a million. Very neat in appearance, he had that happy-to-be-alive attitude that made even his occasional mischievousness delightful.

Mark also talked incessantly. I tried to remind him again and again that talking without permission was not acceptable. What impressed me so much, though, was the sincere response every time I had to correct him for misbehaving. "Thank you for correcting me, Sister!" I didn't know what to make of it at first but before long I became accustomed to hearing it many times a day.

One morning my patience was growing thin when Mark talked once too often. I made a novice-teacher's mistake. I looked at Mark and said, "If you say one more word, I am going to tape your mouth shut!"

It wasn't 10 seconds later when Chuck blurted out, "Mark is talking again." I hadn't asked any of the students to help me watch Mark, but since I had stated the punishment in front of the class, I had to act on it.

I remember the scene as if it had occurred this morning. I walked to my desk, very deliberately opened the drawer and took out a roll of masking tape. Without saying a word, I proceeded to Mark's desk, tore off two pieces of tape and made a big X with them over his mouth. I then returned to the front of the room.

As I glanced at Mark to see how he was doing, he winked at me. That did it! I started laughing. The entire class cheered as I walked back to Mark's desk, removed the tape and shrugged my shoulders. His first words were, "Thank you for correcting me, Sister."

At the end of the year I was asked to teach junior high math. The years flew by, and before I knew it Mark was in my classroom again. He was more handsome than ever and just as polite. Since he had to listen carefully to my instruction in the "new math," he did not talk as much in ninth grade.

One Friday things just didn't feel right. We had worked hard on a new concept all week, and I sensed that the students were growing frustrated with themselves — and edgy with one another. I had to stop this crankiness before it got out of hand. So I asked them to list the names of the other students in the room on two sheets of paper, leaving a space between each name. Then I told them to think of the nicest thing they could say about each of their classmates and write it down.

It took the remainder of the class period to finish the assignment, but as the students left the room, each one handed me their paper. Chuck smiled. Mark said, "Thank you for teaching me, Sister. Have a good weekend."

That Saturday, I wrote down the name of each student on a separate sheet of paper, and I listed what everyone else had said about that individual. On Monday I gave each student his or her list. Some of them ran two pages. Before long, the entire class was smiling. "Really?" I heard whispered. "I never knew that meant anything to anyone!" "I didn't know others liked me so much!"

No one ever mentioned those papers in class again. I never knew if they discussed them after class or with their parents, but it didn't matter. The exercise had accomplished its purpose. The students were happy with themselves and one another again.

That group of students moved on. Several years later, after I had returned from a vacation, my parents met me at the airport. As we were driving home, Mother asked the usual questions about the trip:

How the weather was, my experiences in general. There was a slight lull in the conversation.

Mother gave Dad a sideways glance and simply said, "Dad?"

My father cleared his throat. "The Eklunds called last night," he began.

"Really?" I said. "I haven't heard from them for several years. I wonder how Mark is."

Dad responded quietly. "Mark was killed in Vietnam," he said. "The funeral is tomorrow, and his parents would like it if you could attend." To this day I can still point to the exact spot on I-494 where Dad told me about Mark.

I had never seen a serviceman in a military coffin before. Mark looked so handsome, so mature. All I could think at that moment was, *Mark, I would give all the masking tape in the world if only you could talk to me.*

The church was packed with Mark's friends. Chuck's sister sang "The Battle Hymn of the Republic." Why did it have to rain on the day of the funeral? It was difficult enough at the graveside. The pastor said the usual prayers and the bugler played taps. One by one those who loved Mark took a last walk by the coffin and sprinkled it with holy water.

I was the last one to bless the coffin. As I stood there, one of the soldiers who had acted as a pallbearer came up to me. "Were you Mark's math teacher?" he asked. I nodded as I continued to stare at the coffin. "Mark talked about you a lot," he said.

After the funeral most of Mark's former classmates headed to Chuck's farmhouse for lunch. Mark's mother and father were there, obviously waiting for me. "We want to show you something," his father said, taking a wallet out of his pocket. "They found this on Mark when he was killed. We thought you might recognize it."

Opening the billfold, he carefully removed two worn pieces of notebook paper that had obviously been taped, folded and refolded many times. I knew without looking that the papers were the ones on which I had listed all the good things each of Mark's classmates had said about him. "Thank you so much for doing that," Mark's mother said. "As you can see, Mark treasured it."

Mark's classmates started to gather around us. Chuck smiled rather sheepishly and said, "I still have my list. It's in the top drawer of my desk at home." John's wife said, "John asked me to put his in our wedding album." "I have mine, too," Marilyn said. "It's in my diary." Then Vicki, another classmate, reached into her pocketbook, took out her wallet and showed her worn and frazzled list to the group. "I carry this with me at all times," Vicki said without batting an eyelash. "I think we all saved our lists."

That's when I finally sat down and cried. I cried for Mark and for all his friends who would never see him again.

— Helen P. Mrosla —

You Are a Marvel

Children are one third of our population
and all of our future.
~Select Panel for the Promotion of Child Health, 1981

Each second we live is a new and unique moment of the universe, a moment that will never be again… And what do we teach our children? We teach them that two and two make four, and that Paris is the capital of France.

When will we also teach them what they are?

We should say to each of them: Do you know what you are? You are a marvel. You are unique. In all the years that have passed, there has never been another child like you. Your legs, your arms, your clever fingers, the way you move.

You may become a Shakespeare, a Michelangelo, a Beethoven. You have the capacity for anything. Yes, you are a marvel. And when you grow up, can you then have another who is, like you, a marvel?

You must work — we must all work — to make the world worthy of its children.

— Pablo Casals —

We Learn by Doing

I am learning all the time. The tombstone
will be my diploma.
~Eartha Kitt

Not many years ago I began to play the cello. Most people would say that what I am doing is "learning to play" the cello. But these words carry into our minds the strange idea that there exist two very different processes: (1) learning to play the cello; and (2) playing the cello. They imply that I will do the first until I have completed it, at which point I will stop the first process and begin the second. In short, I will go on "learning to play" until I have "learned to play" and then I will begin to play. Of course, this is nonsense. There are not two processes, but one. We learn to do something by doing it. There is no other way.

—John Holt—

The Hand

A teacher takes a hand, opens a mind,
and touches a heart.
~Author Unknown

A Thanksgiving Day editorial in the newspaper told of a school-teacher who asked her class of first graders to draw a picture of something they were thankful for. She thought of how little these children from poor neighborhoods actually had to be thankful for. But she knew that most of them would draw pictures of turkeys or tables with food. The teacher was taken aback with the picture Douglas handed in — a simple childishly drawn hand.

But whose hand? The class was captivated by the abstract image. "I think it must be the hand of God that brings us food," said one child. "A farmer," said another, "because he grows the turkeys." Finally when the others were at work, the teacher bent over Douglas's desk and asked whose hand it was. "It's your hand, Teacher," he mumbled.

She recalled that frequently at recess she had taken Douglas, a scrubby forlorn child by the hand. She often did that with the children. But it meant so much to Douglas. Perhaps this was everyone's Thanksgiving, not for the material things given to us but for the chance, in whatever small way, to give to others.

— Source Unknown —

The Little Boy

Don't expect anything original from an echo.
~Author Unknown

Once a little boy went to school.
He was quite a little boy.
And it was quite a big school.
But when the little boy
Found that he could go to his room
By walking right in from the door outside,
He was happy. And the school did not seem
Quite so big any more.

One morning,
When the little boy had been in school a while,
The teacher said:

"Today we are going to make a picture."
"Good!" thought the little boy.
He liked to make pictures.
He could make all kinds:
Lions and tigers,
Chickens and cows,
Trains and boats—
And he took out his box of crayons

And began to draw.
But the teacher said:
"Wait! It is not time to begin!"
And she waited until everyone looked ready.

"Now," said the teacher,
"We are going to make flowers."
"Good!" thought the little boy,
He liked to make flowers,
And he began to make beautiful ones
With his pink and orange and blue crayons.

But the teacher said,
"Wait! And I will show you how."
And she drew a flower on the blackboard.
It was red, with a green stem.
"There," said the teacher.
"Now you may begin."

The little boy looked at the teacher's flower.
Then he looked at his own flower,
He liked his flower better than the teacher's.
But he did not say this,
He just turned his paper over
And made a flower like the teacher's.
It was red, with a green stem.

On another day,
When the little boy had opened
The door from the outside all by himself,
The teacher said,
"Today we are going to make something with clay."
"Good!" thought the little boy.
He liked clay.

He could make all kinds of things with clay:
Snakes and snowmen,
Elephants and mice,
Cars and trucks —
And he began to pull and pinch
His ball of clay.

But the teacher said,
"Wait! It is not time to begin!"
And she waited until everyone looked ready.

"Now," said the teacher,
"We are going to make a dish."
"Good!" thought the little boy,
He liked to make dishes,
And he began to make some
That were all shapes and sizes.

But the teacher said,
"Wait! And I will show you how."
And she showed everyone how to make
One deep dish.
"There," said the teacher,
"Now you may begin."

The little boy looked at the teacher's dish
Then he looked at his own.
He liked his dishes better than the teacher's
But he did not say this,
He just rolled his clay into a big ball again,
And made a dish like the teacher's.
It was a deep dish.

And pretty soon
The little boy learned to wait

And to watch,
And to make things just like the teacher.
And pretty soon
He didn't make things of his own anymore.

Then it happened
That the little boy and his family
Moved to another house,
In another city,
And the little boy
Had to go to another school.

This school was even bigger
Than the other one,
And there was no door from the outside
Into his room.
He had to go up some big steps,
And walk down a long hall
To get to his room.

And the very first day
He was there, the teacher said,
"Today we are going to make a picture."

"Good!" thought the little boy,
And he waited for the teacher
To tell him what to do
But the teacher didn't say anything.
She just walked around the room.

When she came to the little boy,
She said, "Don't you want to make a picture?"
"Yes," said the little boy.
"What are we going to make?"
"I don't know until you make it," said the teacher.

"How shall I make it?" asked the little boy.
"Why, any way you like," said the teacher.
"And any color?" asked the little boy.
"Any color," said the teacher,
"If everyone made the same picture,
And used the same colors,
How would I know who made what,
And which was which?"
"I don't know," said the little boy.
And he began to make pink and orange
and blue flowers.

He liked his new school,
Even if it didn't have a door
Right in from the outside!

— Helen E. Buckley —

I Am a Teacher

Appreciation is a wonderful thing. It makes what is
excellent in others belong to us as well.
~Voltaire

I am a Teacher.
I was born the first moment that a question leaped from
  the mouth of a child.
I have been many people in many places.
I am Socrates exciting the youth of Athens to discover
  new ideas through the use of questions.
I am Anne Sullivan tapping out the secrets of the universe
  into the outstretched hand of Helen Keller.
I am Aesop and Hans Christian Andersen revealing truth
  through countless stories.
I am Marva Collins fighting for every child's right to an
  education.
I am Mary McCleod Bethune building a great college for
  my people, using orange crates for desks.
And I am Bel Kaufman struggling to go *Up the Down*
  Staircase.
The names of those who have practiced my profession ring like a
  hall of fame for humanity... Booker T. Washington, Buddha,
  Confucius, Ralph Waldo Emerson, Leo Buscaglia, Moses and
  Jesus.

I am also those whose names and faces have long been forgotten but whose lessons and character will always be remembered in the accomplishments of their students.

I have wept for joy at the weddings of former students, laughed with glee at the birth of their children and stood with head bowed in grief and confusion by graves dug too soon for bodies far too young.

Throughout the course of a day I have been called upon to be an actor, friend, nurse and doctor, coach, finder of lost articles, money lender, taxi driver, psychologist, substitute parent, salesman, politician and a keeper of the faith.

Despite the maps, charts, formulas, verbs, stories and books, I have really had nothing to teach, for my students really have only themselves to learn, and I know it takes the whole world to tell you who you are.

I am a paradox. I speak loudest when I listen the most. My greatest gifts are in what I am willing to appreciatively receive from my students.

Material wealth is not one of my goals, but I am a full-time treasure seeker in my quest for new opportunities for my students to use their talents and in my constant search for those talents that sometimes lie buried in self-defeat.

I am the most fortunate of all who labor.

A doctor is allowed to usher life into the world in one magic moment. I am allowed to see that life is reborn each day with new questions, ideas and friendships.

An architect knows that if he builds with care, his structure may stand for centuries. A teacher knows that if he builds with love and truth, what he builds will last forever.

I am a warrior, daily doing battle against peer pressure, negativity, fear, conformity, prejudice, ignorance and apathy. But I have great allies: Intelligence, Curiosity, Parental Support, Individuality, Creativity, Faith, Love and Laughter all rush to my banner with indomitable support.

And who do I have to thank for this wonderful life I am so fortunate to experience, but you the public, the parents. For you have done me the great honor to entrust to me your greatest contribution to eternity, your children.

And so I have a past that is rich in memories. I have a present that is challenging, adventurous and fun because I am allowed to spend my days with the future.

I am a teacher… and I thank God for it every day.

—John W. Schlatter—

Chapter

5

Chicken Soup
for the Soul

Live Your Dream

*People who say it cannot be done should not
interrupt those who are doing it.*

~George Bernard Shaw

"You've Got Mail" Revisited 25 Years Later

Whatever else anything is, it ought
to begin by being personal.
~Nora and Delia Ephron, You've Got Mail

The first time I watched the movie *You've Got Mail* was right after I graduated from college back in 1998. I was living in West Hollywood working at a small brand development and design firm in Studio City. My soon-to-be-ex-boyfriend (who I moved to LA to be with) was working an intense job with long hours, so I had a lot of time to myself after work. Free time was new for me and, actually, unwelcome. I'd been an intense student, working relentlessly to graduate Yale with honors. Yet suddenly, the nights seemed to stretch on.

I was taking a class in personal essay writing at the UCLA Extension school. The only thing I remember producing was a piece about buying my first bra with my mother at Bergdorf Goodman at age nine and hiding between the silk robes so no one would see me. My first essay had been published in *Seventeen* magazine when I was sixteen years old and since then I'd been determined to become a writer — but knew there was no path directly there. I resolved to take the winding road through life hoping I could get there, somehow.

You've Got Mail allowed me to luxuriate in the dream life of owning The Shop Around the Corner children's bookstore that Meg Ryan's character inherited from her late, beloved and sorely-missed mom. As a lifelong New Yorker, the setting on the Upper West Side, just blocks from where I went to high school, was so familiar it made me smile. Was I in the background somewhere? I ate it all up as I watched the big-box bookstore put the little one out of business while learning that business is, in fact, personal and should be.

Now, in 2023, I just watched *You've Got Mail* again on my flight from New York to Los Angeles, the same route I've crisscrossed more times than should be humanly allowed. (I ended up hightailing it out of LA in 2000 to move back to New York post break-up. There I shared an apartment with my old college roommate again who, on September 11th, 2001, perished in the World Trade Center attacks.)

But this time I'm on my way to LA because my own bookstore, Zibby's Bookshop, is opening in Santa Monica *tomorrow*. I'm now forty-six years old and working just as hard as when I was a student. It took many rejections from 2005 through 2020 of several novels and memoirs for me to finally become a published author (memoirist!).

Along the way, I accidentally created an empire. I started a podcast at the advice of a new friend back in 2018 as a way to "build my platform" and be in a stronger position to sell a book to publishers, my end-goal. The podcast, "Moms Don't Have Time to Read Books," quickly usurped my time, attention and passion. For thirty minutes daily, I interviewed authors one-on-one about their work and their lives which, as an avid reader and lifelong bookworm, was like attending the Academy Awards every afternoon. I grew obsessed. The show shot up the Apple rankings. And interviewing authors came naturally to me, both because I was so legitimately passionate about the topic (their fabulous books!), but also because I have a strong sense of empathy, deep interest in others, and, I'm told, excellent listening skills.

Quite simply: I care about people and their stories, no matter who they are. But to delve deep into *authors'* lives? Dream come true.

Soon, my Harvard Business School degree kicked in and I put on my marketing hat and channeled all my creativity and out-of-the-box thinking to grow the podcast audience, social media, and more. I launched a salon author series in my home, hosted book fairs, launched an online magazine, and, in 2021, decided to start my own publishing company.

Zibby Books launched its first title last week, *My What If Year* by Alisha Fernandez Miranda. I'd reached out to her after she wrote for our online magazine and told her to wait for me because I just might start my own publishing company. She did — and I did. In the past two weeks, the book has been on CNN, MSNBC, *GMA*, ABC-7, PIX-11, NPR, WNYC, *People* magazine, Katie Couric Media, Thrive Global and more. It's hard to believe the success already.

And tomorrow my bookshop opens. It's only 823 square feet but it is already magical, designed to look like my living room and curated by topic and emotion with non-stop author events and conversations. The *LA Times* did an enormous piece about it — and me — that I reread many times just to make sure those kind words were still there in black and white.

I didn't know a lot about the publishing industry the first time I watched *You've Got Mail*, having worked only in advertising, psychology, and marketing roles with one short internship at *Vanity Fair*. This time, I caught all the references. It was like Nora and Delia Ephron had written the movie for me, now, twenty-five years later. Tom Hanks's girlfriend in the film was the head of a publishing company! They threw around events like the PEN gala, author launch events, advances, and so many other words of the word business. The bookstore sales figures were similar to the talk I had with my accountant about our projected sales just last week.

As I hurtle over the country on a plane that happens to be one of the bumpiest I've ever been on (for the first twenty minutes I was shaking, crying and gasping along with other passengers), it takes shape as a metaphor for my career. It was so tough at first that I cried and had to hold the hands of those I loved. Then, it felt like an endless, long journey.

Soon, we'll land. Soon, my store will open. Soon, my career to date, all those ups and downs, turbulence and travel, will have led somewhere quite definitive. The bookstore to me isn't about commerce. It's about community, building a place that others cherish, that helps readers discover books and authors they never would have otherwise without the store — and me. It's a profound responsibility that I absolutely cherish.

So here it comes. The end of the film. The end of the flight. The end of a chapter. But really, this is just the beginning. Who knows where I'll go from here or where my next flight will head. Luckily, like Meg Ryan's character, I also ended up with my Tom Hanks, Kyle, who I'm in love with and who will go on this journey with me.

The credits are rolling.

The next movie is queued up to start.

Here I go.

— Zibby Owens —

My Own Destiny

There is an unseen life that dreams us. It knows our
true direction and destiny. We can trust ourselves more
than we realize and we need have no fear of change.
~John O'Donohue

I was a 22-year-old hotshot — or so I thought. As a publicist for NBC News in New York — the youngest ever, I was told — I was making enough money to rent a nice apartment near Lincoln Center, enjoy manicures and pedicures on weekends, eat out and shop. Not bad for a nice Jewish girl from Miami Beach who had always dreamed of making it in the Big Apple.

I was on a first-name basis with some of the biggest names in broadcast news: Jane Pauley, Maria Shriver and the late Tim Russert. At some point those boldface names benefited from my publicity skills. It was heady stuff and I was on a roll. I envisioned a long and happy career at NBC's iconic 30 Rock headquarters.

Then NBC News hired a new division president. He planned to make big changes, or so I learned abruptly one day when I got a call from a human resources representative who told me to report to the new boss's office. When I walked in, he was sitting behind his big desk. He didn't get up to greet me. Not a good sign.

He clasped his hands behind his head, leaned back in his leather chair and told me that anytime someone took over a company or a division, he or she would want to put his or her mark on things — new protocols, new processes, and a new team.

The light dawned. "Are you firing me?" I interrupted.

"You have 30 minutes to leave the building," he said, matter-of-factly.

My world was crashing, so I quickly went into spin mode, using all the skills I had learned as a high school debate champ. I told him he was making a terrible mistake, and I listed the reasons. I told him that if he talked to anyone internally and externally they would say what a great asset I was, that I really knew my stuff, and that I was one thousand percent committed to NBC News.

He looked at his watch.

Desperate, I asked him to give me a chance to prove myself. "Give me three things to accomplish in three weeks, three months — any timeframe you decide — to prove myself directly to you." All I wanted, I said, was to stay at NBC News.

His response? "You now have 25 minutes to leave the building."

Game over. As I stood up to walk out of his office — trying desperately not to burst into tears — his parting words of wisdom were, "Tory, it's a big world out there, and I suggest you go explore it."

I left in shock. My world as I had known it had come to an end. I thought my career was over. I didn't even get to pack up my office. It was done for me and my boxes were messengered to my apartment later that day.

I walked home, climbed into my pajamas and threw myself an old-fashioned pity party, catered by Haagen-Dazs. The entertainment? Daytime TV, long conversations with my mom in Florida, and lots of sleepless nights filled with self-doubt, wondering what would become of me. My party turned into a misery marathon for months, financed by severance pay, unemployment benefits and a cashed-out 401(k) — something only someone naïve in her twenties would think was a great idea.

With a cool $23,000 in my checking account, going to the ATM never felt scary. That is, until one day I stood at a Citibank machine, stunned that I had run out of money. I'm not sure why a smart girl like me was so surprised: when nothing's coming in and it's all going out, it's inevitable that the funds dry up.

I realized I had two choices: pack my bags and move back home to Miami Beach or snap out of my funk and get another job.

Having no desire to go backwards, I took stock of my situation. First, I told myself: nothing lasts forever. All jobs are temporary and nobody holds onto the same role forever. Second, sometimes you can do everything right and still lose your job. And third, you can take away my business cards, my corporate ID and my paycheck, but *nobody* can strip me of my skills or experience, or my friends and colleagues who'd vouch for me and my talent. Once I discovered that — and truly believed it — it took me just weeks to get hired.

As I began my new job, I reflected on other key lessons, which most notably was that I control my self-worth — and it's up to me to project what I want others to see. It's not about job title or place of employment. It's about me and all that I'm capable of doing, giving and achieving.

I also realized that I never wanted to be on someone else's pay-roll — to leave my destiny in someone else's hands. I resented the notion that, despite all my hard work and commitment, an arrogant man in a suit could take away my paycheck and attempt to rob me of my dignity and self-worth. No matter how hard I tried, I couldn't shake it. I couldn't stomach the specter of getting fired again.

The permanent scar of a pink slip convinced me that I'd feel best running my own shop and signing my own paycheck. I'd bank exclusively on *me*. Everything would be up to *me*. That concept is terrifying for many people, but I found it exhilarating. I still do. It was the most freeing personal move I could have made. Ask anyone who has quit corporate America to go out on their own and many will say the same thing.

— Tory Johnson —

I Think I Can!

Stubbornly persist, and you will find that the limits
of your stubbornness go well beyond
the stubbornness of your limits.
~Robert Brault

Rocky Lyons, the son of New York Jets defensive end Marty Lyons, was five years old when he was driving through rural Alabama with his mother, Kelly. He was asleep on the front seat of their pickup truck, with his feet resting on her lap.

As his mom drove carefully down the winding two-lane country road, she turned onto a narrow bridge. As she did, the truck hit a pothole and slid off the road, and the right front wheel got stuck in a rut. Fearing the truck would tip over, she attempted to jerk it back up onto the road by pressing hard on the gas pedal and spinning the steering wheel to the left. But Rocky's foot got caught between her leg and the steering wheel and she lost control of the pickup truck.

The truck flipped over and over down a 20-foot ravine. When it hit bottom, Rocky woke up. "What happened, Mama?" he asked. "Our wheels are pointing toward the sky."

Kelly was blinded by blood. The gearshift had jammed into her face, ripping it open from lip to forehead. Her gums were torn out, her cheeks pulverized, her shoulders crushed. With one shattered bone sticking out of her armpit, she was pinned against the crushed door.

"I'll get you out, Mama," announced Rocky, who had miraculously escaped injury. He slithered out from under Kelly, slid through the open window and tried to yank his mother out. But she didn't move.

"Just let me sleep," begged Kelly, who was drifting in and out of consciousness.

"No, Mama," Rocky insisted. "You can't go to sleep."

Rocky wriggled back into the truck and managed to push Kelly out of the wreckage. He then told her he'd climb up to the road and stop a car to get help. Fearing that no one would be able to see her little boy in the dark, Kelly refused to let him go alone. Instead they slowly crept up the embankment, with Rocky using his meager 40-pound frame to push his 104-pound mother. They crawled inches at a time. The pain was so great that Kelly wanted to give up, but Rocky wouldn't let her.

To urge his mother on, Rocky told her to think "about that little train," the one in the classic children's story, *The Little Engine That Could,* which managed to get up a steep mountain. To remind her, Rocky kept repeating his version of the story's inspirational phrase: "I know you can, I know you can."

When they finally reached the road, Rocky was able to see his mother's torn face clearly for the first time. He broke into tears. Waving his arms and pleading, "Stop! Please stop!" the boy hailed a truck. "Get my mama to a hospital," he implored the driver.

It took 8 hours and 344 stitches to rebuild Kelly's face. She looks quite different today — "I used to have a straight long nose, thin lips and high cheekbones; now I've got a pug nose, flat cheeks and much bigger lips" — but she has few visible scars and has recovered from her injuries.

Rocky's heroics were big news. But the spunky youngster insists he didn't do anything extraordinary. "It's not like I wanted it to happen," he explains. "I just did what anyone would have done."

Says his mother, "If it weren't for Rocky, I'd have bled to death."

— First heard from Michele Borba —

Rest in Peace: The "I Can't" Funeral

Optimism is the foundation of courage.
~Nicholas Murray Butler

onna's fourth-grade classroom looked like many others I had seen in the past. Students sat in five rows of six desks. The teacher's desk was in the front and faced the students. The bulletin board featured student work. In most respects it appeared to be a traditional elementary classroom. Yet something seemed different that day I entered it for the first time. There seemed to be an undercurrent of excitement.

Donna was a veteran small-town Michigan schoolteacher only two years away from retirement. In addition she was a volunteer participant in a county-wide staff development project I had organized and facilitated. The training focused on language arts ideas that would empower students to feel good about themselves and take charge of their lives. Donna's job was to attend training sessions and implement the concepts being presented. My job was to make classroom visitations and encourage implementation.

I took an empty seat in the back of the room and watched. All the students were working on a task, filling a sheet of notebook paper with thoughts and ideas. The 10-year-old student closest to me was filling her page with "I Can'ts."

"I can't kick the soccer ball past second base."

"I can't do long division with more than three numerals."

"I can't get Debbie to like me."

Her page was half full and she showed no signs of letting up. She worked on with determination and persistence.

I walked down the row glancing at students' papers. Everyone was writing sentences, describing things they couldn't do.

"I can't do 10 push-ups."

"I can't hit one over the left-field fence."

"I can't eat only one cookie."

By this time, the activity engaged my curiosity, so I decided to check with the teacher to see what was going on. As I approached her, I noticed that she too was busy writing. I felt it best not to interrupt.

"I can't get John's mother to come in for a teacher conference."

"I can't get my daughter to put gas in the car."

"I can't get Alan to use words instead of fists."

Thwarted in my efforts to determine why students and teacher were dwelling on the negative instead of writing the more positive "I Can" statements, I returned to my seat and continued my observations. Students wrote for another 10 minutes. Most filled their page. Some started another.

"Finish the one you're on and don't start a new one," were the instructions Donna used to signal the end of the activity. Students were then instructed to fold their papers in half and bring them to the front. When students reached the teacher's desk, they placed their "I Can't" statements into an empty shoebox.

When all of the student papers were collected, Donna added hers. She put the lid on the box, tucked it under her arm and headed out the door and down the hall. Students followed the teacher. I followed the students.

Halfway down the hall the procession stopped. Donna entered the custodian's room, rummaged around and came out with a shovel. Shovel in one hand, shoebox in the other, Donna marched the students out of the school to the farthest corner of the playground. There they began to dig.

They were going to bury their "I Can'ts"! The digging took over 10 minutes because most of the fourth graders wanted a turn. When the hole approached three feet deep, the digging ended. The box of "I Can'ts" was placed in position at the bottom of the hole and quickly covered with dirt.

Thirty-one 10- and 11-year-olds stood around the freshly dug gravesite. Each had at least one page full of "I Can'ts" in the shoebox, four feet under. So did their teacher.

At this point Donna announced, "Boys and girls, please join hands and bow your heads." The students complied. They quickly formed a circle around the grave, creating a bond with their hands. They lowered their heads and waited. Donna delivered the eulogy.

"Friends, we gather today to honor the memory of 'I Can't.' While he was with us on earth, he touched the lives of everyone, some more than others. His name, unfortunately, has been spoken in every public building—schools, city halls, state capitals and yes, even the White House.

"We have provided 'I Can't' with a final resting place and a headstone that contains his epitaph. He is survived by his brothers and sister, 'I Can', 'I Will' and 'I'm Going to Right Away.' They are not as well known as their famous relative and are certainly not as strong and powerful yet.

"Perhaps some day, with your help, they will make an even bigger mark on the world.

"May 'I Can't' rest in peace and may everyone present pick up their lives and move forward in his absence. Amen." As I listened to the eulogy I realized that these students would never forget this day. The activity was symbolic, a metaphor for life. It was a right-brain experience that would stick in the unconscious and conscious mind forever. Writing "I Can'ts," burying them and hearing the eulogy. That was a major effort on the part of this teacher. And she wasn't done yet. At the conclusion of the eulogy she turned the students around, marched them back into the classroom and held a wake.

They celebrated the passing of "I Can't" with cookies, popcorn and fruit juices. As part of the celebration, Donna cut out a large tombstone from butcher paper. She wrote the words "I Can't" at the top and put RIP in the middle. The date was added at the bottom.

The paper tombstone hung in Donna's classroom for the remainder of the year. On those rare occasions when a student forgot and said, "I Can't," Donna simply pointed to the RIP sign. The student then remembered that "I Can't" was dead and chose to rephrase the statement.

I wasn't one of Donna's students. She was one of mine. Yet that day I learned an enduring lesson from her.

Now, years later, whenever I hear the phrase, "I Can't," I see images of that fourth-grade funeral. Like the students, I remember that "I Can't" is dead.

— Chick Moorman —

The 333 Story

Change your thoughts and you change your world.
~Norman Vincent Peale

I was doing a weekend seminar at the Deerhurst Lodge, north of Toronto. On Friday night a tornado swept through a town north of us called Barrie, killing several people and doing millions of dollars of damage. Sunday night, as I was coming home, I stopped the car when I got to Barrie. I got out on the side of the highway and looked around. It was a mess. Everywhere I looked there were smashed houses and cars turned upside down.

That same night Bob Templeton was driving down the same highway. He stopped to look at the disaster just as I had, only his thoughts were different than my own. Bob was the vice president of Telemedia Communications, which owns a string of radio stations in Ontario and Quebec. He thought there must be something he could do for those people with the radio stations his company had.

The following night I was doing another seminar in Toronto. Bob Templeton and Bob Johnson, another vice president from Telemedia, came in and stood in the back of the room. They shared their conviction that there had to be something they could do for the people in Barrie. After the seminar we went back to Bob's office. He was now committed to the idea of helping the people who had been caught in the tornado.

The following Friday he called all the executives at Telemedia into his office. At the top of a flip chart he wrote three 3s. He said to his executives "How would you like to raise 3 million dollars 3 days from now in just 3 hours and give the money to the people in Barrie?" There was nothing but silence in the room.

Finally someone said, "Templeton, you're crazy. There is no way we could do that."

Bob said, "Wait a minute. I didn't ask you if we *could* or even if we *should*. I just asked you if you'd *like* to."

They all said, "Sure, we'd like to." He then drew a large T underneath the 333. On one side he wrote, "Why we can't." On the other side he wrote, "How we can."

"I'm going to put a big X on the 'Why we can't side.' We're not going to spend any time on the ideas of why we can't. That's of no value. On the other side we're going to write down every idea that we can come up with on how we can. We're not going to leave the room until we figure it out." There was silence again.

Finally, someone said, "We could do a radio show across Canada."

Bob said, "That's a great idea," and wrote it down.

Before he had it written, someone said, "You can't do a radio show across Canada. We don't have radio stations across Canada." That was a pretty valid objection. They only had stations in Ontario and Quebec.

Templeton replied, "That's why we can. That stays." But this was a really strong objection because radio stations are very competitive. They usually don't work together and to get them to do so would be virtually impossible according to the standard way of thinking.

All of a sudden someone suggested, "You could get Harvey Kirk and Lloyd Robertson, the biggest names in Canadian broadcasting, to anchor the show." (That would be like getting Tom Brokaw and Sam Donaldson to anchor the show. They are anchors on national TV. They are not going to go on radio.) At that point it was absolutely amazing how fast and furious the creative ideas began to flow.

That was on a Friday. The following Tuesday they had a radio-thon. They had 50 radio stations all across the country that agreed to broadcast it. It didn't matter who got the credit as long as the people in Barrie got the money. Harvey Kirk and Lloyd Robertson anchored the show and they succeeded in raising 3 million dollars in 3 hours within 3 business days!

You see you can do anything if you put your focus on how to do it rather than on why you can't.

— Bob Proctor —

There Are No Vans

No one can whistle a symphony.
It takes a whole orchestra to play it.
~H.E. Luccock

remember one Thanksgiving when our family had no money and no food, and someone came knocking on our door. A man was standing there with a huge box of food, a giant turkey and even some pans to cook it in. I couldn't believe it. My dad demanded, "Who are you? Where are you from?"

The stranger announced, "I'm here because a friend of yours knows you're in need and that you wouldn't accept direct help, so I've brought this for you. Have a great Thanksgiving."

My father said, "No, no, we can't accept this."

The stranger replied, "You don't have a choice," closed the door and left.

Obviously that experience had a profound impact on my life. I promised myself that someday I would do well enough financially so that I could do the same thing for other people. By the time I was 18 I had created my Thanksgiving ritual. I like to do things spontaneously, so I would go out shopping and buy enough food for one or two families. Then I would dress like a delivery boy, go to the poorest neighborhood and just knock on a door. I always included a note that explained my Thanksgiving experience as a kid. The note concluded, "All that I ask in return is that you take good enough care of yourself so that someday you can do the same thing for someone else." I have received more from this annual ritual than I have from any amount of money I've ever earned.

Several years ago I was in New York City with my new wife during Thanksgiving. She was sad because we were not with our family. Normally she would be home decorating the house for Christmas, but we were stuck here in a hotel room.

I said, "Honey, look, why don't we decorate some lives today instead of some old trees?" When I told her what I always do on Thanksgiving, she got excited. I said, "Let's go someplace where we can really appreciate who we are, what we are capable of and what we can really give. Let's go to Harlem!" She and several of my business partners who were with us weren't really enthusiastic about the idea. I urged them: "C'mon, let's go to Harlem and feed some people in need. We won't be the people who are giving it because that would be insulting. We'll just be the delivery people. We'll go buy enough food for six or seven families for 30 days. We've got enough. Let's just go do it! That's what Thanksgiving really is: Giving good thanks, not eating turkey. C'mon. Let's go do it!"

Because I had to do a radio interview first, I asked my partners to get us started by getting a van. When I returned from the interview, they said, "We just can't do it. There are no vans in all of New York. The rent-a-car places are all out of vans. They're just not available."

I said, "Look, the bottom line is that if we want something, we can make it happen! All we have to do is take action. There are plenty of vans here in New York City. We just don't have one. Let's go get one."

They insisted, "We've called everywhere. There aren't any."

I said, "Look down at the street. Look down there. Do you see all those vans?"

They said, "Yeah, we see them."

"Let's go get one," I said. First I tried walking out in front of vans as they were driving down the street. I learned something about New York drivers that day: They don't stop; they speed up.

Then we tried waiting by the light. We'd go over and knock on the window and the driver would roll it down, looking at us kind of leery, and I'd say "Hi. Since today is Thanksgiving, we'd like to know if you would be willing to drive us to Harlem so we can feed some people." Every time the driver would look away quickly, furiously roll up the window and pull away without saying anything.

Eventually we got better at asking. We'd knock on the window, they'd roll it down and we'd say, "Today is Thanksgiving. We'd like to help some underprivileged people, and we're curious if you'd be willing to drive us to an underprivileged area that we have in mind here in New York City." That seemed slightly more effective but still didn't work. Then we started offering people $100 to drive us. That got us even closer, but when we told them to take us to Harlem, they said no and drove off.

We had talked to about two dozen people who all said no. My partners were ready to give up on the project, but I said, "It's the law of averages: somebody is going to say *yes*." Sure enough, the perfect van drove up. It was perfect because it was extra big and would accommodate all of us. We went up, knocked on the window and we asked the driver, "Could you take us to a disadvantaged area? We'll pay you 100 dollars."

The driver said, "You don't have to pay me. I'd be happy to take you. In fact, I'll take you to some of the most difficult spots in the whole city." Then he reached over on the seat and grabbed his hat. As he put it on, I noticed that it said, "Salvation Army." The man's name was Captain John Rondon and he was the head of the Salvation Army in the South Bronx.

We climbed into the van in absolute ecstasy. He said, "I'll take you places you never even thought of going. But tell me something. Why do you people want to do this?" I told him my story and that I wanted to show gratitude for all that I had by giving something back.

Captain Rondon took us into parts of the South Bronx that make Harlem look like Beverly Hills. When we arrived, we went into a store where we bought a lot of food and some baskets. We packed enough for seven families for 30 days. Then we went out to start feeding people. We went to buildings where there were half a dozen people living in one room: "squatters" with no electricity and no heat in the dead of winter surrounded by rats, cockroaches and the smell of urine. It was both an astonishing realization that people lived this way and a truly fulfilling experience to make even a small difference.

You see, you can make anything happen if you commit to it and take action. Miracles like this happen every day — even in a city where "there are no vans."

— Anthony Robbins —

Ask, Ask, Ask

I've got a theory that if you give 100 percent all of the
time, somehow things will work out in the end.
~Larry Bird

The greatest saleswoman in the world today doesn't mind if you call her a girl. That's because Markita Andrews has generated more than eighty thousand dollars selling Girl Scout cookies since she was seven years old.

Going door to door after school, the painfully shy Markita transformed herself into a cookie-selling dynamo when she discovered, at age 13, the secret of selling.

It starts with desire. Burning, white-hot desire.

For Markita and her mother, who worked as a waitress in New York after her husband left them when Markita was eight years old, their dream was to travel the globe. "I'll work hard to make enough money to send you to college," her mother said one day. "You'll go to college and when you graduate, you'll make enough money to take you and me around the world. Okay?"

So at age 13, when Markita read in her Girl Scout magazine that the Scout who sold the most cookies would win an all-expenses-paid trip for two around the world, she decided to sell all the Girl Scout cookies she could — more Girl Scout cookies than anyone in the world, ever.

But desire alone is not enough. To make her dream come true, Markita knew she needed a plan.

"Always wear your right outfit, your professional garb," her aunt advised. "When you are doing business, dress like you are doing business. Wear your Girl Scout uniform. When you go up to people in their tenement buildings at 4:30 or 6:30 and especially on Friday night, ask for a big order. Always smile, whether they buy or not, always be nice. And don't ask them to buy your cookies; ask them to invest."

Lots of other Scouts may have wanted that trip around the world. Lots of other Scouts may have had a plan. But only Markita went off in her uniform each day after school, ready to ask — and keep asking — folks to invest in her dream. "Hi. I have a dream. I'm earning a trip around the world for me and my mom by merchandising Girl Scout cookies," she'd say at the door. "Would you like to invest in one dozen or two dozen boxes of cookies?"

Markita sold 3,526 boxes of Girl Scout cookies that year and won her trip around the world. Since then, she has sold more than 42,000 boxes of Girl Scout cookies, spoken at sales conventions across the country, starred in a Disney movie about her adventure and has coauthored the bestseller, *How to Sell More Cookies, Condos, Cadillacs, Computers... And Everything Else.*

Markita is no smarter and no more extroverted than thousands of other people, young and old, with dreams of their own. The difference is Markita has discovered the secret of selling: Ask, Ask, Ask! Many people fail before they even begin because they fail to *ask* for what they want. The fear of rejection leads many of us to reject ourselves and our dreams long before anyone else ever has the chance — no matter what we're selling.

And everyone is selling something. "You're selling yourself every day — in school, to your boss, to new people you meet," said Markita at 14. "My mother is a waitress: she sells the daily special. Mayors and presidents trying to get votes are selling. One of my favorite teachers was Mrs. Chapin. She made geography interesting, and that's really selling. I see selling everywhere I look. Selling is part of the whole world."

It takes courage to ask for what you want. Courage is not the absence of fear. It's doing what it takes despite one's fear. And, as Markita has discovered, the more you ask, the easier (and more fun) it gets.

Once, on live TV, the producer decided to give Markita her toughest selling challenge. Markita was asked to sell Girl Scout cookies to another guest on the show. "Would you like to invest in one dozen or two dozen boxes of Girl Scout cookies?" she asked.

"Girl Scout cookies? I don't buy any Girl Scout cookies!" he replied. "I'm a Federal Penitentiary warden. I put 2,000 rapists, robbers, criminals, muggers and child abusers to bed every night."

Unruffled, Markita quickly countered, "Mister, if you take some of these cookies, maybe you won't be so mean and angry and evil. And, Mister, I think it would be a good idea for you to take some of these cookies back for every one of your 2,000 prisoners, too."

The warden wrote a check.

—Jack Canfield and Mark Victor Hansen—

Did the Earth Move for You?

Know, then, whatever cheerful and serene
Supports the mind supports the body too.
~John Armstrong

Eleven-year-old Angela was stricken with a debilitating disease involving her nervous system. She was unable to walk and her movement was restricted in other ways as well. The doctors did not hold out much hope of her ever recovering from this illness. They predicted she'd spend the rest of her life in a wheelchair. They said that few, if any, were able to come back to normal after contracting this disease. The little girl was undaunted. There, lying in her hospital bed, she would vow to anyone who'd listen that she was definitely going to be walking again someday.

She was transferred to a specialized rehabilitation hospital in the San Francisco Bay area. Whatever therapies could be applied to her case were used. The therapists were charmed by her undefeatable spirit. They taught her about imaging—about seeing herself walking. If it would do nothing else, it would at least give her hope and something positive to do in the long waking hours in her bed. Angela would work as hard as possible in physical therapy, in whirlpools and in exercise sessions. But she worked just as hard lying there faithfully doing her imaging, visualizing herself moving, moving, moving!

One day, as she was straining with all her might to imagine her legs moving again, it seemed as though a miracle happened: The bed moved! It began to move around the room! She screamed out, "Look what I'm doing! Look! Look! I can do it! I moved, I moved!"

Of course, at this very moment everyone else in the hospital was screaming, too, and running for cover. People were screaming, equipment was falling and glass was breaking. You see, it was an earthquake. But don't tell that to Angela. She's convinced that she did it. And now only a few years later, she's back in school. On her own two legs. No crutches, no wheelchair. You see, anyone who can shake the earth between San Francisco and Oakland can conquer a piddling little disease, can't they?

—Hanoch McCarty—

Tommy's Bumper Sticker

Action is the foundational key to all success.
~Pablo Picasso

little kid down at our church in Huntington Beach came up to me after he heard me talk about the Children's Bank. He shook my hand and said, "My name is Tommy Tighe, I'm six years old and I want to borrow money from your Children's Bank."

I said, "Tommy, that's one of my goals, to loan money to kids. And so far all the kids have paid it back. What do you want to do?"

He said, "Ever since I was four I had a vision that I could cause peace in the world. I want to make a bumper sticker that says, 'PEACE, PLEASE! DO IT FOR US KIDS,' and sign it 'Tommy'."

"I can get behind that," I said. He needed $454 to produce 1,000 bumper stickers. The Mark Victor Hansen Children's Free Enterprise Fund wrote a check to the printer that was printing the bumper stickers.

Tommy's dad whispered in my ear, "If he doesn't pay the loan back, are you going to foreclose on his bicycle?"

I said, "No, knock on wood, every kid is born with honesty, morality and ethics. They have to be taught something else. I believe he'll pay us back." If you have children, let them work for money for someone honest, moral and ethical so they learn the principle early.

We gave Tommy a copy of all of my tapes and he listened to them 21 times each and took ownership of the material. Tommy said, "It says 'Always start selling at the top.'" Tommy convinced his dad to drive him up to Ronald Reagan's home. Tommy rang the bell and the gatekeeper came out. Tommy gave a two-minute, irresistible sales presentation on his bumper sticker. The gatekeeper reached in his pocket, gave Tommy $1.50 and said, "Here, I want one of those. Hold on and I'll get the former President."

I asked, "Why did you ask him to buy?"

He said, "You said in the tapes to ask everyone to buy."

I said, "I did. I did. I'm guilty."

He sent a bumper sticker to Mikhail Gorbachev with a bill for $1.50 in U.S. funds. Gorbachev sent him back $1.50 and a picture that said, "Go for peace, Tommy," and signed it, "Mikhail Gorbachev, President."

Since I collect autographs, I told Tommy, "I'll give you $500 for Gorbachev's autograph."

He said, "No thanks, Mark."

I said, "Tommy, I own several companies. When you get older, I'd like to hire you."

"Are you kidding?" he answered. "When I get older, I'm going to hire you."

The Sunday edition of the *Orange County Register* did a feature section on Tommy's story, the Children's Free Enterprise Bank and me. Marty Shaw, the journalist, interviewed Tommy for six hours and wrote a phenomenal interview. Marty asked Tommy what he thought his impact would be on world peace. Tommy said, "I don't think I am old enough yet; I think you have to be eight or nine to stop all the wars in the world."

Marty asked, "Who are your heroes?"

He said, "My dad, George Burns, Wally Joyner and Mark Victor Hansen." Tommy has good taste in role models.

Three days later, I got a call from Hallmark. A Hallmark franchisee had faxed a copy of the *Register* article. They were having a convention in San Francisco and wanted Tommy to speak. After all, they saw that Tommy had nine goals for himself:

1. Call about cost (baseball card collateral).

2. Have bumper sticker printed.
3. Make a plan for a loan.
4. Find out how to tell people.
5. Get address of leaders.
6. Write a letter to all of the presidents and leaders of other countries and send them all a free bumper sticker.
7. Talk to everyone about peace.
8. Call the newspaper stand and talk about my business.
9. Have a talk with school.

Hallmark wanted my company to book Tommy to speak. While the talk did not happen because the two-week lead time was too short, the negotiation between Hallmark, myself and Tommy was fun, uplifting and powerful.

Joan Rivers called Tommy Tighe to be on her syndicated television show. Someone had also faxed her a copy of the *Register* interview on Tommy.

"Tommy," Joan said, "this is Joan Rivers and I want you on my TV show which is viewed by millions."

"Great!" said Tommy. He didn't know her from a bottle of Vicks.

"I'll pay you $300," said Joan.

"Great!" said Tommy. Having listened repeatedly to and mastered my *Sell Yourself Rich* tapes, Tommy continued selling Joan by saying: "I am only eight years old, so I can't come alone. You can afford to pay for my mom, too, can't you, Joan?"

"Yes!" Joan replied.

"By the way, I just watched a *Lifestyles of the Rich and Famous* show and it said to stay at the Trump Plaza when you're in New York. You can make that happen, can't you, Joan?"

"Yes," she answered.

"The show also said when in New York, you ought to visit the Empire State Building and the Statue of Liberty. You can get us tickets, can't you?"

"Yes…"

"Great. Did I tell you my mom doesn't drive? So we can use your limo, can't we?"

"Sure," said Joan.

Tommy went on *The Joan Rivers Show* and wowed Joan, the camera crew, the live and television audiences. He was so handsome, interesting, authentic and such a great self-starter. He told such captivating and persuasive stories that the audience was found pulling money out of their wallets to buy a bumper sticker on the spot.

At the end of the show, Joan leaned in and asked, "Tommy, do you really think your bumper sticker will cause peace in the world?"

Tommy, enthusiastically and with a radiant smile, said, "So far I've had it out two years and got the Berlin Wall down. I'm doing pretty good, don't you think?"

— Mark Victor Hansen —

If You Don't Ask, You Don't Get – But If You Do, You Do

Problems are not stop signs, they are guidelines.
~Robert Schuller

My wife Linda and I live in Miami, Florida. When we had just started our self-esteem training program called Little Acorns to teach children how to say no to drugs, sexual promiscuity and other self-destructive behavior, we received a brochure for an educational conference in San Diego. As we read the brochure and realized that everybody who is anybody was going to be there, we realized we had to go. But we didn't see how. We were just getting started, we were working out of our home and we had just about exhausted our personal savings with the early stages of the work. There was no way we could afford the airline tickets or any of the other expenses. But we knew we had to be there, so we started asking.

The first thing I did was to call the conference coordinators in San Diego, explain why we just had to be there and ask them if they would give us two complimentary admissions to the conference. When I explained our situation, what we were doing and why we had to be there, they said yes. So now we had the tickets.

I told Linda we had the tickets and we could get into the conference. She said, "Great! But we're in Miami and the conference is in

San Diego. What do we do next?"

So I said, "We've got to get transportation." I called an airline I knew was doing well at the time, Northeast Airlines. The woman who answered happened to be the secretary to the president so I told her what I needed. She put me directly through to the president, Steve Quinto. I explained to him that I had just talked to the conference people in San Diego, they had given us free tickets to the conference but we were stuck on how to get there and would he please donate two round trip tickets from Miami to San Diego. He said, "Of course I will," just like that. It was that fast and the next thing he said really floored me. He said, "Thank you for asking."

I said, "Pardon me?"

He said, "I don't often have the opportunity to do the best thing that I can for the world unless someone asks me to. The best thing I can ever do is to give of myself and you've asked me to do that. That's a nice opportunity and I want to thank you for that opportunity." I was blown away, but I thanked him and hung up the phone. I looked at my wife and said, "Honey, we got the plane tickets." She said, "Great! Where do we stay?"

Next I called the Holiday Inn Downtown Miami and asked, "Where is your headquarters?" They told me it was in Memphis, Tennessee, so I called Tennessee and they patched me through to the person I needed to talk to. It was a guy in San Francisco. He controlled all of the Holiday Inns in California. I then explained to him that we had obtained our plane tickets through the airlines and asked if there were some way he could help us with the lodging for the three days. He asked if it would be okay if he put us up in their new hotel in downtown San Diego as his guest. I said, "Yes, that would be fine."

He then said, "Wait a minute. I need to caution you that the hotel is about a 35-mile drive from the campus where the conference is being held and you'll have to find out how to get there."

I said, "I'll figure it out if I need to buy a horse." I thanked him and I said to Linda, "Well, honey, we've got the admission, we've got the plane tickets and we've got a place to stay. What we need now is a way to get back and forth from the hotel to the campus twice a day."

Next I called National Car Rental, told them the story and asked if they could help me out. They said, "Would a new Olds 88 be okay?" I said it would be.

In one day we had put the whole thing together.

We did wind up buying our own meals for part of the time but before the conference was over, I stood up, told this story at one of the general assemblies and said, "Anyone who wants to volunteer to take us to lunch now and again would be graciously thanked." About 50 people jumped up and volunteered so we wound up having some of the meals thrown in as well.

We had a marvelous time, learned a lot and connected with people like Jack Canfield, who is still on our advisory board. When we returned, we launched the program and it's been growing about 100 percent a year. This last June we graduated our 2,250th family from the Little Acorn training. We've also held two major conferences for educators called *Making The World Safe For Children*, to which we've invited people from all over the world. Thousands of educators have come to get ideas on how to do self-esteem training in their classrooms while they're still teaching the three *Rs*.

The last time we sponsored the conference we invited educators from 81 nations to come. Seventeen nations sent representatives including some ministers of education. Out of that has grown invitations for us to take our program to the following places: Russia, Ukraine, Byelorussia, Kazakhstan, Mongolia, Taiwan, the Cook Islands and New Zealand.

So you see you can get anything you want if you just ask enough people.

— Rick Gelinas —

Rick Little's Quest

Difficult things take a long time,
impossible things a little longer.
~André A. Jackson

At 5 A.M. Rick Little fell asleep at the wheel of his car, hurtled over a 10-foot embankment and crashed into a tree. He spent the next six months in traction with a broken back. Rick found himself with a lot of time to think deeply about his life — something for which the 13 years of his education had not prepared him. Only two weeks after he was discharged from the hospital, he returned home one afternoon to find his mother lying semiconscious on the floor from an overdose of sleeping pills. Rick confronted once again the inadequacy of his formal education in preparing him to deal with the social and emotional issues of his life.

During the following months Rick began to formulate an idea — the development of a course that would equip students with high self-esteem, relationship skills and conflict management skills. As Rick began to research what such a course should contain, he ran across a study by the National Institute of Education in which 1,000 30-year-olds had been asked if they felt their high school education had equipped them with the skills they needed for the real world. Over 80 percent responded, "Absolutely not."

These 30-year-olds were also asked what skills they now wish they had been taught. The top answers were relationship skills: How to get along better with the people you live with. How to find and keep a job. How to handle conflict. How to be a good parent. How to understand the normal development of a child. How to handle financial management. And how to intuit the meaning of life.

Inspired by his vision of creating a class that might teach these things, Rick dropped out of college and set across the country to interview high school students. In his quest for information on what should be included in the course, he asked over 2,000 students in 120 high schools the same two questions:

1. If you were to develop a program for your high school to help you cope with what you're meeting now and what you think you'll be meeting in the future, what would that program include?

2. List the top 10 problems in your life that you wish were dealt with better at home and in school.

Whether the students were from wealthy private schools or inner city ghettos, rural or suburban, the answers were surprisingly the same. Loneliness and not liking themselves topped the list of problems. In addition, they had the same list of skills they wished they were taught as the ones compiled by the 30-year-olds.

Rick slept in his car for two months, living on a total of $60. Most days he ate peanut butter on crackers. Some days he didn't eat at all. Rick had few resources but he was committed to his dream.

His next step was to make a list of the nation's top educators and leaders in counseling and psychology. He set out to visit everyone on his list to ask for their expertise and support. While they were impressed with his approach — asking students directly what they wanted to learn — they offered little help. "You're too young. Go back to college. Get your degree. Go to graduate school, then you can pursue this." They were less than encouraging.

Yet Rick persisted. By the time he turned 20, he had sold his car, his clothes, had borrowed from friends and was $32,000 in debt. Someone suggested he go to a foundation and ask for money.

His first appointment at a local foundation was a huge disappointment. As he walked into the office, Rick was literally shaking with fear. The vice president of the foundation was a huge dark-haired man with a cold stern face. For a half hour he sat without uttering a word while Rick poured his heart out about his mother, the two thousand kids and plans for a new kind of course for high school kids.

When he was through, the vice president pushed up a stack of folders. "Son," he said, "I've been here nearly 20 years. We've funded all these education programs. And they all failed. Yours will, too. The reasons? They're obvious. You're 20 years old, you have no experience, no money, no college degree. Nothing!"

As he left the foundation office, Rick vowed to prove this man wrong. Rick began a study of which foundations were interested in funding projects for teenagers. He then spent months writing grant proposals — working from early morning until late at night. Rick worked for over a year laboriously writing grant proposals, each one carefully tailored to the interests and requirements of the individual foundations. Each one went out with high hopes and each one came back — rejected.

Proposal after proposal was sent out and rejected. Finally, after the 155th grant proposal had been turned down, all of Rick's support began to crumble.

Rick's parents were begging him to go back to college and Ken Greene, an educator who had left his job to help Rick write proposals, said, "Rick, I have no money left and I have a wife and kids to support. I'll wait for one more proposal. But if it's a turndown, I'll have to go back to Toledo and to teaching."

Rick had one last chance. Activated by desperation and conviction, he managed to talk himself past several secretaries and he secured a lunch date with Dr. Russ Mawby, President of the Kellogg Foundation. On their way to lunch they passed an ice cream stand. "Would you like one?" Mawby asked. Rick nodded. But his anxiety got the better of him. He crushed the cone in his hand and, with chocolate ice cream running between his fingers, he made a surreptitious but frantic effort to shake it loose before Dr. Mawby could note what had happened. But Mawby did see it, and bursting into laughter, he went back to the vendor and brought Rick a bunch of paper napkins.

The young man climbed into the car, red-faced and miserable. How could he request funding for a new educational program when he couldn't even handle an ice cream cone?

Two weeks later Mawby phoned. "You asked for $55,000. We're sorry, but the trustees voted against it." Rick felt tears pressing behind his eyes. For two years he had been working for a dream; which would now go down the drain.

"However," said Mawby, "the trustees did vote unanimously to give you $130,000."

The tears came then. Rick could hardly even stammer out a thank you.

Since that time Rick Little has raised over $100,000,000 to fund his dream. The Quest Skills Programs are currently taught in over 30,000 schools in all 50 states and 32 countries. Three million kids per year are being taught important life skills because one 19-year-old refused to take "no" for an answer.

In 1989, because of the incredible success of Quest, Rick Little expanded his dream and was granted $65,000,000, the second largest grant ever given in U.S. history, to create The International Youth Foundation. The purpose of this foundation is to identify and expand successful youth programs all over the world.

Rick Little's life is a testament to the power of commitment to a high vision, coupled with a willingness to keep on asking until one manifests the dream.

—Adapted from Peggy Mann—

The Magic of Believing

*You must have long-range goals to keep you from
being frustrated by short-range failures.*
~Charles C. Noble

'm not old enough to play baseball or football. I'm not eight yet. My mom told me when you start baseball, you aren't going to be able to run that fast because you had an operation. I told Mom I wouldn't need to run that fast. When I play baseball, I'll just hit them out of the park. Then I'll be able to walk.

— Edward J. McGrath, Jr. —
An Exceptional View of Life

Glenna's Goal Book

Success isn't a result of spontaneous combustion.
You must set yourself on fire.
~Arnold H. Glasow

n 1977 I was a single mother with three young daughters, a house payment, a car payment and a need to rekindle some dreams.

One evening I attended a seminar and heard a man speak about the I x V = R Principle. (Imagination mixed with Vividness becomes Reality.) The speaker pointed out that the mind thinks in pictures, not in words. And as we vividly picture in our mind what we desire, it will become a reality.

This concept struck a chord in my heart. I knew the Biblical truth that the Lord gives us "the desires of our heart" (Psalms 37:4) and that "as a man thinketh in his heart, so is he" (Proverbs 23:7). I was determined to take my written prayer list and turn it into pictures. I began cutting up old magazines and gathering pictures that depicted the "desires of my heart." I arranged them in a photo album and waited expectantly.

I was very specific with my pictures. They included:

1. A good-looking man
2. A woman in a wedding gown and a man in a tuxedo
3. Bouquets of flowers (I'm a romantic)
4. Beautiful diamond jewelry (I rationalized that God loved David

and Solomon and they were two of the richest men who ever lived)

5. An island in the sparkling blue Caribbean
6. A lovely home
7. New furniture
8. A woman who had recently become vice president of a large corporation. (I was working for a company that had no female officers. I wanted to be the first woman vice president in that company.)

About eight weeks later, I was driving down a California freeway, minding my own business at 10:30 in the morning. Suddenly a gorgeous red-and-white Cadillac passed me. I looked at the car because it was beautiful. The driver looked at me and smiled, and I smiled back because I always smile. Now I was in deep trouble. Have you ever done that? I tried to pretend that I hadn't looked. "Who me? I didn't look at you!" He followed me for the next fifteen miles. Scared me to death! I drove a few miles, he drove a few miles. I parked, he parked… And eventually I married him!

On the first day after our first date, Jim sent me a dozen roses. Then I found out that he had a hobby. His hobby was collecting diamonds. Big ones! And he was looking for somebody to decorate. I volunteered! We dated for about two years and every Monday morning I received a long-stemmed red rose and a love note from him.

About three months before we were getting married, Jim said to me, "I have found the perfect place to go on our honeymoon. We will go to St. John's down in the Caribbean." I laughingly said, "I never would have thought of that!"

I did not confess the truth about my picture book until Jim and I had been married for almost a year. It was then that we were moving into our gorgeous new home and furnishing it with the elegant furniture that I had pictured. (Jim turned out to be the West Coast wholesale distributor for one of the finest East Coast furniture manufacturers.)

By the way, the wedding was in Laguna Beach, California, and included the gown and tuxedo as realities. Eight months after I created my dream book, I became the vice president of human resources in the company where I worked.

In some sense this sounds like a fairy tale, but it is absolutely true. Jim and I have made many "picture books" since we have been married. God has filled our lives with the demonstration of these powerful principles of faith at work.

Decide what it is that you want in every area of your life. Imagine it vividly. Then act on your desires by actually constructing your personal goal book. Convert your ideas into concrete realities through this simple exercise. There are no impossible dreams.

— Glenna Salsbury —

Another Check Mark on the List

There are many wonderful things that will never be done if you do not do them.
~Charles D. Gill

One rainy afternoon an inspired 15-year-old boy named John Goddard sat down at his kitchen table in Los Angeles and wrote three words at the top of a yellow pad: "My Life List." Under that heading he wrote down 127 goals. Since then he has completed most of those goals. Look at the list of Goddard's goals that appears below. These are not simple or easy goals. They include climbing the world's major mountains, exploring vast waterways, running a mile in five minutes, reading the complete works of Shakespeare and reading the entire *Encyclopedia Britannica*.

Explore:
✓ 1. Nile River
✓ 2. Amazon River
✓ 3. Congo River
✓ 4. Colorado River
   5. Yangtze River, China
   6. Niger River

7. Orinoco River, Venezuela
✓ 8. Rio Coco, Nicaragua

Study Primitive Cultures In:
✓ 9. The Congo
✓ 10. New Guinea
✓ 11. Brazil
✓ 12. Borneo
✓ 13. The Sudan (John was nearly buried alive in a sandstorm.)
✓ 14. Australia
✓ 15. Kenya
✓ 16. The Philippines
✓ 17. Tanganyika (now Tanzania)
✓ 18. Ethiopia
✓ 19. Nigeria
✓ 20. Alaska

Climb:
  21. Mount Everest
  22. Mount Aconcagua, Argentina
  23. Mount McKinley
✓ 24. Mount Huascaran, Peru
✓ 25. Mount Kilimanjaro
✓ 26. Mount Ararat, Turkey
✓ 27. Mount Kenya
  28. Mount Cook, New Zealand
✓ 29. Mount Popocatepetl, Mexico
✓ 30. The Matterhorn
✓ 31. Mount Rainer
✓ 32. Mount Fuji
✓ 33. Mount Vesuvius
✓ 34. Mount Bromo, Java
✓ 35. Grand Tetons
✓ 36. Mount Baldy, California

✓ 37. Carry out careers in medicine and exploration (Studied pre-med and treats illnesses among primitive tribes)

38. Visit every country in the world (30 to go)

✓ 39. Study Navajo and Hopi Indians

✓ 40. Learn to fly a plane

✓ 41. Ride horse in Rose Parade

Photograph:

✓ 42. Iguaçu Falls, Brazil

✓ 43. Victoria Falls, Rhodesia (Chased by a warthog in the process)

✓ 44. Sutherland Falls, New Zealand

✓ 45. Yosemite Falls

✓ 46. Niagara Falls

✓ 47. Retrace travels of Marco Polo and Alexander the Great

Explore Underwater:

✓ 48. Coral reefs of Florida

✓ 49. Great Barrier Reef, Australia (Photographed a 300-pound clam)

✓ 50. Red Sea

✓ 51. Fiji Islands

✓ 52. The Bahamas

✓ 53. Explore Okefenokee Swamp and the Everglades

Visit:

✓ 54. North and South Poles

✓ 55. Great Wall of China

✓ 56. Panama and Suez Canals

✓ 57. Easter Island

✓ 58. The Galapagos Islands

✓ 59. Vatican City (Saw the pope)

✓ 60. The Taj Mahal

✓ 61. The Eiffel Tower

✓ 62. The Blue Grotto

✓ 63. The Tower of London

✓ 64. The Leaning Tower of Pisa
✓ 65. The Sacred Well of Chichén Itzá, Mexico
✓ 66. Climb Ayers Rock in Australia
67. Follow River Jordan from Sea of Galilee to Dead Sea

Swim In:
✓ 68. Lake Victoria
✓ 69. Lake Superior
✓ 70. Lake Tanganyika
✓ 71. Lake Titicaca, South America
✓ 72. Lake Nicaragua

Accomplish:
✓ 73. Become an Eagle Scout
✓ 74. Dive in a submarine
✓ 75. Land on and take off from an aircraft carrier
✓ 76. Fly in a blimp, hot air balloon and glider
✓ 77. Ride an elephant, camel, ostrich and bronco
✓ 78. Skin dive to 40 feet and hold breath two and a half minutes underwater
✓ 79. Catch a 10-pound lobster and a 10-inch abalone
✓ 80. Play flute and violin
✓ 81. Type 50 words a minute
✓ 82. Take a parachute jump
✓ 83. Learn water and snow skiing
✓ 84. Go on a church mission
✓ 85. Follow the John Muir Trail
✓ 86. Study native medicines and bring back useful ones
✓ 87. Bag camera trophies of elephant, lion, rhino, cheetah, cape buffalo and whale
✓ 88. Learn to fence
✓ 89. Learn jujitsu
✓ 90. Teach a college course
✓ 91. Watch a cremation ceremony in Bali

✓ 92. Explore depths of the sea

  93. Appear in a Tarzan movie (He now considers this an irrelevant boyhood dream)

  94. Own a horse, chimpanzee, cheetah, ocelot and coyote (Yet to own a chimp or cheetah)

  95. Become a ham radio operator

✓ 96. Build own telescope

✓ 97. Write a book (On Nile trip)

✓ 98. Publish an article in *National Geographic*

✓ 99. High jump five feet

✓ 100. Broad jump 15 feet

✓ 101. Run a mile in five minutes

✓ 102. Weigh 175 pounds stripped (still does)

✓ 103. Perform 200 sit-ups and 20 pull-ups

✓ 104. Learn French, Spanish and Arabic

  105. Study dragon lizards on Komodo Island (Boat broke down within 20 miles of island)

✓ 106. Visit birthplace of Grandfather Sorenson in Denmark

✓ 107. Visit birthplace of Grandfather Goddard in England

✓ 108. Ship aboard a freighter as a seaman

  109. Read the entire *Encyclopedia Britannica* (Has read extensive parts in each volume)

✓ 110. Read the Bible from cover to cover

✓ 111. Read the works of Shakespeare, Plato, Aristotle, Dickens, Thoreau, Poe, Rousseau, Bacon, Hemingway, Twain, Burroughs, Conrad, Talmage, Tolstoy, Longfellow, Keats, Whittier and Emerson (Not every work of each)

✓ 112. Become familiar with the compositions of Bach, Beethoven, Debussy, Ibert, Mendelssohn, Lalo, Rimski-Korsakov, Respighi, Liszt, Rachmaninoff, Stravinsky, Toch, Tschaikovsky, Verdi

✓ 113. Become proficient in the use of a plane, motorcycle, tractor, surfboard, rifle, pistol, canoe, microscope, football basketball, bow and arrow, lariat and boomerang

✓ 114. Compose music

✓ 115. Play *Clair de Lune* on the piano

✓ 116. Watch fire-walking ceremony (In Bali and Surinam)

✓ 117. Milk a poisonous snake (Bitten by a diamondback during a photo session)

✓ 118. Light a match with a 22 rifle

✓ 119. Visit a movie studio

✓ 120. Climb Cheops' pyramid

✓ 121. Become a member of the Explorers Club and the Adventurers' Club

✓ 122. Learn to play polo

✓ 123. Travel through the Grand Canyon on foot and by boat

✓ 124. Circumnavigate the globe (four times)

   125. Visit the moon ("Some day if God wills")

✓ 126. Marry and have children (Has five children)

✓ 127. Live to see the 21st Century (He will be 75)

—John Goddard—

Look Out, Baby, I'm Your Love Man!

It is better to be prepared for an opportunity and not have one than to have an opportunity and not be prepared.
~Whitney Young, Jr.

Les Brown and his twin brother were adopted by Mamie Brown, a kitchen worker and maid, shortly after their birth in a poverty-stricken Miami neighborhood.

Because of his hyperactivity and nonstop jabber, Les was placed in special education classes for the learning disabled in grade school and throughout high school. Upon graduation, he became a city sanitation worker in Miami Beach. But he had a dream of being a disc jockey.

At night he would take a transistor radio to bed where he listened to the local jive-talking deejays. He created an imaginary radio station in his tiny room with its torn vinyl flooring. A hairbrush served as his microphone as he practiced his patter, introducing records to his ghost listeners.

His mother and brother could hear him through the thin walls and would shout at him to quit flapping his jaws and go to sleep. But Les didn't listen to them. He was wrapped up in his own world, living a dream. One day Les boldly went to the local radio station during his lunch break from mowing grass for the city. He got into the station manager's office and told him he wanted to be a disc jockey.

The manager eyed this disheveled young man in overalls and a straw hat and inquired, "Do you have any background in broadcasting?"

Les replied, "No, sir, I don't."

"Well, son, I'm afraid we don't have a job for you then." Les thanked him politely and left. The station manager assumed that he had seen the last of this young man. But he underestimated the depth of Les Brown's commitment to his goal. You see, Les had a higher purpose than simply wanting to be a disc jockey. He wanted to buy a nicer house for his adoptive mother, whom he loved deeply. The disc jockey job was merely a step toward his goal.

Mamie Brown had taught Les to pursue his dreams, so he felt sure that he would get a job at that radio station in spite of what the station manager had said.

And so Les returned to the station every day for a week, asking if there were any job openings. Finally the station manager gave in and took him on as an errand boy—at no pay. At first, he fetched coffee or picked up lunches and dinner for the deejays who could not leave the studio. Eventually his enthusiasm for their work won him the confidence of the disc jockeys who would send him in their Cadillacs to pick up visiting celebrities such as the Temptations and Diana Ross and the Supremes. Little did any of them know that young Les did not have a driver's license.

Les did whatever was asked of him at the station—and more. While hanging out with the deejays, he taught himself their hand movements on the control panel. He stayed in the control rooms and soaked up whatever he could until they asked him to leave. Then, back in his bedroom at night, he practiced and prepared himself for the opportunity that he knew would present itself.

One Saturday afternoon while Les was at the station, a deejay named Rock was drinking while on the air. Les was the only other person in the building, and he realized that Rock was drinking himself toward trouble. Les stayed close. He walked back and forth in front of the window in Rock's booth. As he prowled, he said to himself. "Drink,

Rock, drink!"

Les was hungry, and he was ready. He would have run down the street for more booze if Rock had asked. When the phone rang, Les pounced on it. It was that station manager, as he knew it would be.

"Les, this is Mr. Klein."

"Yes," said Les. "I know."

"Les, I don't think Rock can finish his program."

"Yes sir, I know."

"Would you call one of the other deejays to come in and take over?"

"Yes, sir. I sure will."

But when Les hung up the telephone, he said to himself, "Now, he must think I'm crazy."

Les did dial the telephone, but it wasn't to call in another deejay. He called his mother first, and then his girlfriend. "You all go out on the front porch and turn up the radio because I'm about to come on the air!" he said.

He waited about 15 minutes before he called the general manager. "Mr. Klein, I can't find nobody," Les said.

Mr. Klein then asked, "Young man, do you know how to work the controls in the studio?"

"Yes sir," replied Les.

Les darted into the booth, gently moved Rock aside and sat down at the turntable. He was ready. And he was hungry. He flipped on the microphone switch and said, "Look out! This is me, LB, triple P — Les Brown, Your Platter Playing Poppa. There were none before me and there will be none after me. Therefore, that makes me the one and only. Young and single and love to mingle. Certified, bona fide, indubitably qualified to bring you satisfaction, a whole lot of action. Look out, baby, I'm your lo-o-ove man!"

Because of his preparation, Les was ready. He wowed the audience and his general manager. From that fateful beginning, Les went on to a successful career in broadcasting, politics, public speaking and television.

— Jack Canfield —

Willing to Pay the Price

Opportunity is a bird that never perches.
~Claude McDonald

When my wife Maryanne and I were building our Greenspoint Mall hair salon 13 years ago, a Vietnamese fellow would stop by each day to sell us doughnuts. He spoke hardly any English, but he was always friendly, and through smiles and sign language we got to know each other. His name was Le Van Vu.

During the day Le worked in a bakery and at night he and his wife listened to audiotapes to learn English. I later learned that they slept on sacks full of sawdust on the floor of the back room of the bakery.

In Vietnam the Van Vu family was one of the wealthiest in Southeast Asia. They owned almost one-third of North Vietnam, including huge holdings in industry and real estate. However, after his father was brutally murdered, Le moved to South Vietnam with his mother, where he went to school and eventually became a lawyer.

Like his father before him, Le prospered. He saw an opportunity to construct buildings to accommodate the ever-expanding American presence in South Vietnam and soon became one of the most successful builders in the country.

On a trip to the North, however, Le was captured by the North Vietnamese and thrown into prison for three years. He escaped by killing five soldiers and made his way back to South Vietnam where he was arrested again. The South Vietnamese government had assumed he was a "plant" from the North.

After serving time in prison, Le got out and started a fishing company, eventually becoming the largest canner in South Vietnam.

When Le learned that the U.S. troops and embassy personnel were about to pull out of his country, he made a life-changing decision.

He took all of the gold he had hoarded, loaded it aboard one of his fishing vessels and sailed with his wife out to the American ships in the harbor. He then exchanged all his riches for safe passage out of Vietnam to the Philippines, where he and his wife were taken into a refugee camp.

After gaining access to the president of the Philippines, Le convinced him to make one of his boats available for fishing and Le was back in business again. Before he left the Philippines two years later en route for America (his ultimate dream), Le had successfully developed the entire fishing industry in the Philippines.

But en route to America, Le became distraught and depressed about having to start over again with nothing. His wife tells of how she found him near the railing of the ship, about to jump overboard.

"Le," she told him, "if you do jump, whatever will become of me? We've been together for so long and through so much. We can do this together." It was all the encouragement that Le Van Vu needed.

When he and his wife arrived in Houston in 1972, they were flat broke and spoke no English. In Vietnam, family takes care of family, and Le and his wife found themselves ensconced in the back room of his cousin's bakery in the Greenspoint Mall. We were building our salon just a couple of hundred feet away.

Now, as they say, here comes the "message" part of this story:

Le's cousin offered both Le and his wife jobs in the bakery. After taxes, Le would take home $175 per week, his wife $125. Their total annual income, in other words, was $15,600. Further, his cousin offered to sell them the bakery whenever they could come up with a $30,000 down payment. The cousin would finance the remainder with a note for $90,000.

Here's what Le and his wife did:

Even with a weekly income of $300, they decided to continue to live in the back room. They kept clean by taking sponge baths for two years in the mall's restrooms. For two years their diet consisted almost entirely of bakery goods. Each year, for two years, they lived on a total, that's right, a total of $600, saving $30,000 for the down payment.

Le later explained his reasoning, "If we got ourselves an apartment, which we could afford on $300 per week, we'd have to pay the rent. Then, of course, we'd have to buy furniture. Then we'd have to have transportation to and from work, so that meant we'd have to buy a car. Then we'd have to buy gasoline for the car as well as insurance. Then we'd probably want to go places in the car, so that meant we'd need to buy clothes and toiletries. So I knew that if we got that apartment, we'd never get our $30,000 together."

Now, if you think you've heard everything about Le, let me tell you, there's more: After he and his wife had saved the $30,000 and bought the bakery, Le once again sat down with his wife for a serious chat. They still owed $90,000 to his cousin, he said, and as difficult as the past two years had been, they had to remain living in that back room for one more year.

I'm proud to tell you that in one year, my friend and mentor Le Van Vu and his wife, saving virtually every nickel of profit from the business, paid off the $90,000 note, and in just three years, owned an extremely profitable business free and clear.

Then, and only then, the Van Vus went out and got their first apartment. To this day, they continue to save on a regular basis, live on an extremely small percentage of their income, and, of course, always pay cash for any of their purchases.

Do you think that Le Van Vu is a millionaire today? I am happy to tell you, many times over.

— John McCormack —

Everybody Has a Dream

*Jumping at several small opportunities may
get us there more quickly than waiting
for one big one to come along.*
~Hugh Allen

S ome years ago I took on an assignment in a southern county
to work with people on public welfare. What I wanted to
do was show that everybody has the capacity to be self-
sufficient and all we have to do is to activate them. I asked
the county to pick a group of people who were on public welfare,
people from different racial groups and different family constel-
lations. I would then see them as a group for three hours every
Friday. I also asked for a little petty cash to work with as I needed
it.

The first thing I said after I shook hands with everybody was,
"I would like to know what your dreams are." Everyone looked at
me as if I were kind of wacky.

"Dreams? We don't have dreams."

I said, "Well, when you were a kid what happened? Wasn't
there something you wanted to do?"

One woman said to me, "I don't know what you can do with
dreams. The rats are eating up my kids."

"Oh," I said. "That's terrible. No, of course, you are very much involved with the rats and your kids. How can that be helped?"

"Well, I could use a new screen door because there are holes in my screen door."

I asked, "Is there anybody around here who knows how to fix a screen door?"

There was a man in the group, and he said, "A long time ago I used to do things like that but now I have a terribly bad back, but I'll try."

I told him I had some money if he would go to the store and buy some screening and go and fix the lady's screen door. "Do you think you can do that?"

"Yes, I'll try."

The next week, when the group was seated, I said to the woman, "Well, is your screen door fixed?"

"Oh, yes," she said.

"Then we can start dreaming, can't we?" She sort of smiled at me.

I said to the man who did the work, "How do you feel?"

He said, "Well, you know, it's a very funny thing. I'm beginning to feel a lot better."

That helped the group to begin to dream. These seemingly small successes allowed the group to see that dreams were not insane. These small steps began to get people to see and feel that something really could happen.

I began to ask other people about their dreams. One woman shared that she always wanted to be a secretary. I said, "Well, what stands in your way?" (That's always my next question.)

She said, "I have six kids, and I don't have anyone to take care of them while I'm away."

"Let's find out," I said. "Is there anybody in this group who would take care of six kids for a day or two a week while this woman gets some training here at the community college?"

One woman said, "I got kids, too, but I could do that."

"Let's do it," I said. So a plan was created and the woman went to school.

The woman who took in the children became a licensed foster care person. In 12 weeks I had all these people off public welfare. I've not only done that once, I've done it many times.

— Virginia Satir —

Follow Your Dream

Don't live down to expectations. Go out there
and do something remarkable.
~Wendy Wasserstein

I have a friend named Monty Roberts who owns a horse ranch in San Ysidro. He has let me use his house to put on fundraising events to raise money for youth at risk programs.

The last time I was there he introduced me by saying, "I want to tell you why I let Jack use my house. It all goes back to a story about a young man who was the son of an itinerant horse trainer who would go from stable to stable, race track to race track, farm to farm and ranch to ranch, training horses. As a result, the boy's high school career was continually interrupted. When he was a senior, he was asked to write a paper about what he wanted to be and do when he grew up.

"That night he wrote a seven-page paper describing his goal of someday owning a horse ranch. He wrote about his dream in great detail and he even drew a diagram of a 200-acre ranch, showing the location of all the buildings, the stables and the track. Then he drew a detailed floor plan for a 4,000-square-foot house that would sit on the 200-acre dream ranch.

"He put a great deal of his heart into the project and the next day he handed it in to his teacher. Two days later he received his paper back. On the front page was a large red F with a note that read, 'See me after class.'

"The boy with the dream went to see the teacher after class and asked, 'Why did I receive an F?'

"The teacher said, 'This is an unrealistic dream for a young boy like you. You have no money. You come from an itinerant family. You have no resources. Owning a horse ranch requires a lot of money. You have to buy the land. You have to pay for the original breeding stock and later you'll have to pay large stud fees. There's no way you could ever do it.' Then the teacher added, 'If you will rewrite this paper with a more realistic goal, I will reconsider your grade.'

"The boy went home and thought about it long and hard. He asked his father what he should do. His father said, 'Look, son, you have to make up your own mind on this. However, I think it is a very important decision for you.'

"Finally, after sitting with it for a week, the boy turned in the same paper, making no changes at all. He stated, 'You can keep the F and I'll keep my dream.'"

Monty then turned to the assembled group and said, "I tell you this story because you are sitting in my 4,000-square-foot house in the middle of my 200-acre horse ranch. I still have that school paper framed over the fireplace." He added, "The best part of the story is that two summers ago that same schoolteacher brought thirty kids to camp out on my ranch for a week. When the teacher was leaving, he said, 'Look, Monty, I can tell you this now. When I was your teacher, I was something of a dream stealer. During those years I stole a lot of kids' dreams. Fortunately you had enough gumption not to give up on yours.'"

Don't let anyone steal your dreams. Follow your heart, no matter what.

—Jack Canfield—

The Box

Opportunity is a parade. Even as one chance passes,
the next is a fife and drum echoing in the distance.
~Robert Brault

When I was a senior in college, I came home for Christmas vacation and anticipated a fun-filled fortnight with my two brothers. We were so excited to be together, we volunteered to watch the store so that my mother and father could take their first day off in years. The day before my parents went to Boston, my father took me quietly aside to the little den behind the store. The room was so small that it held only a piano and a hide-a-bed couch. In fact, when you pulled the bed out, it filled the room and you could sit on the foot of it and play the piano. Father reached behind the old upright and pulled out a cigar box. He opened it and showed me a little pile of newspaper articles. I had read so many Nancy Drew detective stories that I was excited and wide-eyed over the hidden box of clippings.

"What are they?" I asked.

Father replied seriously, "These are articles I've written and some letters to the editor that have been published." As I began to read, I saw at the bottom of each neatly clipped article the name Walter Chapman. "Why didn't you tell me you'd done this?" I asked.

"Because I didn't want your mother to know. She has always told me that since I didn't have much education, I shouldn't try to write. I wanted to run for some political office also, but she told me I shouldn't try. I guess she was afraid she'd be embarrassed if I lost. I just wanted to try for the fun of it. I figured I could write without her knowing it, and so I did. When each item would be printed, I'd cut it out and hide it in this box. I knew someday I'd show the box to someone, and it's you."

He watched me as I read over a few of the articles and when I looked up, his big blue eyes were moist. "I guess I tried for something too big this last time," he added.

"Did you write something else?"

"Yes, I sent some suggestions in to our denominational magazine on how the national nominating committee could be selected more fairly. It's been three months since I sent it in. I guess I tried for something too big."

This was such a new side to my fun-loving father that I didn't quite know what to say, so I tried, "Maybe it'll still come."

"Maybe, but don't hold your breath." Father gave me a little smile and a wink and then closed the cigar box and tucked it into the space behind the piano.

The next morning our parents left on the bus to the Haverhill Depot where they took a train to Boston. Jim, Ron and I ran the store and I thought about the box. I'd never known my father liked to write. I didn't tell my brothers; it was a secret between Father and me. The Mystery of the Hidden Box.

Early that evening I looked out the store window and saw my mother get off the bus — alone. She crossed the Square and walked briskly through the store.

"Where's Dad?" we asked together.

"Your father's dead," she said without a tear.

In disbelief we followed her to the kitchen where she told us they had been walking through the Park Street subway station in the midst of crowds of people when Father had fallen to the floor. A nurse bent over him, looked up at Mother and said simply, "He's dead."

Mother had stood by him stunned, not knowing what to do as people tripped over him in their rush through the subway. A priest said, "I'll call the police," and disappeared. Mother straddled Dad's body for about an hour. Finally an ambulance came and took them both to the morgue where Mother had to go through his pockets and remove his watch. She'd come back on the train alone and then home on the local bus. Mother told us the shocking tale without shedding a tear. Not showing emotion had always been a matter of discipline and pride for her. We didn't cry either and we took turns waiting on the customers.

One steady patron asked, "Where's the old man tonight?"

"He's dead," I replied.

"Oh, too bad," and he left.

I'd not thought of him as the old man, and I was mad at the question, but he was 70 and Mother was only 60. He'd always been healthy and happy and he'd cared for frail Mother without complaining and now he was gone. No more whistling, no more singing hymns while stocking shelves. The "old man" was gone.

On the morning of the funeral, I sat at the table in the store opening sympathy cards and pasting them in a scrapbook when I noticed the church magazine in the pile. Normally I would never have opened what I viewed as a dull religious publication, but just maybe that sacred article might be there and it was.

I took the magazine to the little den, shut the door, and burst into tears. I'd been brave, but seeing Dad's bold recommendations to the national convention in print was more than I could bear. I read and cried and then I read again. I pulled out the box from behind the piano and under the clippings I found a two-page letter to my father from Henry Cabot Lodge, Sr., thanking him for his campaign suggestions.

I didn't tell anyone about my box. It remained a secret.

— Florence Littauer —

Encouragement

It is never too late to be who you might have been.
~George Eliot

Some of the greatest success stories of history have followed a word of encouragement or an act of confidence by a loved one or a trusted friend. Had it not been for a confident wife, Sophia, we might not have listed among the great names of literature the name of Nathaniel Hawthorne. When Nathaniel, a heartbroken man, went home to tell his wife that he was a failure and had been fired from his job in a custom house, she surprised him with an exclamation of joy.

"Now," she said triumphantly, "you can write your book!"

"Yes," replied the man, with sagging confidence, "and what shall we live on while I am writing it?"

To his amazement, she opened a drawer and pulled out a substantial amount of money.

"Where on earth did you get that?" he exclaimed.

"I have always known you were a man of genius," she told him. "I knew that someday you would write a masterpiece. So every week, out of the money you gave me for housekeeping, I saved a little bit. So here is enough to last us for one whole year."

From her trust and confidence came one of the greatest novels of American literature, *The Scarlet Letter.*

— Nido Qubein —

Walt Jones

The big question is whether you are going to be able to say a hearty yes to your adventure.
~Joseph Campbell

No one better epitomizes the fact that success is a journey and not a destination than the many green and growing "human becomings" who do not allow age to be a deterrent to accomplishment. Florence Brooks joined the Peace Corps when she was 64 years of age. Gladys Clappison was living in the dormitory at the University of Iowa working on her Ph.D. in history at age 82. Then there was Ed Stitt, who at age 87, was working on his community college degree program in New Jersey. Ed said it kept him from getting "old-timers' disease" and kept his brain alive.

Probably no one person has stirred my imagination over the years more than Walt Jones of Tacoma, Washington. Walt outlived his third wife to whom he was married for 52 years. When she died, someone said to Walt that it must be sad losing such a long-time friend. His response was, "Well, of course it was, but then again it may be for the best."

"Why was that?"

"I don't want to be negative or say anything to defame her wonderful character, but she kind of petered out on me in the last decade."

When asked to explain, he went on to add, "She just never wanted to do nothin', just kind of became a stick-in-the-mud. Ten years ago when I was 94, I told my wife we ain't never seen nothin' except the beautiful Pacific Northwest. She asked me what was on my mind, and I told her I was thinkin' about buying a motor home and maybe we could visit all 48 of the contiguous states. 'What do you think of that?'

"She said, 'I think you're out of your mind, Walt.'

"'Whydya say that?' I asked.

"'We'd get mugged out there. We'd die and there wouldn't be a funeral parlor.' Then she asked me, 'Who's going to drive, Walter?' and I said, 'I am, Lambie.' 'You'll kill us!' she said.

"I'd like to make footprints in the sands of time before I check out, but you can't make footprints in the sands of time if you're sitting on your butt… unless your intent is to make buttprints in the sands of time."

"So now that she's gone, Walt, what do you intend to do?"

"What do I intend to do? I buried the old gal and bought me a motor home. This is 1976, and I intend to visit all 48 of the states to celebrate our bicentennial."

Walt got to 43 of the states that year selling curios and souvenirs. When asked if he ever picked up hitchhikers, he said, "No way. Too many of them will club you over the head for four bits or sue you for whiplash if you get into an accident."

Walt hadn't had his motor home but a few months and his wife had only been buried for six months when he was seen driving down the street with a rather attractive 62-year-old woman at his side.

"Walt?" he was asked.

"Yeah," he replied.

"Who was the woman sitting by your side? Who's your new lady friend, Walt?"

To which he replied, "Yes, she is."

"Yes she is what?"

"My lady friend."

"Lady friend? Walt, you've been married three times, you're 104 years of age. This woman must be four decades younger than you."

"Well," he responded, "I quickly discovered that man cannot live in a motor home alone."

"I can understand that, Walt. You probably miss having someone to talk to after having had a companion all these years."

Without hesitation Walt replied, "You know, I miss that, too."

"Too? Are you inferring that you have a romantic interest?"

"I just might."

"Walt…"

"What?" he said.

"There comes a time in a person's life when you knock off that stuff."

"Sex?" he replied.

"Yes."

"Why?" he asked.

"Well, because that kind of physical exertion could be hazardous to a person's health."

Walt considered the question and said, "Well, if she dies, she dies."

In 1978 with double digit inflation heating up in our country, Walt was a major investor in a condominium development. When asked why he was taking his money out of a secure bank account and putting it into a condo development, he said, "Ain't you heard? These are inflationary times. You've got to put your money into real property so it will appreciate and be around for your later years when you really need it." How's that for positive thinking?

In 1980 he sold off a lot of his property in and around Pierce County, Washington. Many people thought Walt was cashing in his chips. He assembled his friends and quickly made it clear that he was not cashing in his chips, but he had sold off the property for cash flow. "I took a small down and a 30-year contract. I got four grand a month comin' in until I'm 138."

He celebrated his 110th birthday on the Johnny Carson Show. He walked out resplendent in his white beard and black hat looking a little like the late Colonel Sanders, and Johnny says, "It's good to have you here, Walt."

"It's good to be anywhere at 110, Johnny."

"110?"

"110."

"1-1-0?"

"What's the matter, Carson, you losin' your hearin'? That's what I said. That's what I am. What's the big deal?"

"The big deal is you're within three days of being twice as old as I am."

That would get your attention, wouldn't it? One hundred and ten years of age — a green, growing human becoming. Walt picked up the opening and quickly alluded to Johnny.

"How old would you be if you didn't know the date you were born and there weren't no durned calendar to semi-depress you once a year? Ever heard of people getting depressed because of a calendar date? Oh, Lordy, I hit my 30th birthday. I'm so depressed, I'm over the hill. Oh, no, I hit my 40th birthday. Everybody in my work team dressed in black and sent a hearse to pick me up. Oh, no I'm 50 years old. Half a century old. They sent me dead roses with cobwebs. Johnny, who says you're supposed to roll over and die when you're 65? I have friends more prosperous since they were 75 than they were before. And as a result of a little condominium investment I made a few years ago, I've made more bucks since I was 105 than I did before. Can I give you my definition of depression, Johnny?"

"Go ahead."

"Missing a birthday."

May the story of Walt Jones inspire all of us to remain green and growing every day of our lives.

— Bob Moawad —

Are You Strong Enough to Handle Critics?

No one can make you feel inferior
without your consent.
~Eleanor Roosevelt

t is not the critic who counts, not the man who points out how the strong man stumbles or where the doer of deeds could have done them better. The credit belongs to the man who is actually in the arena, whose face is marred by dust and sweat and blood, who strives valiantly, who errs and comes short again and again because there is no effort without error and shortcomings, who knows the great devotion, who spends himself in a worthy cause, who at best knows in the end the high achievement of triumph and who at worst, if he fails while daring greatly, knows his place shall never be with those timid and cold souls who know neither victory nor defeat.

— Theodore Roosevelt —

Risking

If you don't take risks, you'll have a wasted soul.
~Drew Barrymore

Two seeds lay side by side in the fertile spring soil.

The first seed said, "I want to grow! I want to send my roots deep into the soil beneath me, and thrust my sprouts through the earth's crust above me. I want to unfurl my tender buds like banners to announce the arrival of spring. I want to feel the warmth of the sun on my face and the blessing of the morning dew on my petals!

And so she grew.

The second seed said, "I am afraid. If I send my roots into the ground below, I don't know what I will encounter in the dark. If I push my way through the hard soil above me I may damage my delicate sprouts. What if I let my buds open and a snail tries to eat them? And if I were to open my blossoms, a small child may pull me from the ground. No, it is much better for me to wait until it is safe."

And so she waited.

A yard hen scratching around in the early spring ground for food found the waiting seed and promptly ate it.

MORAL OF THE STORY
Those of us who refuse to risk and grow get swallowed up by life.

— Patty Hansen —

Try Something Different

Fall seven times, stand up eight.
~Japanese Proverb

When we first read the following story, we had just begun teaching a course called "The Million Dollar Forum," a course designed to teach people to accelerate their income up to levels of a million dollars a year or more. Early on we discovered people get locked into a rut of trying harder without trying smarter. Trying harder doesn't always work. Sometimes we need to do something radically different to achieve greater levels of success. We need to break out of our paradigm prisons, our habit patterns and our comfort zones.

***

I'm sitting in a quiet room at the Milcroft Inn, a peaceful little place hidden back among the pine trees about an hour out of Toronto. It's just past noon, late July, and I'm listening to the desperate sounds of a life-or-death struggle going on a few feet away.

There's a small fly burning out the last of its short life's energies in a futile attempt to fly through the glass of the windowpane. The whining wings tell the poignant story of the fly's strategy: *Try harder.*

But it's not working.

The frenzied effort offers no hope for survival. Ironically, the struggle is part of the trap. It is impossible for the fly to try hard enough to succeed at breaking through the glass. Nevertheless, this little insect has staked its life on reaching its goal through raw effort and determination.

This fly is doomed. It will die there on the windowsill.

Across the room, ten steps away, the door is open. Ten seconds of flying time and this small creature could reach the outside world it seeks. With only a fraction of the effort now being wasted, it could be free of this self-imposed trap. The breakthrough possibility is there. It would be so easy.

Why doesn't the fly try another approach, something dramatically different? How did it get so locked in on the idea that this particular route and determined effort offer the most promise for success? What logic is there in continuing until death to seek a breakthrough with more of the same?

No doubt this approach makes sense to the fly. Regrettably, it's an idea that will kill.

Trying harder isn't necessarily the solution to achieving more. It may not offer any real promise for getting what you want out of life. Sometimes, in fact, it's a big part of the problem.

If you stake your hopes for a breakthrough on trying harder than ever, you may kill your chances for success.

— Price Pritchett —

Service with a Smile

The truth brings with it a great measure
of absolution, always.
~R.D. Laing

A man wrote a letter to a small hotel in a Midwest town he planned to visit on his vacation. He wrote:

I would very much like to bring my dog with me. He is well groomed and very well-behaved. Would you be willing to permit me to keep him in my room with me at night?

An immediate reply came from the hotel owner, who said:

I've been operating this hotel for many years. In all that time, I've never had a dog steal towels, bedclothes or silverware or pictures off the walls.

I've never had to evict a dog in the middle of the night for being drunk and disorderly. And I've never had a dog run out on a hotel bill.

Yes, indeed, your dog is welcome at my hotel. And, if your dog will vouch for you, you're welcome to stay here, too.

— Karl Albrecht and Ron Zenke —
Service America

Chapter

6

Chicken Soup for the Soul

Overcoming Obstacles

The greater the obstacle, the more glory in overcoming it.

~Molière

Before It's Too Late

Caregiving often calls us to lean
into love we didn't know possible.
~Tia Walker

Family caregiving is a subject that is very close to my heart since I was a longtime caregiver for my mom Gladyce, who lived to be 93 years old, and my brother Jeff, who had many of the complications of Type II diabetes and also required decades of care.

I grew up in Sacramento, California, where my dad was a cancer surgeon, my mother a stay-at-home mom. My dad was also an avid private pilot and often flew to speak at medical conventions. When I was 14 years old my dad was returning from speaking at a cancer convention when his plane crashed and he was killed. Our world was turned upside down.

When I was in my early twenties, I moved east to New York City to work as a television journalist for ABC-TV. My mom and my brother remained in our hometown of Sacramento. In my early thirties, with my brother's health failing, I found myself financially responsible for their lives.

Unfortunately, we never took the time to sit down and have that important family meeting to make a plan for what would happen when the time came that Mom needed more daily care, or as it happened — that one of them would die.

I learned this lesson the hard way when I got the call that my brother Jeff had died suddenly at age 56. My mother was 88 years old, overcome with grief, and her dementia had suddenly worsened because of the shock of my brother's death. She was unable to cope with even the simplest of matters and I was left with so many questions and so few answers. I wished that I had talked to my mother and brother about their health, their insurance, their banking, their business affairs, and their end-of-life wishes when they were healthy enough to be able to provide me the information.

When I arrived back home in California following my brother's death, knowing I would have to begin acting on my mom's behalf, I began looking for all the important documents. I sifted through thousands of papers trying to find car titles, bank accounts, insurance policies, etc.

My mom had no idea where to even find her driver's license, her passport, or her social security card. How could it be that I was finding stacks of old mail and newspapers, and years of living in every nook and cranny, but not any of the important documents that I needed?

When few could be found, I had to reconstruct my mother's identity so that I could get the documents necessary to run her life. First, a birth certificate and then her marriage license, and with those in hand, I was able to get her a new Social Security card and Medicare card. I had always thought that I had everything under control with my mom and brother. Boy, was I mistaken.

We all know the day will come when we need to step in and deal with the demise of a parent, a spouse, a sibling, or another loved one and we all need to know where all those important papers are. Where is your parents' bank? Is there a safety deposit box? Where's the key and what's the code? I think it's fair to say that most people don't know all this information. And, frankly, you should know it about your spouse as well as your parents.

Frankly, my situation is not all that uncommon. I think it's fair to say most people are not prepared for the day when it falls to them to be a caregiver. As adult children we seem to find it difficult to press our parents to talk about their twilight years and their end-of-life issues. However, dealing with these issues before a crisis hits can make this difficult life event so much easier to manage.

After my brother's death, along with planning a funeral I had to plan a new life for my mom. I had to become an instant expert on senior assisted-living facilities and decide which kind would be best for my mom.

But that was the easy part, trust me. I then had to have that difficult conversation that none of us ever wants to have with our parents—the one where we tell them they must leave the comfort of their home and move into a senior facility. It doesn't matter how pretty or exclusive the place is, it means moving out of the home where they feel safe and secure. Needless to say, my mom didn't want to move. They never do and you can't blame them.

I moved my mom into a fancy assisted-living facility. In my mind, it was where my mom belonged. I thought she would go to the dining room and be a social butterfly with other seniors and then retreat to a beautifully decorated apartment where she could entertain. The problem with my well-meaning plan is that I was making arrangements for the mom that I used to know, and not who she had become. My mom now couldn't remember who people were, and she would get frightened when taken downstairs to the dining room. And for the first time, my mom was afraid of being left alone in an apartment, no matter how pretty it looked. As soon as it would start to get dark, she suffered from sundown syndrome, becoming increasingly frightened as the shadows fell into the darkness of night.

Less than a year later, I was back in California looking for yet another home where Mom would be happy and safe. I tried to talk her into moving back east closer to me; but she still had friends in Sacramento who came to visit her. I found a facility that provided a much higher level of care, where aides would come in throughout the day to assist her. But over the next year she took numerous falls and would end up in the hospital each time. She was having issues with her balance, and with each fall the injuries got worse; first it was a broken toe, then it was a broken rib, then it was staples in the back of the head. Every time it happened, I jumped on an airplane and flew to California.

Finally, after yet another fall, her physician told me that the next fall could be fatal. He recommended I move her to a small residential care facility, a private home with only a few residents, where she would be watched round the clock.

I found a lovely house with six residents, each with their own bedroom. When we visited, the residents were sitting together in the living room, chatting and watching TV, and the care workers were preparing lunch. The home was impeccably clean, and the food being readied in the kitchen smelled yummy. It turned out to be a wonderful environment for Mom.

If there is one thing that I've learned in this journey that would have made taking on the role of caregiver more manageable, it would have been *asking more questions when I could still get answers*. Families need to have these talks, but of course the tendency by most people is to duck the subject. It's like the elephant in the room, yet we just can't get the words out of our mouths: "Hey, what are we going to do with Mom and Dad when Mom and Dad can't take care of themselves?"

My recommendation to everyone is to *call a family meeting* and approach it as you would any other business meeting. Think through the areas that should be discussed and create an agenda. Where do we think Mom and Dad should be living as they age? Is there anyone they might move in with when the time comes? You need to ask these questions. Go down the checklist. Is there a will in place? Do you have a power of attorney for their health and business? Is there an advanced healthcare directive? Do your parents have long-term health care insurance? If not, how will you pay for their care? Do you know their end-of-life wishes?

Many parents are reluctant to have this conversation, and finances can be an especially sensitive topic, but it is essential for all adult children to open this line of communication. Don't make the discussion about what "you are going to have to do for them," since no parent wants to feel like a burden. Make the discussion about what "they want to do and how you might be able to help them towards that end."

It's often best to have an initial meeting without your parents present, so you can be honest and forthcoming about what you are all willing and able to do. Maybe everyone can't help equally, but you can talk about what each of you *could* do. Perhaps one sibling is an accountant and could take care of finances. Is there a stay-at-home mom or an empty nester who could help with day-to-day care? Is there a teenager who loves driving around but needs gas money? There's your chauffeur to doctor's appointments and the runner to the drugstore for Grandma. Discuss your options and have a plan in place — it will mean having the information necessary to help your loved ones when they need your help the most and it often means that you will also be protecting yourself.

I often recommend *interviewing your parents, grandparents, and other relatives on video.* Construct an interview ahead of time; ask them what life was like when you were a child and what life was like for them when they were young. Ask about when your parents met, courted, got married — this kind of video recording of your family history is priceless.

Make sure that you also ask family members about childhood illnesses or family health issues that might affect your own health risks. Once you have them talking, then you can ask about their wishes for their older life. Ask questions like: How do you envision your Golden Years? Where do you hope to live as you get older and need more care? And when the day comes, what kind of funeral do you want? Some may think this is morbid, but it's not. Avoiding these issues can create an incredible emotional and sometimes financial burden for adult children.

Any way you slice it, caregiving can be a difficult role, no matter how much you love your mom, your dad, or whoever you're caring for. It can devastate families and marriages as well as your health. Studies have shown that the constant stress of providing care can take as many as ten years off a person's life. People often report that their caregiver role has resulted in less time for family and friends, and many report giving up vacations, hobbies, and social activities.

Caregiving also has a major impact in the workplace. More than half of those working caregivers say they need to go into work late, leave early or take time off during the day to provide the care. Some report having to take a leave of absence, shift from full time to part time, quit work entirely, lose their job benefits, turn down promotions, or choose early retirement.

Caregiving will never be easy emotionally, but it doesn't have to be such a financial and legal struggle. We just need to take steps to be prepared.

Without a Durable Power of Attorney, you cannot conduct business for them and if you do not have permission to ask questions of their physicians, doctors cannot give you vital medical information. Without an "Advanced Health Care Directive" you won't know their wishes if faced with tough decisions when their life is in the balance. And when the day comes that you must handle their death, if they don't have a will, you won't know how they wish to be buried, or how they wish to distribute their belongings.

I hope that by sharing my caregiving journey I have helped you to be better prepared. In closing, I think the most important lesson I learned through my years of caregiving, is just to *keep the love connection going*. Just tell them that you love them again and again and again.

—Joan Lunden—

One Step Removed

My piece of bread only belongs to me when
I know that everyone else has a share,
and that no one starves while I eat.
~Leo Tolstoy

orn in Sicily, Italy, I eventually became one of six boys living the rough and tumble life, unless my father was home. He lived by an unwritten rule of intolerance. When he got fed up with the noise threshold, that was it; no army could stand in the way of his wrath. I didn't know it until many years later, that his seemingly impetuous anger stemmed from his being in World War II and serving a one-and-a-half year stint in a POW camp.

We moved to the United States when I was three, as some of my uncles and relatives emigrated before us, eventually making Chicago our home. I took a "two-year vacation" before I began helping my brothers with their paper route at age five. I would get up as early as 4:30 A.M. to help them. When the weather was more decent, I would get up as late as 5:30 A.M. seven days a week. Neither snow, rain, nor storm would delay us. The papers had to be delivered.

Money was tight. My mother took care of six boys and my father worked in a factory. He took the bus to work every day, and to save the five cents the bus transfer would have cost he walked the additional miles to work regardless of the weather. One time I heard him reluctantly confess to my mother that it was so cold that he anted up the five cents for the transfer. As a teenager looking for a better job, I once walked the same route that my father walked every day, and it was a very long tedious walk to the main avenue.

I did my part to help my parents, always giving them every penny I made. In the beginning it was a few dollars every few weeks, working a few hours a day. I delivered the papers in time to go home, have breakfast, and then walk a few miles to school regardless of the weather, never taking a bus.

At eight I earned responsibility for my own route and cart of papers, except on some Sundays as the *Chicago Tribune* was so thick and heavy that I literally could not budge the giant cart. I delivered the papers regardless of the weather. The brutal wind would at times cause me to hang onto my cart tightly to avoid being blown away, and at times it made it hard to breathe.

When the Chicago winters were even worse than normal, the wind-chill would take us to another level of freezing. Then, I wore two pairs of socks, two pants, three different undershirts and sweaters, a winter jacket, a hat and two pairs of gloves. After a few hours of delivering papers, I was usually frozen stiff. I would lie on our radiator to defrost myself upon arriving home.

When I wasn't delivering one hundred or so heavy Sunday papers, I delivered the regular weekday papers in a bag thrown over my shoulder. On heavier paper days, my shoulders would ache badly, causing me to switch shoulders constantly from the intense pain that would set in. The faster I delivered them, the less weight, the less the ache. You can imagine my excitement when in my teens we had enough money to get a bicycle to deliver the newspapers. That was a gift from God.

One day I overheard my dad talking with my mom about the fact that he made $75 a week. That motivated me to always deliver the papers no matter how I felt or how much I wanted to stop and sleep in. I never gave up.

At fourteen, after ten years of paper delivery, I went into fast food. To get hired I needed a physical. I found a doctor, looked up the route, and took a train to and from. I got the physical and got hired. I always took care of things myself. I don't even think my parents ever knew that I did that. You took care of things on your own, that was my mentality on everything.

Once I got the fast-food job, I made a proclamation to my parents. Henceforth, I would pay everything myself in terms of school, books, clothes and so forth. I kept my money and learned as best I could how to manage the five to ten dollars a week that I made. It was fun.

That was the foundation which set my course in life.

At nineteen, I started working in corporate America. One of my first jobs was as a professional typist. However, I had never typed anything before, except for using a public typewriter at the local post office a few times when addressing envelopes.

This did not deter me. I went to the library and got a book on how to type. I practiced until I became the best and fastest typist at the company, being able to type faster than the machines would let me. Eventually I worked out the pace just perfectly so that no two keys would ever get jammed. My typing skills entertained my co-workers.

Later, I put myself through college, while continuing to work and help support my family. I graduated *summa cum laude*. That was my mentality — to do it right.

Eventually I started a lead generation company in the early 2000s and got tired of the ups and downs of constant changes in rules and regulations. I then decided to try podcasting, though I had no broadcasting or radio background. Like everything before, I educated myself on how to podcast. With the help of Michael Benner, a radio personality, as my mentor I began in fall 2015. I had zero audience, but I jumped in with both feet and learned as I'd always done.

By the next year, I was getting 25,000 downloads per episode and I started a second show on VoiceAmerica. In a year my show was #1 at VoiceAmerica and still is to this day. By my seventh year I busted through the sound barrier of 35 million listens.

Throughout my adult life, I've helped take care of others in need. At first, it was participating in toy drives for the children in hospitals during the holidays.

Then one year my wife and I noticed a growing number of people without homes in our neighborhood and thought, "Why not help them out?" They needed food and basic supplies. In fact, some had children and pets with them. I called them "our neighbors" instead of calling them "homeless people." Thus "Breakfast With Our Neighbors" began one Christmas Eve.

I put out social media posts asking people for help and my goodness, did we get help! On the day of the event, people showed up with tents, clothing, sleeping bags, food galore, supplies like crazy… You name it, we had it. The press showed up and we made front page of the Opinion section of the *OC Register*.

Eventually we established The Southgate Foundation to focus on helping the elderly, invalids, orphans, widows and widowers. With other volunteers we've passed out over 130,000 meals to date, plus clothing, everyday-living items and so forth. With God's help, we do what we can to help others. After all, I know what it's like to be one paycheck away from having no home. Our neighbors are just like us, one step removed.

— Tony D'Urso —

Love Is All You Need

*If you find it in your heart to care for somebody else,
you will have succeeded.*
~Maya Angelou

I entered the principal's office, and at fifteen years young, I had no idea what would happen next. "So, what are you going to do?" said Sister Bernadine.

"I'm going to get married... because I love him."

The next words seemingly came from underneath Sister Bernadine's breath as she solemnly said, "You don't even know what love is." Her comment startled me.

My next class happened to be religion, and another nun stood at the head of the room. Sister Cynthia had no idea what had just transpired in the principal's office. What I remember is Sister Cynthia's warm embrace as she hugged me at the end of class, saying, "Everything is going to be all right." This positive nudge forged my path as that hug sent warmth to the marrow in my bones; I did not overly dwell on Sister Bernadine's comment until thirty years later.

***

Once my pregnancy became obvious, the school administrators instructed me to drop out.

Being a teenage mother came with challenges, but I never thought about missing out on anything. The baby had to be fed, the house cleaned. My husband Scott came home every night for dinner.

With two GEDs (respectively) as collateral, we opened a small grocery store in what was considered the most challenging area of New Orleans. Some people probably felt sorry for us hustling so hard inside neighborhoods that other people would never care to drive through; however, our fresh eyes saw a golden opportunity. The neighborhood in which we worked to make a living blessed us with more knowledge than we ever could have received in any business college classroom. We did what needed to be done to the best of our ability, and within twenty years we had ten grocery stores employing over three hundred people. Recognizing the basic and vital need of people to have nearby stores gave us the motivation we needed.

We thought we were doing everything right until Hurricane Katrina. It was a game changer.

My grandmother, Laureta, drowned in the St. Rita's nursing home catastrophe, and all of our businesses were submerged in water, as was everything else around us.

There are times in life when the needs are so great that you could become paralyzed with fear. To keep your sanity in times of suffering is to not peer too far into the future. We did what needed to be done. Clean up, get up, go to sleep, wake up, and do it all over again.

I never dreamed I'd be running after pickup trucks trying to get people to work for us, but there I was. I walked along the parking lots where roofing crews waited to be picked up, and I'd just say to them, "Hey, y'all, do you want a better paying job that treats you well? We're hiring!" It didn't take long before we had fulltime crews of more than thirty workers repairing roofs all over the city.

Of course, I would never want to go through a hurricane of such magnitude ever again, but in a strange way, it was like operating a tiny piece of paradise in Hell. Everyone worked together to place thousands of roofs on the homes of fellow New Orleanians, and it didn't take long before we became one of the top private construction companies in the city.

This was our season of construction. We slowly pulled ourselves from the pit of financial ruin, and it had all begun by working with the community to recognize their needs.

Then, sometimes, life is kind enough to offer a second chance.

I never had the chance to get a college degree, but at the age of 43 I had the opportunity. While I was having dinner at home, I wondered out loud if I had gotten too old for school. My son said, "Mom, you're going to be 50 years old with a degree or not; it's up to you to make it happen." The words coming from my child made perfect sense. The next day, I enrolled in Tulane's School of Continuing Studies — and it was love at first lecture.

Those days were filled with deep readings, reflection, and weekly tests. The professors pushed me to think about things I did not normally think about, and four years later, I was on my way to a master's degree at Harvard Divinity School.

***

The week before graduation, a young man on campus asked if I would share my secret to success. He'd asked some other people whom he regarded as successful the same thing, inviting them to join him and a few other Harvard seniors for a casual conversation in Harvard Yard. When the day came, the Yard was filled with inquisitive students, all curious to learn the reasons for our success in life. As one of the few women in the group, I could tell the young man expected a long answer, which was why my one-word answer perplexed him.

"Love,'" I said.

"That's it?'" he asked.

"Yup, that's the reason." It's the answer I knew in my heart was most true.

I was unconditionally loved as a child; I had never been concerned about failure or coming up against the word "no." I had every confidence in the world that I would succeed at whatever I put my heart into. Even when Scott and I told my parents that I was pregnant, the love they showed me was limitless. Sure, they were disappointed, and the tears that welled up in their eyes spoke of the dreams they'd had for me, but their love was unwavering. Because of that love, I faced the world with unparalleled confidence.

When a person is loved, I told the young man, they're not afraid to make mistakes. They automatically have a leg up with the decisions they need to make in life because they believe not only in what they're doing, they believe in themselves.

Today, I teach world religions at a small Catholic university and operate a non-profit literacy project inside a po'boy shop in the heart of New Orleans. The "Eat and Read at Melba's" literacy project has garnered attention from some of the best writers in the world, such as Colson Whitehead, Sister Helen Prejean, Professor Eddie Glaude, Jr., Walter Isaacson, Matthew McConaughey, Professor Benjamin Friedman, and journalist Christina Lamb, as they visited to share their books with New Orleanians. Even President Bill Clinton, First Lady Hillary and Chelsea Clinton and *The Today Show* have visited to recognize what we're doing to develop lifelong learners. We have offered 18,500 free books to date.

Thirty years earlier, Sister Bernadine was both right and wrong for what she said to me. At the time, I did not understand the different depths of love and how its action contributes to the wellbeing of people. While her attitude was wrong, I don't blame her. I believe her comment about love helped to build my understanding of love in ways I never thought possible.

Love is a powerful thing.

Scott and I are married, still. Our two children have given us five beautiful grandchildren.

If you do what needs to be done to the best of your ability, day by day, your life and loves fall into place.

— Jane Wolfe —

The Blank Page

Be patient and tough; someday
this pain will be useful to you.
~Ovid

When you make an observation, you have an obligation. This is the piece of poetry that I try to live by. It's the mantra that led me through rural Pennsylvania to conduct a creative writing workshop in prison — the pen.

As I pulled up to the jail — a colorless lump of concrete strangled with jagged concertina wire — rain fell, flickering like old film. I remembered how my life had been transformed by a single blank page. Remembered how I showed up to Crefeld, an alternative school in Philadelphia, as a troubled teen who'd been expelled from everywhere else. Remembered how Stacey, the English teacher, placed a blank sheet of paper down in front of me and told me, simply, "Write."

"Write what?" I asked her.

Stacey's response — "anything you want" — changed my life.

I stared at the blank page, an ocean of white glowing with possibility. Its blankness begged me to tell a story — dared me to share my own.

But I couldn't. I froze, terrified and uncomfortable. There were things I wanted to say, but my pen was stuck, my words trapped like water under an ice block. The distance between my mind and the page felt like it could've been measured in light-years.

"It's like there's a wall," I said.

"Every wall is a door," Stacey replied. "You don't need to be great to get started, but you need to get started to be great." Stacey transformed her observation of me into an obligation to me.

Finally, I gripped the pen. My hand shook and trembled like it was freezing. Then it hit me: a silence louder than all the music I'd ever heard. I took a breath, then exhaled — deep, like I just rose from under water.

I stared so deep into the page that I saw myself. Then I felt something I'd never felt before: purpose. I realized that I am the blank page, that we are all blank pages.

Because the blank page was the starter pistol that triggered my purpose, helping to take me from a juvenile delinquent to an award-winning writer, filmmaker, and professor, it was my hope to share the power and possibility of creative writing with the prisoners. I remembered the words of my mentor, Maya Angelou: "When you get, give. When you learn, teach."

Inside I huddled with an intense group of inmates, all young men, all bent on not being broken. After the workshop, I was taken to visit the cellblock where they spent the bulk of their days and nights. On my way out, I noticed that Jordan, a participant in the workshop who was suffering from writer's block, had the only cell whose bed did not have a mattress.

"No mattress?" I asked, puzzled.

"I have one, but I don't sleep on it," he told me.

"What do you sleep on?" I pried.

"The hard floor, the steel frame, anywhere but not on this," he asserted as he hunched beneath the bunk and flashed a flimsy mattress. "See," he started, as he reburied the cot, "I can't sleep on that. It's too comfortable and I don't trust comfort in a place like this."

For Jordan, certain comforts numbed him to the raspy reality of where he really was. He used his discomfort to remind him of where he was and where he wanted to go. I remembered my initial discomfort with the blank page, my writer's block, and thought about where I am now. Then I thought about Jordan's struggles, both on the page and off, and how through discomfort, tremendous growth is possible.

When you make an observation, you have an obligation.
Before I left, I handed Jordan a blank page.

— MK Asante —

Obstacles

Wherever there is a human being, there is an
opportunity for a kindness.
~Seneca

We who lived in the concentration camps can remember the men who walked through the huts comforting others, giving away their last piece of bread. They may have been few in number, but they offer sufficient proof that everything can be taken from a man but one thing: The last of his freedoms — to choose one's attitude in any given set of circumstances, to choose one's own way.

—Viktor E. Frankl—
Man's Search for Meaning

Consider This

*To change one's life: Start immediately. Do it
flamboyantly. No exceptions.*
~William James

Consider this:

- After Fred Astaire's first screen test, the memo from the testing direc-
tor of MGM, dated 1933, said, "Can't act! Slightly bald! Can dance
a little!" Astaire kept that memo over the fireplace in his Beverly
Hills home.
- An expert said of Vince Lombardi: "He possesses minimal football
knowledge. Lacks motivation."
- Socrates was called, "An immoral corrupter of youth."
- When Peter J. Daniel was in the fourth grade, his teacher, Miss
Phillips, constantly said, "Peter J. Daniel, you're no good, you're a
bad apple and you're never going to amount to anything." Peter was
virtually illiterate until he was 26. A friend stayed up with him all
night and read him a copy of *Think and Grow Rich.* Now he owns
the street corners he used to fight on and just published his latest
book: *Miss Phillips, You Were Wrong!*
- Louisa May Alcott, the author of *Little Women*, was encouraged to
find work as a servant or seamstress by her family.
- Beethoven handled the violin awkwardly and preferred playing his
own compositions instead of improving his technique. His teacher

called him hopeless as a composer.

- The parents of the famous opera singer Enrico Caruso wanted him to be an engineer. His teacher said he had no voice at all and could not sing.
- Charles Darwin, father of the theory of evolution, gave up a medical career and was told by his father, "You care for nothing but shooting, dogs and rat catching." In his autobiography, Darwin wrote, "I was considered by all my masters and by my father, a very ordinary boy, rather below the common standard in intellect."
- Walt Disney was fired by a newspaper editor for lack of ideas. Walt Disney also went bankrupt before he built Disneyland.
- Thomas Edison's teachers said he was too stupid to learn anything.
- Albert Einstein did not speak until he was four years old and didn't read until he was seven. His teacher described him as "mentally slow, unsociable and adrift forever in his foolish dreams." He was expelled and was refused admittance to the Zurich Polytechnic School.
- Louis Pasteur was only a mediocre pupil in undergraduate studies and ranked 15th out of 22 in chemistry.
- Isaac Newton did very poorly in grade school.
- The sculptor Rodin's father said, "I have an idiot for a son." Described as the worst pupil in the school, Rodin failed three times to secure admittance to the school of art. His uncle called him uneducable.
- Leo Tolstoy, author of *War and Peace*, flunked out of college. He was described as "both unable and unwilling to learn."
- Playwright Tennessee Williams was enraged when his play *Me, Vasha* was not chosen in a class competition at Washington University where he was enrolled in English XVI. The teacher recalled that Williams denounced the judges' choices and their intelligence.
- F. W. Woolworth's employers at the dry goods store said he had not enough sense to wait upon customers.
- Babe Ruth, considered by sports historians to be the greatest athlete of all time and famous for setting the home run record, also holds the record for strikeouts.
- Winston Churchill failed sixth grade. He did not become Prime Minister of England until he was 66, and then only after a lifetime

of defeats and setbacks. His greatest contributions came when he was a "senior citizen."

- Eighteen publishers turned down Richard Bach's 10,000-word story about a "soaring" seagull, *Jonathan Livingston Seagull*, before Macmillan finally published it in 1970. By 1975 it had sold more than 7 million copies in the U.S. alone.
- Richard Hooker worked for seven years on his humorous war novel, *M*A*S*H*, only to have it rejected by more than a dozen publishers before Morrow decided to publish it. It became a runaway bestseller, spawning a blockbuster movie and a highly successful television series.

—Jack Canfield and Mark Victor Hansen—

John Corcoran – The Man Who Couldn't Read

To the uneducated an A is just three sticks.
~A.A. Milne

For as long as John Corcoran could remember, words had mocked him. The letters in sentences traded places, vowel sounds lost themselves in the tunnels of his ears. In school he'd sit at his desk, stupid and silent as a stone, knowing he would be different from everyone else forever. If only someone had sat next to that little boy, put an arm around his shoulder and said, "I'll help you. Don't be scared."

But no one had heard of dyslexia then. And John couldn't tell them that the left side of his brain, the lobe humans use to arrange symbols logically in a sequence, had always misfired.

Instead, in second grade they put him in the "dumb" row. In third grade a nun handed a yardstick to the other children when John refused to read or write and let each student have a crack at his legs. In fourth grade his teacher called on him to read and let one minute of quiet pile upon another until the child thought he would suffocate. Then he was passed on to the next grade and the next. John Corcoran never failed a year in his life.

In his senior year, John was voted homecoming king, went steady with the valedictorian and starred on the basketball team. His mom kissed him when he graduated — and kept talking about college. College? It would be insane to consider. But he finally decided on the University of Texas at El Paso where he could try out for the basketball team. He took a deep breath, closed his eyes... and recrossed enemy lines.

On campus John asked each new friend: Which teachers gave essay tests? Which gave multiple choice? The minute he stepped out of a class, he tore the pages of scribble from his notebook, in case anyone asked to see his notes. He stared at thick textbooks in the evening so his roommate wouldn't doubt. And he lay in bed, exhausted but unable to sleep, unable to make his whirring mind let go. John promised he'd go to Mass 30 days straight at the crack of dawn, if only God would let him get his degree.

He got the diploma. He gave God his 30 days of Mass. Now what? Maybe he was addicted to the edge. Maybe the thing he felt most insecure about — his mind — was what he needed most to have admired. Maybe that's why, in 1961, John became a teacher.

John taught in California. Each day he had a student read the textbook to the class. He gave standardized tests that he could grade by placing a form with holes over each correct answer and he lay in bed for hours on weekend mornings, depressed.

Then he met Kathy, an A student and a nurse. Not a leaf, like John. A rock. "There's something I have to tell you, Kathy," he said one night in 1965 before their marriage, "I... I can't read."

"He's a teacher," she thought. He must mean he can't read well. Kathy didn't understand until years later when she saw John unable to read a children's book to their 18-month-old daughter. Kathy filled out his forms, read and wrote his letters. Why didn't he simply ask her to teach him to read and write? He couldn't believe that anyone could teach him.

At age 28 John borrowed $2,500, bought a second house, fixed it up and rented it. He bought and rented another. And another. His business got bigger and bigger until he needed a secretary, a lawyer and a partner.

Then one day his accountant told him he was a millionaire. Perfect.

Who'd notice that a millionaire always pulled on the doors that said PUSH or paused before entering public bathrooms, waiting to see which one the men walked out of?

In 1982 the bottom began to fall out. His properties started to sit empty and investors pulled out. Threats of foreclosures and lawsuits tumbled out of envelopes. Every waking moment, it seemed, he was pleading with bankers to extend his loans, coaxing builders to stay on the job, trying to make sense of the pyramid of paper. Soon he knew they'd have him on the witness stand and the man in black robes would say: "The truth, John Corcoran. Can't you even read?"

Finally in the fall of 1986, at age 48, John did two things he swore he never would. He put up his house as collateral to obtain one last construction loan. And he walked into the Carlsbad City Library and told the woman in charge of the tutoring program, "I can't read."

Then he cried.

He was placed with a 65-year-old grandmother named Eleanor Condit. Painstakingly — letter by letter, phonetically — she began teaching him. Within 14 months, his land-development company began to revive. And John Corcoran was learning to read.

The next step was confession: a speech before 200 stunned businessmen in San Diego. To heal, he had to come clean. He was placed on the board of directors of the San Diego Council on Literacy and began traveling across the country to give speeches.

"Illiteracy is a form of slavery!" he would cry. "We can't waste time blaming anyone. We need to become obsessed with teaching people to read!"

He read every book or magazine he could get his hands on, every road sign he passed, out loud, as long as Kathy could bear it. It was glorious, like singing. And now he could sleep.

Then one day it occurred to him — one more thing he could finally do. Yes, that dusty box in his office, that sheaf of papers bound by ribbon... a quarter-century later, John Corcoran could read his wife's love letters.

— Gary Smith —

Don't Be Afraid to Fail

Don't look where you fall, but where you slipped.
~African Proverb

You've failed many times, although you may not remember.

You fell down the first time you tried to walk.

You almost drowned the first time you tried to swim, didn't you?

Did you hit the ball the first time you swung a bat?

Heavy hitters, the ones who hit the most home runs, also strike out a lot.

R. H. Macy failed seven times before his store in New York caught on.

English novelist John Creasey got 753 rejection slips before he published 564 books.

Babe Ruth struck out 1,330 times, but he also hit 714 home runs.

Don't worry about failure.

Worry about the chances you miss when you don't *even try.*

— United Technologies Corporation©1981 —

Abraham Lincoln Didn't Quit

*The sense of obligation to continue is present
in all of us. A duty to strive is the duty of us all.
I felt a call to that duty.*
~Abraham Lincoln

Probably the greatest example of persistence is Abraham Lincoln. If you want to learn about somebody who didn't quit, look no further.

Born into poverty, Lincoln was faced with defeat throughout his life. He lost eight elections, twice failed in business and suffered a nervous breakdown.

He could have quit many times — but he didn't and because he didn't quit, he became one of the greatest presidents in the history of our country.

Lincoln was a champion and he never gave up. Here is a sketch of Lincoln's road to the White House:

1816 His family was forced out of their home. He had to work to support them.

1818 His mother died.

1831 Failed in business.

1832 Ran for state legislature — lost.

1832 Also lost his job — wanted to go to law school but couldn't get in.

1833 Borrowed some money from a friend to begin a business and by the end of the year he was bankrupt. He spent the next 17 years of his life paying off this debt.

1834 Ran for state legislature again — won.

1835 Was engaged to be married, sweetheart died and his heart was broken.

1836 Had a total nervous breakdown and was in bed for six months.

1838 Sought to become speaker of the state legislature — defeated.

1840 Sought to become elector — defeated.

1843 Ran for Congress — lost.

1846 Ran for Congress again — this time he won — went to Washington and did a good job.

Ran for re-election to Congress — lost.

Sought the job of land officer in his home state — rejected.

1854 Ran for Senate of the United States — lost.

1856 Sought the Vice Presidential nomination at his party's national convention — got less than 100 votes.

1858 Ran for U.S. Senate again — again he lost.

1860 Elected President of the United States.

The path was worn and slippery. My foot slipped from under me, knocking the other out of the way, but I recovered and said to myself, "It's a slip and not a fall."
~Abraham Lincoln after losing a Senate race

— Source Unknown —

Lesson from a Son

If passion drives you, let reason hold the reins.
~Benjamin Franklin

My son Daniel's passion for surfing began at the age of 13. Before and after school each day, he donned his wet suit, paddled out beyond the surf line and waited to be challenged by his three- to six-foot companions. Daniel's love of the ride was tested one fateful afternoon.

"Your son's been in an accident," the lifeguard reported over the phone to my husband Mike.

"How bad?"

"Bad. When he surfaced to the top of the water, the point of the board was headed toward his eye."

Mike rushed him to the emergency room and they were then sent to a plastic surgeon's office. He received 26 stitches from the corner of his eye to the bridge of his nose.

I was on an airplane flying home from a speaking engagement while Dan's eye was being stitched. Mike drove directly to the airport after they left the doctor's office. He greeted me at the gate and told me Dan was waiting in the car.

"Daniel?" I questioned. I remember thinking the waves must have been lousy that day.

"He's been in an accident, but he's going to be fine."

A traveling working mother's worst nightmare had come true. I ran to the car so fast the heel of my shoe broke off. I swung open the door, and my youngest son with the patched eye was leaning forward with both arms stretched out toward me crying, "Oh, Mom, I'm so glad you're home."

I sobbed in his arms telling him how awful I felt about not being there when the lifeguard called.

"It's okay, Mom," he comforted me. "You don't know how to surf anyway."

"What?" I asked, confused by his logic.

"I'll be fine. The doctor says I can go back in the water in eight days."

Was he out of his mind? I wanted to tell him he wasn't allowed to go near water again until he was 35, but instead I bit my tongue and prayed he would forget about surfing forevermore.

For the next seven days he kept pressing me to let him go back on the board. One day after I emphatically repeated "No" to him for the 100th time, he beat me at my own game.

"Mom, you taught us never to give up what we love."

Then he handed me a bribe—a framed poem by Langston Hughes that he bought "because it reminded me of you."

Mother to Son

Well, son, I'll tell you:
Life for me ain't been no crystal stair. It's had tacks in it.
And splinters,
And boards torn up,
And places with no carpet on the floor—
Bare.
But all the time
I'se been a-climbin' on,
And reachin' landin's
And turnin' corners,
And sometimes goin' in the dark
Where there ain't been no light.

So, boy, don't you turn back,
Don't you set down on the steps
'Cause you finds it's kinder hard.
Don't you fall now —
For I'se still goin', honey,
I'se still climbin'
And life for me ain't been no crystal stair.

I gave in.

Back then Daniel was a just a boy with a passion for surfing.
Now he's a man with a responsibility. He ranks among the top 25 pro
surfers in the world.

I was tested in my own back yard on an important principle that
I teach audiences in distant cities: "Passionate people embrace what
they love and never give up."

— Danielle Kennedy —

Failure? No! Just Temporary Setbacks

To see things in the seed, that is genius.

~Lao-tzu

If you could come to my office in California to visit with me today, you would notice across one side of the room a beautiful old-fashioned Spanish tile and mahogany soda fountain with nine leather-covered stools (the kind they used to have in the old drugstores). Unusual? Yes. But if those stools could speak, they would tell you a story about the day I almost lost hope and gave up.

It was a recession period after World War II and jobs were scarce. Cowboy Bob, my husband, had purchased a small dry cleaning business with borrowed money. We had two darling babies, a tract home, a car and all the usual time payments. Then the bottom fell out. There was no money for the house payments or anything else.

I felt that I had no special talent, no training, no college education. I didn't think much of myself. But I remembered someone in my past who thought I had a little ability — my Alhambra High School English teacher. She inspired me to take journalism and named me advertising manager and feature editor of the school paper. I thought, "Now if I could write a 'Shoppers Column' for the small weekly newspaper in our rural town, maybe I could earn that house payment."

I had no car and no babysitter. So I pushed my two children before me in a rickety baby stroller with a big pillow tied in the back. The wheel kept coming off, but I hit it back on with the heel of my shoe and kept going. I was determined that my children would not lose their home as I often had done as a child.

But at the newspaper office, there were no jobs available. Recession. So I caught an idea. I asked if I might buy advertising space at wholesale and sell it at retail as a "Shoppers Column." They agreed, telling me later that they mentally gave me about a week of pushing that beat-up heavily laden stroller down those country roads before I gave up. But they were wrong.

The newspaper column idea worked. I made enough money for the house payment and to buy an old used car that Cowboy Bob found for me. Then I hired a high school girl to babysit from three to five each afternoon. When the clock struck three, I grabbed my newspaper samples and flew out of the door to drive to my appointments.

But on one dark rainy afternoon every advertising prospect I had worked on turned me down when I went to pick up their copy.

"Why?" I asked. They said they had noticed that Ruben Ahlman, the President of the Chamber of Commerce and the owner of the Rexall drugstore did not advertise with me. His store was the most popular in town. They respected his judgment. "There must be something wrong with your advertising," they explained.

My heart sank. Those four ads would have made the house payment. Then I thought, I will try to speak with Mr. Ahlman one more time. Everyone loves and respects him. Surely he will listen. Every time I had tried to approach him in the past, he had refused to see me. He was always "out" or unavailable. I knew that if he advertised with me, the other merchants in town would follow his lead.

This time, as I walked into the Rexall drugstore, he was there at the prescription counter in the back. I smiled my best smile and held up my precious "Shoppers Column" carefully marked in my children's green Crayola. I said, "Everyone respects your opinion, Mr. Ahlman. Would you just look at my work for a moment so that I can tell the other merchants what you think?"

His mouth turned into in an upside-down U. Without saying a word he emphatically shook his head, "NO!"

Suddenly all of my enthusiasm left me. I made it as far as the beautiful old soda fountain at the front of the drugstore, feeling that I didn't have the strength to drive home. I didn't want to sit at the soda fountain without buying something, so I pulled out my last dime and ordered a cherry Coke. I wondered desperately what to do. Would my babies lose their home as I had so many times when I was growing up? Was my journalism teacher wrong? Maybe that talent she talked about was just a dud. My eyes filled with tears.

A soft voice beside me on the next soda fountain stool said, "What is the matter, dear?" I looked up into the sympathetic face of a lovely gray-haired lady. I poured out my story to her, ending it with, "But Mr. Ahlman, who everyone respects so much, will not look at my work."

"Let me see that Shoppers Column," she said. She took my marked issue of the newspaper in her hands and carefully read it all the way through. Then she spun around on the stool, stood up, looked back at the prescription counter and in a commanding voice that could be heard down the block, said, "Ruben Ahlman, come *here!*" The lady was Mrs. Ahlman!

She told Ruben to buy the advertising from me. His mouth turned up the other way in a big grin. Then she asked me for the names of the four merchants who had turned me down. She went to the phone and called each one. She gave me a hug and told me they were waiting for me and to go back and pick up their ads.

Ruben and Vivian Ahlman became our dear friends, as well as steady advertising customers. I learned that Ruben was a darling man who bought from everyone. He had promised Vivian not to buy any more advertising. He was just trying to keep his word to her. If I had only asked others in town, I might have learned that I should have been talking to Mrs. Ahlman from the beginning. That conversation on the stools of the soda fountain was the turning point. My advertising business prospered and grew into four offices, with 285 employees serving 4,000 continuous-contract advertising accounts.

Later when Mr. Ahlman modernized the old drugstore and removed the soda fountain, my sweet husband Bob bought it and installed it in my office. If you were here in California, we would sit on the soda fountain stools together. I'd pour you a cherry Coke and remind you to never give up, to remember that help is always closer than we know.

Then I would tell you that if you can't communicate with a key person, search for more information. Try another path around. Look for someone who can communicate for you in a third person endorsement. And, finally, I would serve you these sparkling, refreshing words of Bill Marriott of the Marriott Hotels:

Failure? I never encountered it.

All I ever met were temporary setbacks.

— Dottie Walters —

For Me to Be More Creative, I Am Waiting for...

*We should be taught not to wait for inspiration to
start a thing. Action always generates inspiration.
Inspiration seldom generates action.*
~Frank Tibolt

1. Inspiration
2. Permission
3. Reassurance
4. The coffee to be ready
5. My turn
6. Someone to smooth the way
7. The rest of the rules
8. Someone to change
9. Wider fairways
10. Revenge
11. The stakes to be lower
12. More time
13. A significant relationship to:
   (a) improve
   (b) terminate
   (c) happen

14. The right person
15. A disaster
16. Time to almost run out
17. An obvious scapegoat
18. The kids to leave home
19. A Dow Jones of 1500
20. The lion to lie down with the lamb
21. Mutual consent
22. A better time
23. A more favorable horoscope
24. My youth to return
25. The two-minute warning
26. The legal profession to reform
27. Richard Nixon to be re-elected
28. Age to grant me the right of eccentricity
29. Tomorrow
30. Jacks or better
31. My annual checkup
32. A better circle of friends
33. The stakes to be higher
34. The semester to start
35. My way to be clear
36. The cat to stop clawing the sofa
37. An absence of risk
38. The barking dog next door to leave town
39. My uncle to come home from the service
40. Someone to discover me.
41. More adequate safeguards
42. A lower capital gains rate
43. The statue of limitations to run out
44. My parents to die (Joke!)
45. A cure for herpes/AIDS
46. The things that I do not understand or approve of to go away
47. Wars to end
48. My love to rekindle

49. Someone to be watching
50. A clearly written set of instructions
51. Better birth control
52. The ERA to pass
53. An end to poverty, injustice, cruelty, deceit, incompetence, pestilence, crime and offensive suggestions
54. A competing patent to expire
55. Chicken Little to return
56. My subordinates to mature
57. My ego to improve
58. The pot to boil
59. The new credit card
60. The piano tuner
61. This meeting to be over
62. My receivables to clear
63. The unemployment checks to run out
64. Spring
65. My suit to come back from the cleaners
66. My self-esteem to be restored
67. A signal from Heaven
68. The alimony payments to stop
69. The gems of brilliance buried within my first bumbling efforts to be recognized, applauded and substantially rewarded so that I can work on the second draft in comfort
70. A reinterpretation of *Robert's Rules of Order*
71. Various aches and pains to subside
72. Shorter lines at the bank
73. The wind to be freshen
74. My children to be thoughtful, neat, obedient and self-supporting
75. Next season
76. Someone else to screw up
77. My current life to be declared a dress rehearsal with some script changes permitted before opening night
78. Logic to prevail
79. The next time around

80. You to stand out of my light
81. My ship to come in
82. A better deodorant
83. My dissertation to be finished
84. A sharp pencil
85. The check to clear
86. My wife, film or boomerang to come back
87. My doctor's approval, my father's permission, my minister's bless-
    ing or my lawyer's okay
88. Morning
89. California to fall into the ocean
90. A less turbulent time
91. The Iceman to Cometh
92. An opportunity to call collect
93. A better write-off
94. My smoking urges to subside
95. The rates to go down
96. The rates to go up
97. The rates to stabilize
98. My grandfather's estate to be settled
99. Weekend rates
100. A cue card
101. You to go first

—David B. Campbell—

Everybody Can Do Something

The basic difference between an ordinary man and
a warrior is that a warrior takes everything as a
challenge, while an ordinary man takes everything
either as a blessing or a curse.
~Don Juan

Roger Crawford had everything he needed to play tennis—except two hands and a leg. When Roger's parents saw their son for the first time, they saw a baby with a thumb-like projection extended directly out of his right forearm and a thumb and one finger stuck out of his left forearm. He had no palms. The baby's arms and legs were shortened, and he had only three toes on his shrunken right foot and a withered left leg, which would later be amputated.

The doctor said Roger suffered from ectrodactylism, a rare birth defect affecting only one out of 90,000 children born in the United States. The doctor said Roger would probably never walk or care for himself.

Fortunately, Roger's parents didn't believe the doctor.

"My parents always taught me that I was only as handicapped as I wanted to be," said Roger. "They never allowed me to feel sorry for myself or take advantage of people because of my handicap. Once I got into trouble because my school papers were continually late," explained Roger, who had to hold his pencil with both "hands" to write slowly. "I asked Dad to write a note to my teachers, asking for a two-day extension on my assignments. Instead, Dad made me start writing my paper two days early!"

Roger's father always encouraged him to get involved in sports, teaching Roger to catch and throw a volleyball, and play backyard football after school. At age 12, Roger managed to win a spot on the school football team.

Before every game, Roger would visualize his dream of scoring a touchdown. Then one day he got his chance. The ball landed in his arms and off he ran as fast as he could on his artificial leg toward the goal line, his coach and teammates cheering wildly. But at the 10-yard line, a guy from the other team caught up with Roger, grabbing his left ankle. Roger tried to pull his artificial leg free, but instead it ended up being pulled off.

"I was still standing up," recalls Roger. "I didn't know what else to do so I started hopping towards the goal line. The referee ran over and threw his hands into the air. Touchdown! You know, even better than the six points was the look on the face of the other kid who was holding my artificial leg."

Roger's love of sports grew and so did his self-confidence. But not every obstacle gave way to Roger's determination. Eating in the lunchroom with the other kids watching him fumble with his food proved very painful to Roger, as did his repeated failure in typing class. "I learned a very good lesson from typing class," said Roger. "You can't do *everything* — it's better to concentrate on what you can do."

One thing Roger could do was swing a tennis racket. Unfortunately, when he swung it hard, his weak grip usually launched it into space. By luck, Roger stumbled upon an odd-looking tennis racket in a sports shop and accidentally wedged his finger between its double-barred handle when he picked it up. The snug fit made it possible for Roger to swing, serve and volley like an able-bodied player. He practiced every day and was soon playing — and losing — matches.

But Roger persisted. He practiced and practiced and played and played. Surgery on the two fingers of his left hand enabled Roger to grip his special racket better, greatly improving his game. Although he had no role models to guide him, Roger became obsessed with tennis and in time he started to win.

Roger went on to play college tennis, finishing his tennis career with 22 wins and 11 losses. He later became the first physically handicapped tennis player to be certified as a teaching professional by the United States Professional Tennis Association. Roger now tours the country, speaking to groups about what it takes to be a winner, no matter who you are.

"The only difference between you and me is that you can see my handicap, but I can't see yours. We *all* have them. When people ask me how I've been able to overcome my physical handicaps, I tell them that I haven't overcome anything. I've simply learned what I can't do — such as play the piano or eat with chopsticks — but more importantly, I've learned what I *can* do. Then I do what I can with all my heart and soul."

—Jack Canfield—

Yes, You Can

Experience is not what happens to a man. It is
what a man does with what happens to him.
~Aldous Huxley

What if at age 46 you were burned beyond recognition in a terrible motorcycle accident, and then four years later were paralyzed from the waist down in an airplane crash? Then, can you imagine yourself becoming a millionaire, a respected public speaker, a happy newlywed and a successful businessperson? Can you see yourself going whitewater rafting? Skydiving? Running for political office?

W. Mitchell has done all these things and more after two horrible accidents left his face a quilt of multicolored skin grafts, his hands fingerless and his legs thin and motionless in a wheelchair.

The 16 surgeries Mitchell endured after the motorcycle accident burned more than 65 percent of his body left him unable to pick up a fork, dial a telephone or go to the bathroom without help. But Mitchell, a former Marine, never believed he was defeated. "I am in charge of my own spaceship," he said. "It's my up, my down. I could choose to see this situation as a setback or a starting point." Six months later he was piloting a plane again.

Mitchell bought himself a Victorian home in Colorado, some real estate, a plane and a bar. Later he teamed up with two friends and co-founded a wood-burning stove company that grew to be Vermont's second largest private employer.

Then four years after the motorcycle accident, the plane Mitchell was piloting crashed back onto the runway during takeoff, crushing Mitchell's 12 thoracic vertebrae and permanently paralyzing him from the waist down. "I wondered what the hell was happening to me. What did I do to deserve this?"

Undaunted, Mitchell worked day and night to regain as much independence as possible. He was elected Mayor of Crested Butte, Colorado, to save the town from mineral mining that would ruin its beauty and environment. Mitchell later ran for Congress, turning his odd appearance into an asset with slogans such as, "Not just another pretty face."

Despite his initially shocking looks and physical challenges, Mitchell began whitewater rafting, fell in love and married, earned a master's degree in public administration and continued flying, environmental activism and public speaking.

Mitchell's unshakable Positive Mental Attitude has earned him appearances on the *Today Show* and *Good Morning America* as well as feature articles in *Parade*, *Time*, *The New York Times* and other publications.

"Before I was paralyzed, there were 10,000 things I could do," Mitchell says. "Now there are 9,000. I can either dwell on the 1,000 I lost or focus on the 9,000 I have left. I tell people that I have had two big bumps in my life. If I have chosen not to use them as an excuse to quit, then maybe some of the experiences you are having which are pulling you back can be put into a new perspective. You can step back, take a wider view and have a chance to say, 'Maybe that isn't such a big deal after all.'"

Remember: "It's not what happens to you, it's what you do about it."

— Jack Canfield and Mark Victor Hansen —

Run, Patti, Run

Follow your passion, and success will follow you.
~Terri Guillemets

A
t a young and tender age, Patti Wilson was told by her doctor that she was an epileptic. Her father, Jim Wilson, is a morning jogger. One day she smiled through her teenage braces and said, "Daddy what I'd really love to do is run with you every day, but I'm afraid I'll have a seizure."

Her father told her, "If you do, I know how to handle it so let's start running!"

That's just what they did every day. It was a wonderful experience for them to share and there were no seizures at all while she was running. After a few weeks, she told her father, "Daddy, what I'd really love to do is break the world's long-distance running record for women."

Her father checked the *Guinness Book of World Records* and found that the farthest any woman had run was 80 miles. As a freshman in high school, Patti announced, "I'm going to run from Orange County up to San Francisco." (A distance of 400 miles.) "As a sophomore," she went on, "I'm going to run to Portland, Oregon." (Over 1,500 miles.) "As a junior I'll run to St. Louis. (About 2,000 miles.) "As a senior I'll run to the White House." (More than 3,000 miles away.)

In view of her handicap, Patti was as ambitious as she was enthusiastic, but she said she looked at the handicap of being an epileptic as simply "an inconvenience." She focused not on what she had lost, but on what she had *left*. That year she completed her run to San Francisco wearing a T-shirt that read "I Love Epileptics." Her dad ran every mile at her side, and her mom, a nurse, followed in a motor home behind them in case anything went wrong. In her sophomore year Patti's classmates got behind her. They built a giant poster that read, "Run, Patti, Run!" (This has since become her motto and the title of a book she has written.) On her second marathon, en route to Portland, she fractured a bone in her foot. A doctor told her she had to stop her run. He said, "I've got to put a cast on your ankle so that you don't sustain permanent damage."

"Doc, you don't understand," she said. "This isn't just a whim of mine, it's a magnificent obsession! I'm not just doing it for me, I'm doing it to break the chains on the brains that limit so many others. Isn't there a way I can keep running?" He gave her one option. He could wrap it in adhesive instead of putting it in a cast. He warned her that it would be incredibly painful, and he told her, "It will blister." She told the doctor to wrap it up.

She finished the run to Portland, completing her last mile with the governor of Oregon. You may have seen the headlines: "Super Runner, Patti Wilson Ends Marathon For Epilepsy On Her 17th Birthday."

After four months of almost continuous running from the West Coast to the East Coast, Patti arrived in Washington and shook the hand of the President of the United States. She told him, "I wanted people to know that epileptics are normal human beings with normal lives."

I told this story at one of my seminars not long ago, and afterward a big teary-eyed man came up to me, stuck out his big meaty hand and said, "Mark, my name is Jim Wilson. You were talking about my daughter, Patti." Because of her noble efforts, he told me, enough money had been raised to open up 19 multi-million-dollar epilepsy centers around the country.

If Patti Wilson can do so much with so little, what can you do to outperform yourself in a state of total wellness?

— Mark Victor Hansen —

The Power of Determination

Perseverance is not a long race; it is
many short races one after another.
~Walter Elliott

The little country schoolhouse was heated by an old-fashioned, potbellied coal stove. A little boy had the job of coming to school early each day to start the fire and warm the room before his teacher and his classmates arrived.

One morning they arrived to find the schoolhouse engulfed in flames. They dragged the unconscious little boy out of the flaming building more dead than alive. He had major burns over the lower half of his body and was taken to the nearby county hospital.

From his bed the dreadfully burned, semi-conscious little boy faintly heard the doctor talking to his mother. The doctor told his mother that her son would surely die — which was for the best, really — for the terrible fire had devastated the lower half of his body.

But the brave boy didn't want to die. He made up his mind that he would survive. Somehow, to the amazement of the physician, he did survive. When the mortal danger was past, he again heard the doctor and his mother speaking quietly. The mother was told that since the fire had destroyed so much flesh in the lower part of his body, it would almost be better if he had died, since he was doomed to be a lifetime cripple with no use at all of his lower limbs.

Once more the brave boy made up his mind. He would not be a

cripple. He would walk. But, unfortunately, from the waist down he had no motor ability. His thin legs just dangled there, all but lifeless.

Ultimately, he was released from the hospital. Every day his mother would massage his little legs, but there was no feeling, no control, nothing. Yet his determination that he would walk was as strong as ever.

When he wasn't in bed, he was confined to a wheelchair. One sunny day his mother wheeled him out into the yard to get some fresh air. This day, instead of sitting there, he threw himself from the chair. He pulled himself across the grass, dragging his legs behind him.

He worked his way to the white picket fence bordering their lot. With great effort, he raised himself up on the fence. Then, stake by stake, he began dragging himself along the fence, resolved that he would walk. He started to do this every day until he wore a smooth path all around the yard beside the fence. There was nothing he wanted more than to develop life in those legs.

Ultimately through his daily massages, his iron persistence and his resolute determination, he did develop the ability to stand up, then to walk haltingly, then to walk by himself — and then — to run.

He began to walk to school, then to run to school, to run for the sheer joy of running. Later in college he made the track team.

Still later in Madison Square Garden this young man who was not expected to survive, who would surely never walk, who could never hope to run — this determined young man, Dr. Glenn Cunningham, ran the world's fastest mile!

— Burt Dubin —

Faith

Trouble and perplexity drive me to prayer and
prayer drives away perplexity and trouble.
~Philip Melanchthen

We're a rugged breed, us quads. If we weren't, we wouldn't be around today. Yes, we're a rugged breed. In many ways, we've been blessed with a savvy and spirit that isn't given to everybody.

And let me say that this refusal of total or full acceptance of one's disability all hooks up with one thing — faith, an almost divine faith.

Down in the reception room of the Institute of Physical Medicine and Rehabilitation, over on the East River at 400 East 34th Street in New York City, there's a bronze plaque that's riveted to the wall. During the months of coming back to the Institute for treatment — two or three times a week — I rolled through that reception room many times, coming and going. But I never quite made the time to pull over to one side and read the words on that plaque that were written, it's said, by an unknown Confederate soldier.

Then one afternoon, I did. I read it and then I read it again. When I finished it for the second time, I was near to bursting — not in despair, but with an inner glow that had me straining to grip the arms of my wheelchair. I'd like to share it with you.

A Creed For Those Who Have Suffered

I asked God for strength, that I might achieve.
I was made weak, that I might learn humbly to obey...

I asked for health, that I might do great things.
I was given infirmity, that I might do better things...

I asked for riches, that I might be happy.
I was given poverty, that I might be wise...

I asked for power, that I might have the praise of men.
I was given weakness, that I might feel the need of God...

I asked for all things, that I might enjoy life.
I was given life, that I might enjoy all things...

I got nothing I asked for — but everything I had hoped for. Almost despite myself, my unspoken prayers were answered.

I am, among men, most richly blessed!

—Roy Campanella—

She Saved 219 Lives

Every day you either see a scar or courage.
Where you dwell will define your struggle.
~Dodinsky

Mrs. Betty Tisdale is a world-class heroine. When the war in Vietnam heated up back in April of 1975, she knew she had to save the 400 orphans who were about to be put on the streets. She had already adopted five orphaned Vietnamese girls with her former pediatrician husband, Col. Patrick Tisdale, who was a widower and already had five children.

As a U.S. Naval doctor in Vietnam in 1954, Tom Dooley had helped refugees flee from the communist north. Betty says, "I really feel Tom Dooley was a saint. His influence changed my life forever." Because of Dooley's book, she took her life savings and traveled to Vietnam 14 times on her vacations to visit and work in the hospitals and orphanages he had founded. While in Saigon, she fell in love with the orphans at An Lac (Happy Place), run by Madame Vu Thi Ngai, who was later evacuated by Betty the day Vietnam fell, and returned with her to Georgia to live with Betty and her ten children.

When Betty, a do-it-now and invent-solutions-as- problems-arise kind of person, realized the 400 children's plight, she went into warp-speed action. She called Madame Ngai and said, "Yes! I'll come and get the children and get them all adopted." She didn't know how she would do it. She just knew that she'd do it. Later, in a movie of the evacuation, "The Children of An Lac," Shirley Jones portrayed Betty.

In moments she began to move mountains. She raised the necessary money in many different ways, even including accepting green stamps. She simply decided to do it and she did it. She said, "I visualized all those babies growing up in good homes in America, not under communism." That kept her motivated.

She left for Vietnam from Fort Benning, Georgia, on Sunday, arrived on Tuesday in Saigon, and miraculously and sleeplessly conquered every obstacle to airlift 400 children out of Saigon by Saturday morning. However, upon her arrival, the head of Vietnam's social welfare, Dr. Dan, suddenly announced he would only approve children under ten years old and all the children must have birth certificates. She quickly discovered war orphans are fortunate to simply be alive. They don't have birth certificates.

Betty went to the hospital pediatric department, obtained 225 birth certificates, and quickly created birth dates, times and places for the 219 eligible babies, toddlers and youngsters. She says, "I have no idea when, where and to whom they were born. My fingers just created birth certificates." Birth certificates were the only hope they had to depart the place safely and have a viable future with freedom. It was now or never.

Now she needed a place to house the orphans once they were evacuated. The military at Fort Benning resisted, but Betty brilliantly and tenaciously persisted. Try as she might, she could not get the Commanding General on the phone, so she called the office of the Secretary of the Army, Bo Callaway. His duty, too, was not answering Betty's calls, no matter how urgent and of life-saving importance they were.

However, Betty was not to be beaten. She had come too far and done too much to be stopped now. So since he was from Georgia, she called his mother and pleaded her case. Betty enrolled her with her heart and asked her to intercede. Virtually overnight, the Secretary of the Army, her son, responded and arranged that a school at Fort Benning be used as the interim home for the orphans of An Lac.

But the challenge of how to get the children out was still to be accomplished. When Betty arrived in Saigon, she went to Ambassador Graham Martin immediately and pleaded for some sort of transportation for the children. She had tried to charter a Pan Am plane, but Lloyd's of London had raised the insurance so high that it was impossible to negotiate at this time. The Ambassador agreed to help if all the papers were cleared through the Vietnamese government. Dr. Dan signed the last manifest, literally, as the children were boarding the two Air Force planes.

The orphans were malnourished and sickly. Most had never been away from the orphanage. They were scared. She had recruited soldiers and the ABC crew to help strap them in, transport them and feed them. You can't believe how deeply and permanently those volunteers' hearts were touched that beautiful Saturday as 219 children were transported to freedom. All the volunteers cried with joy and appreciation that they had tangibly contributed to another's freedom.

Chartering airlines home from the Philippines was a huge hassle. There was a $21,000 expense for a United Airlines plane. Dr. Tisdale guaranteed payment because of his love for the orphans. Had Betty had more time, she could have probably got it for free! But time was a factor so she moved quickly.

Every child was adopted within one month of arriving in the United States. The Tressler Lutheran Agency in York, Pennsylvania, which specializes in getting handicapped children adopted, found a home for each orphan.

Betty has proven over and over again that you can do anything at all if you are simply willing to ask, to not settle for a "no," to do whatever it takes and to persevere.

As Dr. Tom Dooley once said, "It takes ordinary people to do extraordinary things."

—Jack Canfield and Mark Victor Hansen—

Are You Going to Help Me?

Hope is faith holding out its hand in the dark.
~George Iles

In 1989 an 8.2 earthquake almost flattened Armenia, killing over 30,000 people in less than four minutes.

In the midst of utter devastation and chaos, a father left his wife securely at home and rushed to the school where his son was supposed to be, only to discover that the building was as flat as a pancake.

After the initial shock, he remembered the promise he had made to his son: "No matter what, I'll always be there for you!" And tears began to fill his eyes. As he looked at the pile of debris that once was the school, it looked hopeless, but he kept remembering his commitment to his son.

He began to concentrate on where he walked his son to class at school each morning. Remembering his son's classroom would be in the back right corner of the building, he rushed there and started digging through the rubble.

As he was digging, other forlorn parents arrived, clutching their hearts, saying: "My son!" "My daughter!" Other well-meaning parents tried to pull him off what was left of the school saying:

"It's too late!"

"They're dead!"

"You can't help!"

"Go home!"

"Come on, face reality, there's nothing you can do!"

"You're just going to make things worse!"

To each parent he responded with one line: "Are you going to help me now?" And then he proceeded to dig for his son, stone by stone.

The fire chief showed up and tried to pull him off the school's debris, saying "Fires are breaking out, explosions are happening everywhere. You're in danger. We'll take care of it. Go home."

To which this loving, caring father responded, "Are you going to help me now?"

The police came and said, "You're angry, distraught and it's over. You're endangering others. Go home. We'll handle it!"

To which he replied, "Are you going to help me now?" No one helped.

Courageously he proceeded alone because he needed to know for himself: "Is my boy alive or is he dead?"

He dug for eight hours… 12 hours… 24 hours… 36 hours… then, in the 38th hour, he pulled back a boulder and heard his son's voice. He screamed his son's name, *"ARMAND!"*

He heard back, "Dad! It's me, Dad! I told the other kids not to worry. I told them that if you were alive, you'd save me and when you saved me, they'd be saved. You promised, 'No matter what, I'll always be there for you!' You did it, Dad!"

"What's going on in there? How is it?" the father asked.

"There are 14 of us left out of 33, Dad. We're scared, hungry, thirsty and thankful you're here. When the building collapsed, it made a wedge, like a triangle, and it saved us."

"Come on out, boy!"

"No, Dad! Let the other kids out first, because I know you'll get me! No matter what, I know you'll be there for me!"

— Mark Victor Hansen —

Just One More Time

Faith is the bird that sings when the dawn is still dark.
~Rabindranath Tagore

There's a 19th-century English novel set in a small Welsh town in which every year for the past 500 years the people all gather in church on Christmas Eve and pray. Shortly before midnight, they light candle lanterns and, singing carols and hymns, they walk down a country path several miles to an old abandoned stone shack. There they set up a crèche scene, complete with manger. And in simple piety, they kneel and pray. Their hymns warm the chilly December air. Everyone in town capable of walking is there.

There is a myth in that town, a belief that if all citizens are present on Christmas Eve, and if all are praying with perfect faith, then and only then, at the stroke of midnight, the Second Coming will be at hand. And for 500 years they've come to that stone ruin and prayed. Yet the Second Coming has eluded them.

One of the main characters in this novel is asked, "Do you believe that He will come again on Christmas Eve in our town?"

"No," he answers, shaking his head sadly, "no, I don't."

"Then why do you go each year?" he asked.

"Ah," he says smiling, "what if I were the only one who wasn't there when it happened?"

Well, that's very little faith he has, isn't it? But it is some faith. As it says in the New Testament, we need only have faith as small as a grain of mustard seed to get into the Kingdom of Heaven. And sometimes, when we work with disturbed children, at-risk youth, troubled teens, alcoholic or abusive or depressed and suicidal partners, friends or clients… it is at those moments that we need that small bit of faith that kept that man coming back to the stone ruin on Christmas Eve. Just one more time. Just this next time, perhaps I'll make the breakthrough then.

We sometimes are called upon to work with people for whom others have abandoned all hope. Perhaps we have even come to the conclusion that there's no possibility of change or growth. It's at that time that, if we can find the tiniest scrap of hope, we may turn the corner, achieve a measurable gain, save someone worth saving. Please go back, my friend, just this one more time.

— Hanoch McCarty —

There Is Greatness All Around You — Use It

*Individual commitment to a group effort — that is
what makes a team work, a company work,
a society work, a civilization work.*
~Vince Lombardi

There are many people who could be Olympic champions, All-Americans who have never tried. I'd estimate five million people could have beaten me in the pole vault the years I won it, at *least* five million. Men who were stronger, bigger and faster than I was could have done it, but they never picked up a pole, never made the feeble effort to pick their legs off the ground to try to get over the bar.

Greatness is all around us. It's easy to be great because great people will help you. What is fantastic about all the conventions I go to is that the greatest in the business will come and share their ideas, their methods and their techniques with everyone else. I have seen the greatest salesmen open up and show young salesmen exactly how they did it. They don't hold back. I have also found it true in the world of sports.

I'll never forget the time I was trying to break Dutch Warmerdam's record. I was about a foot below his record, so I called him on the phone. I said, "Dutch, can you help me? I seem to have leveled off. I can't get any higher."

He said, "Sure, Bob, come on up to visit me and I'll give you all I got." I spent three days with the master, the greatest pole vaulter in the world. For three days, Dutch gave me everything that he'd seen. There were things that I was doing wrong and he corrected them. To make a long story short, I went up eight inches. That great guy gave me the best that he had. I've found that sports champions and heroes willingly do this just to help you become great, too.

John Wooden, the great UCLA basketball coach, has a philosophy that every day he is supposed to help someone who can never reciprocate. That's his obligation.

When in college working on his masters thesis on scouting and defensive football, George Allen wrote up a 30-page survey and sent it out to the great coaches in the country. Eighty-five percent answered it completely.

Great people will share, which is what made George Allen one of the greatest football coaches in the world. Great people will tell you their secrets. Look for them, call them on the phone or buy their books. Go where they are, get around them, talk to them. It is easy to be great when you get around great people.

— Bob Richards, Olympic Athlete —

Chapter
7

Chicken Soup
for the Soul

Eclectic Wisdom

This life is a test.
It is only a test.
Had it been
an actual life
You would have received
Further instructions on
Where to go and what to do!

~Found on a bulletin board

Gratitude Makes You Stronger

When we give cheerfully and accept gratefully,
everyone is blessed.
~Maya Angelou

"Thank you." It's one of the first things we are taught to say when we are youngsters. In a civilized society, it's part of being a polite person.

But then there's *ingratitude*, and most of us have experienced that, too — extending ourselves on someone's behalf and the gesture not being acknowledged. When you have experienced ingratitude, you never forget it.

It's been years since my son invited a friend to spend the day with him at the local amusement park. When we pulled up in front of his house after a long and fun-filled day, the boy jumped out of the car and ran inside. "He didn't say *thank you!*" my son said in amazement. I too was stunned — I sat behind the wheel of the car, speechless. Both of us still remember that boy's omission, and we wonder how that lack of thankfulness has affected him.

"Thank you" is the grease that keeps society functioning. But *saying* thank you and *being* thankful are two very different things. The former is part of being mannerly, the latter — well, it's the secret to a life of happiness and success.

For one thing, people will like you better. *Ingratitude* is one of the most disliked traits in people. It acts as a repellent. No one wants to be around ingrates. Gratitude, on the other hand, is right up there in the top ten percent of qualities people appreciate. Being likable is just the beginning. The list of consequences that come from being grateful is so long and so upbeat that it sounds more like the sales pitch of a cheesy infomercial than research-proven outcomes. Greater optimism. Higher energy. Increased creativity. Longer lifespan. Boldness in the face of challenge. Higher immune response. Greater tolerance. Increased cognitive skills.

I learned all of this as the result of being bored at work. It was during a news cycle when it seemed the stories making headlines all fell into the category of "Young Stars Having Meltdowns." Britney Spears was in her head-shaving/tattoo-getting phase and Lindsay Lohan was just beginning her string of run-ins with the law. It didn't take much time or many brain cells to write my scripts for the broadcast and, frankly, I had time on my hands.

I decided to spend some of that time looking into a hunch I had always had: that my life went better when I focused on what was going right for me, rather than lamenting the things that went wrong. This was *not* a novel idea. Charles Dickens once said, "*Reflect upon your present blessings, of which every man has plenty; not on your past misfortunes of which all men have some.*"

What I wanted to know was: Is there anything to it? Is there actually any proof that counting your blessings, looking on the bright side, practicing gratitude — whatever you call it — actually produces quantifiable benefits? I came at it with a reporter's mindset. Do the research, examine the facts, talk to the experts. I shared what I learned in a book I wrote called *Thank You Power: Making the Science of Gratitude Work for You*. I learned that not only was there peer-reviewed scientific research into the consequences of a grateful mindset, those consequences were life altering in a variety of life affirming ways.

Being grateful puts you in a positive frame of mind. Psychologists call it the "upward spiral." Just as focusing on all the things that went wrong during the day leaves you cranky and ill-tempered, acknowledging what went right — call them blessings or "good things" — has the reverse effect. One positive thought prompts another positive thought, which is followed by a pleasant memory and so on. Each thought spirals upward into another happy moment and your mood climbs along with your thoughts.

The reason this happens is multifold. Your attention is focused on actual events that occurred — giving a concrete realness to moments most of us would likely forget or overlook if not being deliberate about recollecting them. Since the majority of most people's grateful moments involve other people — tallying those moments underscores the relationships that give life meaning, which is particularly important in today's electronically isolated existence. It also boosts one's self-esteem. "If all this good stuff is happening to me, I must deserve it."

Common sense dictates these would probably be likely outcomes of recalling positive past moments. That finding didn't surprise me. But some of the other results documented by researchers really got me excited. One professor I consulted found that when people feel appreciated, they go the extra mile on your behalf. Her experiment found that when busy physicians were given a small token of gratitude — a little bag of candy in this case — they were more elastic in their thinking and willing to consult other doctors to confirm their diagnoses. The doctors who didn't get the extra "thank you" tended to be methodical in their approach and sometimes ignored facts that didn't fit with their preliminary diagnosis.

Gratitude also helps "take care of emotional business of negative things in our lives," says psychology professor Philip Watkins, Ph.D. of Eastern Washington State University. Grateful people are able to remember past positive events, even in the aftermath of trauma. Finding things for which one can be grateful helps make the memory of a difficult experience less intrusive. Other research has found a connection between the kind of positive emotions created by gratitude and resilience. Grateful people are better able to weather life's storms.

Those positive emotions can *also* help you solve life's problems. There is a clear connection between feeling upbeat and making cognitive connections and associations. One fascinating study found that when little children were asked to recall a moment that made them so happy that they wanted to dance, they were better able to remember information they'd just been taught than children who did not get the "happy dance" prompt. That bit of research prompted me to tell my own children to think of a happy memory just before taking a challenging test at school. I figured it couldn't hurt, and the data indicated it just might help a lot!

Equally important, gratitude can help take the edge off stress. Counting one's blessings elevates one's mood, which studies have shown can reduce the physical effects of stress. Six out of ten millennials say they are trying to reduce stress in their lives, and more than half say stress has kept them awake at night. One researcher I spoke with conducted a study in which participants were wired up so their blood pressure, heart rate and stress hormones could be measured. Then they were asked to present an impromptu speech that would count for a majority of their course grade, which put them all in a high-stress state. The participants who were given a visual cue that summoned up a positive mindset were shown to quickly de-stress in a way that those given neutral or negative visual images did not. Gratitude can have a similar impact.

The good news is you can *become* more grateful even if it doesn't come naturally for you. Hearing other people's stories of gratitude is one way to do it. In a letter he wrote in 1771, Thomas Jefferson commented, "When an… act of charity or of gratitude, for instance, is presented to our sight or imagination, we are deeply impressed with its beauty and feel a strong desire in ourselves of doing charitable and grateful acts also."

Being thankful CAN change your life — in just ONE way: It can make your life better.

— Deborah Norville —

What Made You Smile Today?

It takes a lot of energy to be negative.
You have to work at it. But smiling is painless.
I'd rather spend my energy smiling.
~Eric Davis

Several years ago, Jack, a good friend of mine was having trouble with his manipulative, drug-abusing twenty-something daughter.

He told me, "I really should be in touch with her, but every time I try, she lies to me, complains or lays a 'poor me' trip on me. But then I got the idea to text her every day at 5 P.M. with this message, 'Hey honey, it's Dad. What made you smile today?' Because I figured everyone smiles about something: a piece of pizza, a shower, even just going to the bathroom… At first she tried to manipulate me to get money and I texted back, 'Oh no, no, no. That ship sailed a long time ago. No more money.'

"Nevertheless, I continued every day. And then one day six weeks later she texted back, 'If you really want to know, it was knowing that you'd text me.' I got emotional because that was the first time we connected without her wanting anything other than that.

"Two months later, she was off drugs and alcohol. Maybe she was using them because she felt like a burden to me that I resented. It wasn't her that was the burden, it was her lying and manipulation," Jack explained.

There was something about asking that simple question that triggered an idea in me.

I then went on a mission whenever someone served me at a fast-food restaurant or I interacted with a cashier at a supermarket or warehouse store or a TSA agent at the airport. I noticed that even though they had nametags, they were often faceless to the public, largely ignored beyond their function.

Every day when I was served by someone like that, I checked first to see how busy/stressed they might be. If there was some breathing room, and after they rang me up or provided their service, I looked at their nametag and said the following, "Hi Mary, my name is Mark. Thank you. I have a question for you." Sometimes they would startle, worried they did something wrong, and I would say, "No, no. You didn't do anything wrong. Mary, what made you smile today?"

Nearly always, they would do a doubletake, and look up at the ceiling to reflect on this gift of having been appreciated *and* seen as a person. Then they would look at me with a twinkle in their eye and respond, "My grandchild," "My puppy," "It's a beautiful day," and occasionally, "*You* made me smile."

After that I took it a step further and bought 2,000 wristbands that said #WMYST (What Made You Smile Today). I would then add to my interaction, pulling out two wristbands and say to my unsuspecting new friend, "You have a great smile. Here is a wristband to wear to remind you to think of what made you smile today; and here is a second one to give to someone else because I'd like you to pay this forward and see the effect it has on them *and* on you."

I wondered what made this little exercise so powerful and so easy. I realized that most people do have something that makes them smile each day; you just need to bring it to their attention to re-experience and re-appreciate it. I also realized that "What made you smile today?" is not as heavy-handed as, "What are you grateful for?" The latter runs the risk of causing some people to feel you are accusing them of not being grateful enough.

I also discovered that not only did this exercise make them smile, it made me smile too, because I had just given a gift to someone who could not help me be more successful or make money. They did something more important. They made me feel more worthwhile as a person because I just made another human being a little happier without being so focused on myself.

There may be another reason that doing this caused the person who asked "What made you smile today?" to be as happy as the recipient of the question. Over the years in my psychotherapy practice, when I have drilled down with depressed patients to figure out what was really going on, some replied, "I don't think I deserve to be happy, because to be honest all I think about is myself. I am totally self-absorbed and self-centered and maybe, just maybe, someone who doesn't care about anyone but themselves doesn't deserve to be happy."

You don't have to be depressed to feel that sometimes you are a little bit too self-absorbed and are not very caring about your fellow human beings. Doing this exercise temporarily relieves you of that self-absorption and the shame that accompanies it. And relief from that shame can also be a source of happiness for you.

Also, being a psychiatrist and passionate about neuroscience, I realized that there may be some neurophysiology at play. When you ask someone "What made you smile today?" and they pause to think about it, they feel a small burst of dopamine, the pleasure hormone, at re-experiencing something pleasurable. That dopamine can also spontaneously cross over into appreciating you for caring, and the experience of that releases oxytocin in both of you. Oxytocin is a hormone associated with emotional connection and it does something else also. It helps lower cortisol, which is the hormone associated with stress. When stress goes down, a part of your brain having to do with processing fearful and threatening stimuli called the amygdala calms down. When that happens your mind relaxes and can think more clearly, which also is pleasurable and releases more dopamine.

Isn't it amazing what a simple "What made you smile today?" can do?

— Dr. Mark Goulston —

In a Heartbeat

It is not flesh and blood, but heart
which makes us fathers and sons.
~Friedrich von Schiller

I swore I would never play golf. The game is the direct opposite of everything I'm wired to do. I'm blessed with many things, but one of them isn't patience. Patience I have to work at. What I love is speed — fast boats, fast cars, fast results. During the three decades I've been helping transform the quality of people's lives, my message has always been the same: You can change in a heartbeat. How? You can change your focus. If you change the stories you tell yourself, you can change the meaning of what happens to you.

The story I always told myself about golf was that it was slow and boring. But my boys started to play golf, and I wanted to do things with them, so I took up golf. Even though I hated it. But then I thought: "Why spend the time if you're not going to enjoy the game?"

I focused on what I liked about the sport. Golf courses are built in some of the most beautiful places in the world, so I could enjoy the view. Then a buddy pointed out that I could play by my own rules. If I didn't want to play all eighteen holes, I could play six. I could play only the best, most scenic holes. Pretty soon I was thinking, "Hey, this sport is great!"

When you learn to change your focus, it helps you feel gratitude for what you already have — and that is truly the key to happiness.

What I am most grateful for in my life is my beautiful wife, Sage. She has given me more joy than everything else combined. And the only people I love as much as my wife and my children are my father-in-law and mother-in-law. I had four fathers, all of them dead, and my mother has passed, too. So Sage's parents are my mother and father.

So once I learned to love golf, I wanted to share it with my Pops. He's a very strong man, a good, honorable man who spent his life in the lumber business and never had time for something like golf. But I got him playing and before long he was hooked.

One day he said to me, "Tony, let's go play golf!" Then he named a golf course that was a two-hour drive away, and not a particularly great course. I had to catch a flight to London first thing the next morning, but I could see how much he wanted to go, and I loved him so much I didn't want to let him down. So off we went.

When we got there the course was even uglier than I'd expected, and I wasn't playing well. Then suddenly, just as we were about to tee off, three deer came prancing out of the woods and stopped right in front of us. They stood there staring, and we stared back. It was a perfect moment, suspended in time. Then, just as suddenly, the deer took off and were gone.

As we walked back to the car I remember thinking, "You know, you'll never know how long you're going to have the people you love."

I immediately forgot the game and the lousy course, and Pops and I started having an even better time together. When we pulled up to the last hole, my father jumped out of the car and said "I'll go first." He took two steps, then spun around and looked at me. His eyes rolled back in his head until all I could see were the whites, then he toppled over like a big tree falling in a clear cut, crashing straight back and smacking his head on the ground. In that moment everything in my world changed, and it happened unbelievably fast.

I didn't know what to do. I'd never been trained in CPR. But I knew he would die if I didn't do *something*. My whole nervous system started speeding up and I remembered from somewhere that I had to clear his airway and pull back his tongue to keep him from suffocating. I did that, but there was no breath in him. So I started giving him mouth-to-mouth, like I'd seen in the movies, but it wasn't working. He was limp and changing color. I screamed for help but there was nobody who could hear me. Terrible thoughts were rushing through my mind. "If I hadn't taken him golfing we wouldn't be here in this godforsaken place! I can't let him die right in front of me, without his wife and daughter by his side!"

Then something popped into my head out of nowhere, a random CNN news show that I'd seen years ago, that I had no reason to be watching. They were talking about people who could have been saved if they'd been given chest compressions instead of mouth-to-mouth resuscitation. There is already oxygen in the blood, and intense chest compressions can force it into the brain, and it's the brain that you've got to keep alive. So I started chest compressions, but it wasn't working. After three or four minutes he was still lifeless.

I was going crazy now, and I just snapped and started shouting, "You're not dying now! Not on my watch! You are going to be with your family!" I said a prayer and then started to smash his chest, pounding down with incredible ferocity. I pumped and pumped and then all of a sudden he coughed. And then there was a breath. He still couldn't open his eyes. He couldn't speak, so I grabbed his hand and I said, "Squeeze my arm right here if you understand what I'm saying right now." He squeezed it.

Finally help arrived, and we eventually got my father to a hospital. There was no brain damage, and they never could tell us what happened or why. There had been some kind of arrhythmia, followed by cardiac arrest. His heart had stopped, and then he came back to life.

There are many ways to tell this story. I wanted to blame myself for teaching my father to play golf and then taking him somewhere so far from help. But then I thought: Who did I think I was? Who put me in charge of what happens? A better way to look at it was to consider the timing of his heart attack as a gift. What if we didn't play golf, and he was driving his car when he passed out? What if he was in his workshop, alone when it happened? I wouldn't have been there to save him.

For some people, when an ambulance races by and just misses

them, the story they come up with is, "I was almost killed." Other people say, "Wow, God protected me today." The quality of your life is not the quality of your events, it is the meaning you attached to your events.

The story I choose to tell myself is that my father is alive and God guided it. I got to be part of that process, so I get more time with him. I'm going to value every moment we have together, even more than before. And we'll be spending some of that time playing golf.

— Anthony Robbins —

To Connect, Must We Disconnect?

The danger of the past was that men became slaves. The danger of the future is that man may become robots.
~Erich Fromm

As the founder of the Agape International Spiritual Center, I tweet and have friended on Facebook thousands of local members and global live streamers. Added to that are social networking conveniences like texting and calling, which keep me connected to staff and family. Oh yes, I definitely enjoy and appreciate the benefits of technology. After all, I couldn't write this piece without it, nor could I stay in touch as required when traveling to speaking engagements, conferences, and so on. Recently—and in a spirit of honesty it was *not* by choice—I discovered what a shock it is to the system to be cut off, without warning, from all the mechanisms and systems we depend upon to communicate efficiently and effectively.

Here's how it all unfolded. Agape's website was down for over a week. At the same time I was having challenges with my home computer so couldn't access e-mail or the Internet. "Oh well," I comforted myself, "there's always texting and calling." That's when things escalated. After a hunt worthy of a search and rescue team, my cell phone was nowhere to be found. I had to laugh at myself when I observed a slight panic arising at feeling disconnected from the outside world. It was a good time to have cultivated the tools of an accomplished yogi: clairvoyance, telepathic communication, and bilocation. Not being quite there, I had no other choice but to use my household landline, which felt about as antiquated as sending messages via carrier pigeon!

The upside of my predicament is that by forcibly having been put on "pause," I couldn't deny how devouring social media can be. What seemed like utterly natural forms of communicating one moment, when placed under an introspective microscope, revealed not only their addictive potential but also how their misuse is creating what I call a "high-tech, low-touch" society. Interruption technologies have become the norm. Just go out to dinner and see how children are occupied playing games on their iPads while their parents text and talk on the phone, all of them rarely sharing eye contact or personal conversation.

Neurologists, sociologists, psychologists and other pundits are issuing warnings about the Age of Distraction in which we live. They aren't casting blame on social media itself; how can they since it is we who have self-responsibility for how and when we use it? We hear in the news about accidents caused by a metro engineer texting or a driver injuring someone — sometimes fatally — by texting just one trivial word. Perhaps T. S. Eliot realized the timelessness of his words when he wrote, "We are distracted from distraction by distraction."

The message that was driven home to me is that there is a time to disconnect, to curb the insatiable appetite for where the next click might lead. Simply put, equal commitment must be given to connecting to the "inner-net." Just as in the outer world we learn to adjust to ever-advancing technology, so must we equally participate in the inner world of ever-evolving consciousness. Practices such as meditation, affirmative prayer and visioning keep us centered, present to the now moment. They synchronize body, mind and spirit and are the antidote to the seduction of distraction, constant interruption and multi-tasking. Above all, they awaken the Essential Self. And for that there exists no technological substitute.

— Michael Bernard Beckwith —

How to Give Up Bad Habits

Habits are at first cobwebs, then cables.
~Spanish Proverb

Throughout my life I've given up many bad habits. Most recently I got off coffee. Letting go of coffee was not easy. In fact, strange as it may sound, it was even harder than when I got sober eight years ago and gave up drugs and alcohol. Caffeine was my last drug, and because it wasn't killing me I continued to give myself permission to drink it.

One of the main reasons we stay stuck in habits we know don't serve us is because of our permission-giving thoughts, such as *One cup of coffee a day won't kill me.* Or, *I only drink on weekends.* These thoughts keep us convinced that there is nothing wrong with our behavior even though deep down we know it isn't right.

In many cases we use our bad habits to avoid dealing with something much more difficult. In my case, I was using coffee as a final vice. As a sober woman I felt I deserved to have something I could turn to when I felt I needed a jolt. This habit seemed harmless, but when I got honest with myself it became clear that I was just using the coffee as another drug. Upon genuinely reviewing my behavior I came to realize that I had to stop giving myself permission to drink coffee and that it was time to change the habit.

Transitioning out of a bad habit can be really uncomfortable at first. To help you ease into the process, I've outlined the three steps that worked for me when I put down the coffee.

Step One: Keep it in the day
One of the main reasons we get tripped up when we try to change a habit is that we start future tripping. For instance, when I was first letting go of coffee I'd project onto the future with thoughts such as, *What will I do when I'm in Europe and I want a cappuccino?* What helped me most during these future flip-outs was to simply keep it in the day. I would tell myself, *I don't need to worry about tomorrow. Today I choose not to drink coffee.* One day at a time I've stayed committed.

Step Two: Change your breath pattern
The moment we change our breath pattern we change our energy, thereby changing our experience. Whenever you notice yourself about to relapse into your negative behavior, take a long, deep breath. As you change your breath you change your energy. Your calm and centered energy will support you in positive behavior and stop you from indulging in your bad habit.

Step Three: Make it joyful
Letting go of a negative habit doesn't have to be torturous. In fact, it can be joyful. To really create change we need more than just willpower: We must find the joy and curiosity in it. Letting go of a bad habit is really just creating a new habit. In that new habit you can find happiness. In my case, I chose not to dwell on the loss of coffee and instead I fell in love with organic tea and have become a tea connoisseur. When you find joy in creating a new habit you can effortlessly let go of the bad one.

If you're ready to let go of that nasty vice, use these three steps. Keep it in the day, breathe through the transition and find joy in creating new habits.

— Gabrielle Bernstein —

The Two Saddest Words

Precaution is better than cure.
~Edward Coke

Two of the saddest words in the English language are "if only."
I live my life with the goal of never having to say those words,
because they convey regret, lost opportunities, mistakes, and
disappointment. And sometimes the words "if only" go with terrible tragedies. Think about how many times you have heard about
something awful happening, accompanied by "if only he had called
her back to make sure she was okay…" or "if only I had investigated
that noise…" or "if only they had made sure the gate to the pool
clicked behind them…"

My father-in-law is famous in our family for saying, "Take the
extra minute to do it right." He must be doing something right, since
he's 91 years old and still making a lot of sense.

I always try to live by the "extra minute" rule. Sometimes it only
takes seconds to make sure I write something down correctly, or check
something on the Internet, or move an object out of the way before
it trips someone. And of course when my children were young, and
prone to all kinds of mishaps, I lived and breathed the extra minute
rule. I always thought about what I could do to avoid an "if only"
moment, whether it was something minor like moving a cup full of
hot coffee away from the edge of a counter, or something that required
a little more work such as taping padding onto the sharp corners of

a glass coffee table.

I just read a news story about a student pilot who was thrown from an airplane when its canopy lifted off. The instructor, who was belted in, was fine. The student, whose seatbelt was not fastened, fell from the sky and his body was found on the ground somewhere in Tennessee. Imagine how many people are in mourning, and how terrified that man must have been as he fell from the plane and realized he was going to die. Imagine the chorus of "if only" coming from his family. If only he had been wearing his seatbelt... How simple would that have been?

I don't move my car one inch until I hear the seatbelt click on every passenger. I unplug the iron when I leave the laundry room for "just a minute." I'd hate to get distracted, not return to the laundry room, and start a fire with that forgotten iron. Imagine the "if only" I'd be saying then. After I realized that I could not be trusted with a teakettle — I left it boiling on the stove for an hour — I threw it out and bought an electric teakettle that shuts itself off. And I am paranoid about fireplace ashes. I wait till they are two weeks old, then shovel them into a bag on garbage collection day and put the bag 20 feet away from the house in the middle of the driveway.

When my teenage son was first driving, I worried that enforcing his curfew too strictly would cause him to speed and have an accident. A boy in the next town was killed when he drove too fast trying to make it home by midnight. So my son and I agreed on a plan — if he missed curfew he would just lose double those minutes the next night out. Ten minutes late meant 20 minutes shaved off the curfew the next time, consequences that were not so onerous that they would cause him to rush home.

When I was in a car accident a few years ago, resulting in spinal surgery and permanent nerve damage, I handled it well emotionally, because I wasn't the driver who was at fault. There was no "if only" thinking for me, and it's a lot easier to forgive someone else than it is to forgive yourself.

I don't only avoid those "if only" moments when it comes to safety. It's equally important to avoid "if only" in our personal relationships.

We all know people who lost a loved one and bemoaned the fact that they had foregone an opportunity to say "I love you" or "I forgive you." When my father announced he was going to the eye doctor across from my office on Good Friday, I told him that it was a holiday for Chicken Soup for the Soul and I wouldn't be here. But then I thought about the fact that he's 84 years old and I realized that I shouldn't give up an opportunity to see him. I called him and told him I had decided to go to work on my day off after all. When my husband's beloved, elderly uncle pocket-dialed me several times yesterday with his new cell phone, I urged my husband to call him back, invoking the "if only" possibility. My husband called him and was glad that he did. Now if anything happens, my husband won't have to say, "If only I had called him back that day."

I know there will still be occasions when I have to say "if only" about something, but my life is definitely more serene because of my policy of doing everything possible to avoid that eventuality. And even though it takes an extra minute to do something right, or it occasionally takes an hour or two in my busy schedule to make a personal connection, I know that I'm doing the right thing. I'm buying myself peace of mind and that's the best kind of insurance for my emotional wellbeing.

— Amy Newmark —

You've Got Yourself a Deal!

If love does not know how to give and take without restrictions,
it is not love, but a transaction that never fails
to lay stress on a plus and a minus.
~Emma Goldman

When Marita was 13, it was the era of tie-dyed T-shirts and frayed jeans. Even though I had grown up in the Depression and had no money for clothes, I had never dressed this poorly. One day I saw her out in the driveway rubbing the hems of her new jeans with dirt and rocks. I was aghast at her ruining these pants I had just paid for and ran out to tell her so. She continued to grind on as I recounted my soap opera of childhood deprivation. As I concluded without having moved her to tears of repentance, I asked why she was wrecking her new jeans. She replied without looking up, "You can't wear new ones."

"Why not?"

"You just can't, so I'm messing them up to make them look old." Such total loss of logic! How could it be the style to ruin new clothes?

Each morning as she would leave for school I would stare at her and sigh, "My daughter looking like that." There she'd stand in her father's old T-shirt, tie-dyed with big blue spots and streaks. Fit for a duster, I thought. And those jeans — so low-slung I feared if she took a deep breath, they'd drop off her rear. But where would they go? They were so tight and stiff they couldn't move. The frayed bottoms, helped by the rocks, had strings that dragged behind her as she walked.

One day after she had left for school, it was as if the Lord got my attention and said, "Do you realize what your last words are to Marita each morning? 'My daughter looking like that.' When she gets to school and her friends talk about their old-fashioned mothers who complain all the time, she'll have your constant comments to contribute. Have you ever looked at the other girls in junior high? Why not give them a glance?"

I drove over to pick her up that day and observed that many of the other girls looked even worse. On the way home I mentioned how I had overreacted to her ruining her jeans. I offered a compromise: "From now on you can wear anything you want to school and with your friends, and I won't bug you about it."

"That'll be a relief."

"But when I take you out with me to church or shopping or to my friends, I'd like you to dress in something you know I like without my having to say a word."

She thought about it.

Then I added, "That means you get 95 percent your way and I get 5 percent for me. What do you think?"

She got a twinkle in her eye as she put out her hand and shook mine. "Mother, you've got yourself a deal!"

From then on I gave her a happy farewell in the morning and didn't bug her about her clothes. When I took her out with me, she dressed properly without fussing. We had ourselves a deal!

— Florence Littauer —

Take a Moment to Really See

Intuition is a spiritual faculty and does not explain,
but simply points the way.
~Florence Scovel Shinn

We have all heard the expression: "Remember to stop and smell the roses." But, how often do we really take time out of our hectic fast-paced lives to notice the world around us? Too often we get caught up in our busy schedules, thoughts of our next appointment, the traffic or life in general, to even realize there are other people nearby.

I am as guilty as anyone of tuning out the world in this manner, especially when I am driving on California's overcrowded streets. A short time ago, however, I witnessed an event that showed me how being wrapped up in my own little world has kept me from being fully aware of the bigger world picture around me.

I was driving to a business appointment and, as usual, I was planning in my mind what I was going to say. I came to a very busy intersection where the stoplight had just turned red. "All right," I thought to myself, "I can beat the next light if I race ahead of the pack."

My mind and car were on autopilot, ready to go, when suddenly my trance was broken by an unforgettable sight. A young couple, both blind, were walking arm-in-arm across this busy intersection with cars whizzing by in every direction. The man was holding the hand of a little boy, while the woman was clutching a baby sling to her chest, obviously carrying a child. Each of them had a white cane extended, searching for clues to navigate them across the intersection.

Initially I was moved. They were overcoming what I felt was one of the most feared handicaps — blindness. "Wouldn't it be terrible to be blind?" I thought. My thought was quickly interrupted by horror when I saw that the couple was not walking in the crosswalk, but was instead veering diagonally, directly toward the middle of the intersection. Without realizing the danger they were in, they were walking right smack into the path of oncoming cars. I was frightened for them because I didn't know if the other drivers understood what was happening.

As I watched from the front line of traffic (I had the best seat in the house), I saw a miracle unfold before my eyes. *Every* car in *every* direction came to a simultaneous stop. I never heard the screech of brakes or even the peep of a car horn. Nobody even yelled, "Get out of the way!" Everything froze. In that moment, time seemed to stand still for this family.

Amazed, I looked at the cars around me to verify that we were all seeing the same thing. I noticed that everyone's attention was also fixed on the couple. Suddenly the driver to my right reacted. Craning his head out of his car, he yelled, "To your right. To your right!" Other people followed in unison, shouting, "To your right!"

Never skipping a beat, the couple adjusted their course as they followed the coaching. Trusting their white canes and the calls from some concerned citizens, they made it to the other side of the road. As they arrived at the curb, one thing struck me — they were still arm-in-arm.

I was taken aback by the emotionless expressions on their faces and judged that they had no idea what was really going on around them. Yet I immediately sensed the sighs of relief exhaled by everyone stopped at that intersection.

As I glanced into the cars around me, the driver on my right was mouthing the words "Whew, did you see that?" The driver to the left of me was saying, "I can't believe it!" I think all of us were deeply moved by what we had just witnessed. Here were human beings stepping outside themselves for a moment to help four people in need.

I have reflected back on this situation many times since it happened and have learned several powerful lessons from it. The first is: "Slow down and smell the roses." (Something I had rarely done up until then.) Take time to look around and really see what is going on in front of you right now. Do this and you will realize that this moment is all there is; more importantly, this moment is all that you have to make a difference in life.

The second lesson I learned is that the goals we set for ourselves can be attained through faith in ourselves and trust in others, despite seemingly insurmountable obstacles.

The blind couple's goal was simply to get to the other side of the road intact. Their obstacle was eight lanes of cars aimed straight at them. Yet, without panic or doubt, they walked forward until they reached their goal.

We too can move forward in attaining our goals, putting blinders on to the obstacles that would stand in our way. We just need to trust our intuition and accept the guidance of others who may have greater insight.

Finally, I learned to really appreciate my gift of sight, something I had taken for granted all too often.

Can you imagine how different life would be without your eyes? Try to imagine for a moment, walking into a busy intersection without being able to see. How often we forget the simple yet incredible gifts we have in our life.

As I drove away from that busy intersection, I did so with more awareness of life and compassion for others than I had arrived there with. Since then I have made the decision to really see life as I go about my daily activities and use my God-given talents to help others less fortunate.

Do yourself a favor as you walk through life: Slow down and take the time to really *see*. Take a moment to see what is going on around you right now, right where you are. You may be missing something wonderful.

—Jeffrey Michael Thomas—

If I Had My Life to Live Over

Go for it now. The future is promised to no one.
~Wayne Dyer

I'd dare to make more mistakes next time.
I'd relax. I would limber up.
I would be sillier than I have been this trip.
I would take fewer things seriously.
I would take more chances.
I would take more trips.
I would climb more mountains and swim more rivers.
I would eat more ice cream and less beans.
I would perhaps have more actual troubles but I'd have fewer imaginary ones.
You see, I'm one of those people who live sensibly and sanely hour after hour, day after day.
Oh, I've had my moments and if I had it to do over again, I'd have more of them. In fact, I'd try to have nothing else. Just moments.
One after another, instead of living so many years ahead of each day.
I've been one of those people who never go anywhere without a thermometer, a hot water bottle, a raincoat and a parachute.
If I had it to do again, I would travel lighter next time.

If I had my life to live over, I would start barefoot earlier in the spring and stay that way later in the fall.

I would go to more dances.
I would ride more merry-go-rounds.
I would pick more daisies.

—Nadine Stair (age 85)—

Sachi

*In my soul, I am still that small child
who did not care about anything else
but the beautiful colors of a rainbow.*
~Papiha Ghosh

Soon after her brother was born, little Sachi began to ask her parents to leave her alone with the new baby. They worried that like most four-year-olds, she might feel jealous and want to hit or shake him, so they said no. But she showed no signs of jealousy. She treated the baby with kindness and her pleas to be left alone with him became more urgent. They decided to allow it.

Elated, she went into the baby's room and shut the door, but it opened a crack—enough for her curious parents to peek in and listen. They saw little Sachi walk quietly up to her baby brother, put her face close to his and say quietly, "Baby, tell me what God feels like. I'm starting to forget."

—Dan Millman—

The Dolphin's Gift

*I would maintain that thanks are the highest form
of thought; and that gratitude is happiness
doubled by wonder.*
~G.K. Chesterton

I was in about 40 feet of water, alone. I knew I should not have gone alone, but I was very competent and just took a chance. There was not much current, and the water was so warm, clear and enticing. When I got a cramp, I realized at once how foolish I was. I was not too alarmed, but *was* completely doubled up with stomach cramps. I tried to remove my weight belt, but I was so doubled up I could not get to the catch. I was sinking and began to feel more frightened, unable to move. I could see my watch and knew there was only a little more time on the tank before I would be out of air. I tried to massage my abdomen. I wasn't wearing a wet suit, but couldn't straighten out and couldn't get to the cramped muscles with my hands.

I thought, "I can't go like this! I have things to do!" I just couldn't die anonymously this way with no one to even know what happened to me. I called out in my mind, "Somebody, something, help me!"

I was not prepared for what happened. Suddenly I felt a prodding from behind me under the armpit. I thought, "Oh no, sharks!" I felt real terror and despair. But my arm was being lifted forcibly. Around into my field of vision came an eye — the most marvelous eye I could ever imagine. I swear it was smiling. It was the eye of a big dolphin. Looking into that eye, I knew I was safe.

It moved farther forward, nudging under and hooking its dorsal fin below my armpit with my arm over its back. I relaxed, hugging it, flooded with relief. I felt that the animal was conveying security to me, that it was healing me as well as lifting me toward the surface. My stomach cramps went away as we ascended and I relaxed with security, but I felt very strongly that it healed me too.

At the surface it drew me all the way into shore. It took me into water so shallow that I began to be concerned that it might be beached, and I pushed it back a little deeper, where it waited, watching me, I guess to see if I was all right.

It felt like another lifetime. When I took off the weight belt and oxygen tank, I just took everything off and went naked back into the ocean to the dolphin. I felt so light and free and alive, and just wanted to play in the sun and the water in all that freedom. The dolphin took me back out and played around in the water with me. I noticed that there were a lot of dolphins there, farther out.

After a while it brought me back to shore. I was very tired then, almost collapsing and he made sure I was safe in the shallowest water. Then he turned sideways with one eye looking into mine. We stayed that way for what seemed like a very long time, timeless I guess, in a trance almost, with personal thoughts from the past going through my mind. Then he made just one sound and went out to join the others. And all of them left.

— Elizabeth Gawain —

The Touch of the Master's Hand

*To send light into the darkness of men's hearts — such
is the duty of the artist.*
~Schumann

'Twas battered and scarred, and the auctioneer
Thought it scarcely worth his while
To waste much time on the old violin,
But held it up with a smile.
"What am I bidden, good folks," he cried,
"Who'll start the bidding for me?"
"A dollar, a dollar," then, two! Only two?
"Two dollars, and who'll make it three?
"Three dollars, once; three dollars, twice;
Going for three…" But no,
From the room, far back, a gray-haired man
Came forward and picked up the bow;
Then, wiping the dust from the old violin,
And tightening the loose strings,
He played a melody pure and sweet
As a caroling angel sings.

The music ceased, and the auctioneer,
With a voice that was quiet and low,
Said: "What am I bid for the old violin?"
And he held it up with the bow.
"A thousand dollars, and who'll make it two?
Two thousand! And who'll make it three?
Three thousand, once; three thousand, twice;
And going and gone," said he.
The people cheered, but some of them cried,
"We do not quite understand
What changed its worth?"
Swift came the reply:
"The touch of a master's hand."

And many a man with life out of tune,
And battered and scarred with sin,
Is auctioned cheap to the thoughtless crowd,
Much like the old violin.
A "mess of potage," a glass of wine;
A game — and he travels on.
He is "going" once, and "going" twice,
He's "going" and almost "gone."
But the Master comes and the foolish crowd
Never can quite understand
The worth of a soul and the change that's wrought
By the touch of the Master's hand.

— Myra B. Welch —

Afterword

The overarching theme in this book is positive thinking. You've read story after story about how people have used positive thinking to navigate difficult situations, reorient their lives, and improve their personal relationships. We all want to go about our days with a positive outlook—but we don't always know how to do it.

It's our job at Chicken Soup for the Soul to focus on finding stories for you that are positive and uplifting and helpful. Before I became publisher of Chicken Soup for the Soul fifteen years ago, I spent six months getting to know the company, and I read 100 of the old titles. After reading all of those books and tens of thousands of stories submitted for our more recent books, the thing that has struck me the most is the resilience of the human spirit. We try to show you that in all our books.

I've learned how strong people are and how tough they are, and I've read about them overcoming challenges and moving on with their lives, even after horrible things have happened. It's inspiring to be in my job and read all these stories from people just like us—regular people—who've done extraordinary things that I couldn't imagine doing. All those powerful new thought leaders who contributed the bonus stories to this 30th Anniversary Edition of *Chicken Soup for the Soul* were ordinary people at one time—they became extraordinary due to events in their own lives… and because they used their positive thinking!

What I've learned is that we are all capable of handling a lot. And our ability to handle things seems to expand when we need it to.

Norman Vincent Peale said it best: "Change your thoughts and you change your world." Now that makes a lot of sense, because the world you see is colored by *how* you see it. I find myself acting a lot more optimistic and grounded today than I was years ago, and I think it's because of the good examples I see in our books — stories from people from all walks of life showing such can-do spirit, such resilience, and such a positive attitude despite their circumstances. I see ordinary people turning into *extraordinary* people, and I see how we all have that capability inside ourselves.

I've picked up some great advice from the thousands of stories that we have published about living life in a positive way, and I'd like to share seven tips with you:

1. Pursue at least one of your passions. If you have a job that just pays the bills, okay then, that is just your job, but that doesn't have to be what you *do*. Find some time to do what you actually love to do. I've heard that you should think back to what you loved to do when you were ten years old and you should try to do that now. For me, it was two things: reading, and hiking in the woods behind our house. And now I do just that — I read for work, I read for pleasure, and when the weather and time permits, my husband and I go hiking on the trails in our neighborhood.

2. Do something that has meaning to you and gives you purpose. Ralph Waldo Emerson said, "Make yourself necessary to somebody." You lift yourself when you lift others. We have thousands of stories from people who found that doing some kind of volunteer work practically saved their lives — it turned everything around for them to be giving back, to feel valued by other people, no matter what their own circumstances. Doing good for others is incredibly good for you.

3. Count your blessings. We get more stories than we could possibly publish about people who have purposefully turned their attitudes

around by keeping a journal. Some people write down one good thing that happened to them each day, even if it's something like "there was no line at Starbucks this morning." Other people make themselves write down three good things that happen to them each day. It may sound hokey, but it works, and we hear about these gratitude journals all the time. It's been scientifically proven that people who keep track of the "good things" in their lives are healthier and more productive, and they get along better with other people.

4. Smile at everyone. No matter what kind of day you are having, smile. We have countless stories from people who tried this, including one woman who saw herself by accident in a mirror and wondered who that grouchy lady was. She had an epiphany when she realized she was looking at her own reflection and she resolved to start smiling no matter how she felt inside. She started getting smiles back, people treated her differently, and she started acting like the non-grouchy person who she wished she really was.

5. Keep learning. Have you ever noticed how energized you feel when you learn something new? Of course, you are already doing that by reading this book. My parents were still reading books to learn history in their eighties, and they were traveling and watching documentaries on television. They never stopped learning, and they talked about what they have learned with great enthusiasm.

6. Take the long-term view. Think about your legacy, not the day to day. No matter what is happening now, what are you leaving the world. What has been your contribution? For me, that legacy is our children, despite the fact that my name is on the front cover of dozens of books. No matter how hard I work, or how much I enjoy it, my most important lifetime achievement will always be the two children I gave birth to and my two stepchildren. Our four amazing fully-grown children and five grandchildren (and their significant others and even their dogs) are what make us happy. I know that my face glows when someone asks about the kids, no matter what else is happening.

7. And finally, take some time for yourself. Sometimes, I don't get home from work till eight o'clock and I'm dead tired, but before I go into the house to start what I call the second shift, I just sit in the car for an extra minute in the garage, listening to the end of an interesting news report or a song. Or I go for a walk on the weekend, with no phone, and I listen to my thoughts instead of music or a podcast. That's "me" time. No matter how tired I am, or how late I go to bed, I take half an hour to read. That's "me" time too. You've already given yourself the gift of some "me" time by reading this book. While you read the powerful stories in this book, you recharged your batteries, gained perspective on your current issues, and remembered what you're grateful for in your life.

— Amy Newmark —
Publisher, Editor-in-Chief, and Coauthor
Chicken Soup for the Soul

Meet the Contributors of the Bonus Stories

MK Asante is a bestselling author and award-winning filmmaker who CNN calls "a master storyteller and major creative force." The author of four celebrated books, Asante is a recipient of the Langston Hughes Award. His latest book, *Buck*, is a critically acclaimed memoir about his youth in Philadelphia. He is a distinguished professor of creative writing and film at Morgan State University. He can be reached at mkasante.com.

Michael Bernard Beckwith is the founder of the Agape International Spiritual Center headquartered in Los Angeles. He is the author of *Spiritual Liberation*, *Life Visioning*, and originator of the Life Visioning Process. He has appeared on *The Oprah Show*, *Larry King Live*, *Tavis Smiley* and his own PBS special, *The Answer Is You*.

Gabrielle Bernstein is the New York Times bestselling author of the book, *May Cause Miracles*. Her earlier titles include, *Spirit Junkie* and *Add More ~ing to Your Life*. Gabrielle was recently featured on Oprah's *Super Soul Sunday* as a next generation thought leader. She is the founder of the social networking site HerFuture.com for women to inspire, empower and connect.

Kris Carr is a New York Times bestselling author and health advocate. Her books and film include the groundbreaking *Crazy Sexy Cancer* series, *Crazy Sexy Diet*, and *Crazy Sexy Kitchen*. Kris regularly lectures at medical schools, hospitals, wellness centers, and corporations. Her TV appearances include: the *Today* show, *Good Morning America, CBS Evening News* and *The Oprah Winfrey Show*. Find out more at www.kriscarr.com.

Deepak Chopra, MD is the author of more than 70 books with 21 New York Times bestsellers. He is the founder of the Chopra Foundation, co-founder and Chairman of the Board of The Chopra Center for Wellbeing, founder of The Chopra Well on YouTube, Adjunct Professor at Kellogg School of Management at Northwestern University, Adjunct Professor at Columbia Business School, Columbia University, and Senior Scientist with The Gallup Organization.

Lori Deschene is the founder of tinybuddha.com, a community blog about wisdom that draws a million monthly readers. She runs the site as a group effort because she believes we're all students and teachers. She is the author of *Tiny Buddha: Simple Wisdom for Life's Hard Questions* and the upcoming *Tiny Buddha's Guide to Self-Love.*

Tony D'Urso interviews those who made it to the top of their category (calling them "Elite Entrepreneurs") and who share their wisdom and advice with the audience. The Tony D'Urso Show is the #1 show on VoiceAmerica. Breaking the sound barrier at 35 million all-time listens and downloads, Tony helps millions of entrepreneurs learn from the success of others. Learn more at tonydurso.com.

After anchoring the news for twenty years at WCBS in New York City, **Pat Farnack** has retired. She continues, however, to anchor and produce the daily WCBS Health & Well-Being Report. She has worked in San Francisco, Philadelphia and New York, in television, radio, and in print, beginning her career in Berwick, Pennsylvania in the early seventies.

Dr. Mark Goulston is a psychiatrist and author/co-author of nine books, including, *Just Listed* and *Get Out of Your Own Way.* He is the host of the "My Wakeup Call" podcast and co-host of "Hurt Less, Live More with JJ and Dr. Mark" on UK Health Radio.

Eric Handler is the co-founder and publisher of positivelypositive. com — an online multimedia platform known for its creative content designed to inspire readers to live fully, connected and ignite the fire inside of them. Positively Positive has millions of monthly readers.

Darren Hardy is a celebrated speaker, mentor to business luminaries and Publisher and Founding Editor of *SUCCESS*, the award-winning magazine serving to empower small business owners and entrepreneurial-minded achievers. Read his monthly letter, marketing and sales advice from thought leaders, inspiring feature stories and step-by-step guides for maximizing your potential at SUCCESS.com and DarrenHardy.com.

Robert Holden's work on psychology and spirituality has been featured on *Oprah*, *Good Morning America*, a PBS special *Shift Happens!*, and in two major BBC-TV documentaries, *The Happiness Formula* and *How to Be Happy*. He is author of *Happiness NOW!*, *Shift Happens!*, *Authentic Success*, *Be Happy* and *Loveability*. Robert also hosts a weekly show on Hay House Radio called *Shift Happens!* www.robertholden.org

Tory Johnson has built two multi-million-dollar businesses—Women For Hire and Spark & Hustle—while serving as a *Good Morning America* contributor, New York Times bestselling author, contributing editor to *SUCCESS* magazine and a popular speaker. Her seventh book, *The Shift*, will be published in September 2013.

Mastin Kipp is the founder of TheDailyLove.com, a website, daily e-mail and Twitter account that serves soulful inspiration to a new generation. Hosting Mastin on her weekly show *Super Soul Sunday*, Oprah dubbed him an "up and coming thought leader of the next generation of spiritual thinkers." Mastin's book, *Float: An Achiever's Journey from Crisis to Grace*, is due out from Hay House in early 2014.

Steve Leder is the Senior Rabbi of Wilshire Boulevard Temple in Los Angeles and the author of the bestseller *The Beauty of What Remains* and the NY Times Best Seller *For You When I Am Gone*.

An award-winning journalist and bestselling author, **Joan Lunden** has been a trusted voice in American homes for forty years. At the helm of *Good Morning America* for nearly two decades, she is the longest running female host ever on early morning television. Currently she hosts the PBS series, *Second Opinion with Joan Lunden*.

Brad Meltzer is the #1 New York Times bestselling author of *The Lightning Rod*, *The Escape Artist*, and a dozen other bestselling thrillers.

He also writes non-fiction books like *The Nazi Conspiracy*, about a secret plot to kill FDR, Stalin, and Winston Churchill at the height of WWII. He also coauthors the *Ordinary People Change the World* kids book series. To learn more, please go to www.BradMeltzer.com.

Two-time Emmy Award winner **Deborah Norville** is Anchor of *Inside Edition*, the country's top-rated and most honored syndicated newsmagazine. She is currently the longest serving anchor on American television and an inductee into the Broadcasting + Cable Hall of Fame. Her book, *Thank You Power: Making the SCIENCE of Gratitude Work for YOU*, was a New York Times bestseller. She is also the coauthor of the bestselling *Chicken Soup for the Soul: The Power of Gratitude*.

Nick Ortner is the New York Times bestselling author of *The Tapping Solution: A Revolutionary System for Stress-Free Living* and the bestselling documentary by the same name. He teaches and writes about "EFT" or "Tapping" a technique that has shown to be effective for pain relief, limiting beliefs, weight loss, fears and phobias and more.

Laura Owens co-hosts one of the top self-help podcasts in the world, "Nobody Told Me!" She is a passionate public speaker who fearlessly advocates to eliminate the stigma facing domestic violence victims. You can hear more of her story in her popular TEDx talk, "The Lifesaving Power of Kindness to Strangers."

Zibby Owens is the CEO of Zibby Media, which includes the publishing house Zibby Books, an online magazine, *Zibby Mag*, Zibby Classes, Zibby Retreats, an audiobook and podcast company, Zibby Audio, and Zibby's Book Club. She's the owner of Santa Monica-based Zibby's Bookshop, a regular Contributor to *Good Morning America*, author of the memoir *Bookends: A Memoir of Love, Loss, and Literature*, and author of a children's book, *Princess Charming*. She lives between New York (mostly) and LA with her four kids and husband Kyle Owens of Morning Moon Productions. She always has a book nearby.

For more than 35 years, **Anthony Robbins** has devoted his life to helping people from around the world discover and develop their own unique qualities of greatness. Considered the nation's leader in peak performance and a recognized authority on the psychology of leadership, personal transformation and organizational turnaround, he has been honored consistently for his strategic intellect and humanitarian endeavors.

don Miguel Ruiz is the international bestselling author of *The Four Agreements* (a New York Times bestseller for seven years), *The Mastery of Love*, *The Voice of Knowledge*, and *The Fifth Agreement*. Today, he continues to share ancient Toltec wisdom through lectures and journeys to sacred sites around the world.

Sophfronia Scott writes nonfiction books including *The Seeker and the Monk*, *Love's Long Line*, and *This Child of Faith*, and novels including *Wild, Beautiful, and Free*, *Unforgivable Love*, and *All I Need to Get By*. She is founding director of Alma College's Master of Fine Arts (MFA) in Creative Writing.

Jane Wolfe is the founder of the Eat and Read literacy project in New Orleans. An adjunct professor of World Religions at University of Holy Cross, she holds a Master's in Theological Studies from the Harvard Divinity School and a B.A. in History & Religious Studies from Tulane.

Meet the Contributors of the Original Stories

Bios as of 1993, the year of publication of the original book:

Wally "Famous" Amos is the founder of Famous Amos Cookies and author of the book and cassette album *The Power... In You.* Wally resides in Maui, Hawaii. He can be reached by writing to P.O. Box 897, Kailua, HI 96734 or call (808) 261-6075.

Joe Batten, C.P.A.E., is a professional speaker and a successful businessperson who knows how to inspire confidence in organizations in good economic times and bad. His 35 years as an author, consultant and speaker have earned him the title of Corporate Mentor. Joe wrote the bestselling book: *Tough Minded Management.* Joe is a man who loves life and laughter and translates that warmth and passion to every audience. You can reach Joe by writing to 4505 S.W. 26th St., Des Moines, IA 50321-2813. Call (515) 285-8069 or fax (515) 285-5672.

Gene Bedley is a retired principal, recipient of the PTA's 1985 National Educator of the Year Award and the Milken Family Foundation's 1994 Educator of the Year, and author of numerous books on creating a positive classroom environment. He can be reached at 14252 East Mall, Irvine, California 92714 or call (714) 551-6690.

Michele Borba is a prolific author on building self-esteem in elementary classrooms. She is a member of the board of trustees of the

National Council for Self-Esteem. Her best book is *Esteem Builders,* a collection of 379 classroom activities. You can reach her by writing 840 Prescott Drive, Palm Springs, California 92262 or call (619) 323-5387.

Helice Bridges is a recognized and dynamic speaker and trainer who travels internationally doing self-esteem training and workshops for schools, organizations and businesses. She is Chairperson of the Board for Difference Makers, Inc. and can be reached at P.O. Box 2115, Del Mar, California 92014 or call (800) 887-8422 or (760) 634-1851.

Les Brown is a highly acclaimed speaker who talks to Fortune 500 companies and conducts personal and professional seminars around the country. He is well known to television audiences through his PBS specials, all of which are available on audiocassette and videotape. He can be reached by writing Les Brown Unlimited, 2180 Penobscot Building, Detroit, Michigan 48226 or call (800) 733-4226.

Dr. Helen E. Buckley is a retired professor of English from the State University College of New York at Oswego and former teacher of writing for children at Syracuse University's Continuing Education Department. She is a contributor to professional journals as well as the author of 16 children's books, including: *Grandfather and I, Grandmother and I* and *Someday with My Father.*

Dan Clark is a professional motivational speaker who has conducted thousands of talks for high school students, parents and corporations. He can be reached at P.O. Box 8689, Salt Lake City, Utah 84108 or call (801) 532-5755.

Alan Cohen is a prolific and dynamic speaker and author. Our favorite book of his is *The Dragon Doesn't Live Here Anymore.* He can be reached at P.O. Box 98509, Des Moines, WA 98198 or call (800) 462-3013.

Roger Crawford is a dynamic motivational speaker. His book is entitled *Playing From The Heart.* He can be reached by writing 1050 St. Andrews Drive, Byron, California 94514 or call (510) 634-8519.

Stan Dale, formerly the voice of "The Shadow" and the announcer/narrator of "The Lone Ranger," "Sgt. Preston" and "The Green Hornet" radio shows, is the Director/Founder of the Human Awareness Institute in San Mateo, California, an organization dedicated to "creating a world where everyone wins." He conducts "Sex, Love and Intimacy Workshops" around the world. Stan is the author of *Fantasies Can Set You Free* and *My Child, My Self: How To Raise The Child You Always Wanted To Be*. Both books are also available on cassette from The Human Awareness Institute, 1720 S. Amphlett Blvd., Suite 128, San Mateo, California 94402 or call (800) 800-4117 or (415) 571-5524.

Burt Dubin is the developer of the Speaking Success System, a powerful instrument for helping aspiring and professional speakers position, package, promote and present themselves. "You are a master — an absolute master — I recommend your system without reservations," says Jos J. Charbonneau, C.S.P., C.P.A.E. Burt may be reached at Personal Achievement Institute, 1 Speaking Success Road, Kingman, Arizona 86402-6543 or call (800) 321-1225.

Charles Faraone is one of the world's great huggers. He runs workshops and speaks on hugging, spirituality and single life. He can be reached at Once Upon A Planet, P.O. Box 610220, Bayside, NY 11361-0220 or by calling (516) 883- 4932. For newsletter and Free Hug Coupons, send a self-addressed, stamped envelope to Let's Hug!, P.O. Box 610220, Bayside, NY 11361-0220.

Patricia Fripp, C.S.P., C.P.A.E., is a "speaker for all reasons." She is past president of the National Speakers Association and is one of the most dynamic speakers we know. She can be reached at 527 Hugo Street, San Francisco, California 94122 or call (415) 753-6556.

Bobbie Gee, C.S.P., is recognized as one of America's most outstanding female speakers. She is the author of the book *Winning the Image Game* (Pagemill Press) and two cassette albums *Life Doesn't Have To Be A Struggle* and *Image Power*. You can contact her at Bobbie Gee Enterprises, 1540 S. Coast Highway, Suite 206, Laguna Beach, California 92651 or call (800) 462-4386 or (714) 497-1915.

Rick Gelinas is the President of the Lucky Acorns Delphi Foundation in Miami Florida. He is a master educator and has dedicated his life to making a difference to children. You can reach him at 5888 S.W. 77 Terrace, Miami Florida 33143 or call (305) 667-7756.

John Goddard is an adventurer, explorer and world-class motivational speaker. He can be reached at 4224 Beulah Drive, La Canada,

California 91101 or call (818) 790-7094.

Patty Hansen is Administrative Director of Look Who's Talking. She can be reached at P.O. Box 7665, Newport Beach, California 92658 or call (714) 759-9304.

Danielle Kennedy, M.A., is a celebrated author, world-class sales trainer, inspirationalist and award-winning saleswoman. She holds an Honorary Degree in the Humanities from Clarke College and a Masters in Professional Writing from the University of Southern California. She lectures in 100 cities a year on sales, marketing and leadership. Her bestselling books include *How To List And Sell Real Estate In The '90s* (Prentice Hall) and *Kennedy On Doubling Your Income In Real Estate Sales* (John Wiley). She is married and has eight children. She can be reached at 219 S. El Camino Real, San Clemente, California 92672 or call (714) 498-8033.

Florence Littauer, C.S.P., C.P.A.E., is one of the most wonderful people we know. She is an inspiring writer and teacher. Our favorite book of hers is *Little Silver Boxes*. She can be reached at 1611 S. Rancho Santa Fe Rd., Ste. F2 San Marcos, California 92069 or call (760) 471-0233.

Rick Little over the last 16 years has participated in a wide range of efforts to improve the social and economic conditions of children and youth. In 1975 he founded Quest International and served as its president for 15 years. Mr. Little has co-authored books with leading authorities on youth including Dr. Charlie W. Shedd. In 1990 Rick Little founded the International Youth Foundation with major support from the W.K. Kellogg Foundation. He now serves as Secretary General to the International Youth Foundation, whose goal is to identify and fund replicable youth programs that have demonstrated success. The foundation currently focuses on programs in Southern Africa, Poland, Ecuador, Mexico, Bangladesh, Thailand and the Philippines.

Hanoch McCarty, Ed.D., is a professional speaker, trainer and consultant specializing in motivation, productivity and self-esteem enhancement. Hanoch is one of the most sought-after speakers in the nation because he combines humor and moving stories with practical skills that can be put to work immediately. His books and videotape programs include *Stress and Energy* and *Self-Esteem: The Bottom Line.*

He can be reached at P.O. Box 66, Galt, California 95632 or call (800) 231-7353.

Dan Millman is a former world champion gymnast, university coach and bestselling author whose eight books, including *Way of the Peaceful Warrior, No Ordinary Moments, The Life You Were Born to Live, The Inner Athlete* and *The Laws of Spirit* have inspired millions of people worldwide. For the past decade, Dan has trained people from all walks of life and all over the world, including health and business professionals, therapists, educators and others involved in the fields of peak performance and personal growth. He and his family live in Northern California. Contact him at: www.danmillman.com.

W. Mitchell, C.P.A.E., is one of the most inspirational speakers we have ever met. His tape program is entitled *It's Not What Happens To You, It's What You Do About It.* He can be reached at 12014 W. 54th Drive, #100, Arvada, Colorado 80002 or call (303) 425-1800.

Robert A. Moawad is Chairman and Chief Executive Officer of Edge Learning Institute with offices in Tacoma, Washington, and Tempe, Arizona. Edge is a professional development firm dedicated to assisting organizations achieve greater levels of productivity, quality and customer satisfaction. Bob is a dynamic "edu-tainer." He has an impressive ability to inspire and have an impact on an audience by blending colorful illustrations with solid principles. This has made Bob one of the most sought-after keynote speakers in the nation. Since 1973 he has assisted more than two million people, including some of the most respected leaders in business, government and education. He can be contacted by writing Edge Learning Institute, 2217 N. 30th, #200, Tacoma, Washington 98403 or call (206) 272-3103.

Chick Moorman is the director of the Institute for Personal Power, a consulting firm dedicated to providing high-quality professional development activities for educators and parents. Every year he crisscrosses the country conducting over 100 workshops on cooperative learning, enhancing self-esteem and developing positive attitudes. His mission is to help people experience a greater sense of personal power in their lives so they can in turn empower others. His latest book, *Where the Heart Is: Stories of Home and Family*, celebrates family strength, love, tolerance, hope and commitment. It can be ordered from Personal Power Press, P.O. Box 5985, Saginaw, MI 48603 or call (517) 791-3533.

Michael J. Murphy, Ed.D., DFP, is a family therapist and author of *Popsicle Fish and Other Fathering Stories.* For information or presentations, contact The Family Consultation Team, 349 Old Plymouth Road, P.O. Box 300, Sagamore Beach, MA 02562 or call (508) 833-3800.

Victor H. Nelson, S.T.M., is a therapist and pastoral counselor in private practice. His address is 505 Evergreen Street West, Lafayette, Indiana 47906.

Price Pritchett, Ph.D., holds a doctorate in psychology and is past president of the Dallas Psychological Association. He is the CEO of Pritchett & Associates, Inc., a Dallas-based consulting firm specializing in organizational change. Dr. Pritchett has authored 11 books on individual and organizational effectiveness, including *You2: A High Velocity Formula For Multiplying Your Personal Effectiveness In Quantum Leaps.* You can contact Dr. Pritchett at 200 Crescent Court, Suite 1080, Dallas, Texas 75201 or call (214) 855-8999 or (800) 992-5922.

Bobbie Probstein is a writer and photographer whose new book, *Healing Now,* has been widely praised. It is invaluable for anyone affected by illness or preparing for surgery. Her first book, an autobiography, *Return to Center,* is in its third printing. She may be reached at 28 Shoal Dr., Corona Del Mar, CA 92625.

Bob Proctor is the President of Bob Proctor Seminars and the founder of the Million Dollar Forum in Ontario, Canada. Bob is the author of *You Were Born Rich* and conducts Born Rich Seminars all over the world. Bob's seminars empower people to create the life they've always dreamed about. You can contact him at Million Dollar International, 211 Consumers Road, Suite 201, Willowdale, Ontario, Canada M2J 4G8 or call (416) 498-6700.

Nido Qubein, C.S.P., C.P.A.E., is past president of the National Speakers Association and is an outstanding speaker on sales, management and marketing. His many books include *Get The Best From Yourself, Communicate Like A Pro* and *Professional Selling Techniques.* He can be reached at Creative Services, Inc., P.O. Box 6008, High Point, North Carolina 27262-6008 or call (919) 889-3010.

Anthony Robbins, nationally recognized as the leader in the field of human-development training, is the author of two bestsellers, *Unlimited Power* and *Awaken the Giant Within: How to Take Immediate Control of Your Mental, Emotional, Physical and Financial Destiny!* During the past decade more than a million people have invested in and benefited from his seminars, audiotapes, videotapes and books. He is the founder of nine companies, a consultant to businesses and governments in the U.S. and abroad, and a committed philanthropist with the creation of The Anthony Robbins Foundation. For more information on products and services, call Robbins Research International, Inc. at 1-800-445-8183 or write the company at 9191 Towne Centre Drive, Suite 600, San Diego, California 92122.

Pamela Rogers earned her Masters Degree in Education from the University of Pennsylvania in 1990 and teaches second grade at Reynolds Elementary School in Philadelphia. She studies acting when she's not teaching.

Glenna Salsbury, C.S.P., C.P.A.E., graduated from Northwestern University in Evanston, Illinois, obtained her Masters Degree from UCLA and, 16 years later, earned a Masters of Theology from Fuller Seminary. In 1980 Glenna founded her own company that provides keynote presentations and personal growth seminars. In her personal life, Glenna is married to Jim Salsbury, a former Detroit Lion and Green Bay Packer and has three daughters. Call or write to obtain her powerful six-pack tape album entitled, *Passion, Power and Purpose.* She can be reached at 9228 North 64th Place, Paradise Valley, Arizona 85253 or call (602) 483-7732.

Jack Schlatter, a former teacher, is currently a motivational speaker. He can be reached at P.O. Box 577, Cypress, California 90630 or call (714) 879-7271.

Lee Shapiro is a former trial attorney and judge who left law practice because he never received a standing ovation from a jury! He is now a speaker and professor specializing in ethics in management, keynote addresses and people skills. He can be reached at 5700-12 Baltimore Drive, La Mesa, California 91942 or (619) 668-9036.

Frank Siccone, Ed.D., is the director of the Siccone Institute in San Francisco. He is a consultant to numerous schools and businesses. His books include *Responsibility: The Most Basic R* and *101 Ways To Develop Student Self-Esteem And Responsibility* with Jack Canfield (Allyn & Bacon). He can be reached at the Siccone Institute, 2151 Union Street, San Francisco, California 94123 or call (415) 922-2244.

Cindy Spitzer is a freelance writer who helped us rewrite several of our most difficult and important stories. She can be reached at 5027 Berwyn Road, College Park, Maryland 20740.

Jeffrey Michael Thomas is a regional vice-president for Van Kampen Merritt, a professional money management firm. He is a member of the National Speakers Association and speaks on topics ranging from financial management to fundraising for various charities through his company, J. Michael Thomas & Associates. Mr. Thomas lives and works in Tustin, California, and he is currently seeking a seat on the Tustin City Council. He can be reached at (714) 544-1352.

Pamela Truax is the author of *Small Business Pitfalls And Bridges*. She can be reached at 2073 Columbia Way, Vista, California 92083 or call (619) 598-6008.

Dottie Walters is President of the Walters International Speakers Bureau in California. She sends paid speakers all over the world and is heavily involved in presentation training. She is the author, with her daughter Lilly, of the new Simon and Schuster book, *Speak And Grow Rich*, and is founder and administrator of the International Group of Agents and Bureaus. Dottie publishes Sharing Ideas, the largest news magazine in the world for paid professional speakers. You can write her at P.O. Box 1120, Glendora, California 91740 or call (818) 335-8069 or fax (818) 335-6127.

Bettie Youngs is President of Instruction & Professional Development, Inc., a resource and consulting firm providing in-service to school districts. Bettie is a former Iowa Teacher-of-the-Year, is currently Professor at San Diego State University and Executive Director of the Phoenix Foundation. She is the author of 14 books including *The Educator's Self-Esteem: It's Criteria #1, The 6 Vital Ingredients Of Self-Esteem And*

How To Develop Them In Students and *Safeguarding Your Teenager From The Dragons Of Life*. She can be reached at 3060 Racetrack View Drive, Del Mar, California 92014 or call (619) 481-6360.

Meet Our Authors

Jack Canfield is the co-creator of the *Chicken Soup for the Soul* series, which *Time* magazine has called "the publishing phenomenon of the decade." Jack is also the coauthor of many other bestselling books.

Jack is the CEO of the Canfield Training Group in Santa Barbara, California, and founder of the Foundation for Self-Esteem in Culver City, California. He has conducted intensive personal and professional development seminars on the principles of success for more than a million people in 23 countries, has spoken to hundreds of thousands of people at more than 1,000 corporations, universities, professional conferences and conventions, and has been seen by millions more on national television shows.

Jack has received many awards and honors, including three honorary doctorates and a Guinness World Records Certificate for having seven books from the *Chicken Soup for the Soul* series appearing on the New York Times bestseller list on May 24, 1998.

You can reach Jack at www.jackcanfield.com.

Mark Victor Hansen is the co-founder of Chicken Soup for the Soul, along with Jack Canfield. He is a sought-after keynote speaker, bestselling author, and marketing maven. Mark's powerful messages of possibility, opportunity, and action have created powerful change in thousands of organizations and millions of individuals worldwide.

Mark is a prolific writer with many bestselling books in addition to the *Chicken Soup for the Soul* series. Mark has had a profound influence in the field of human potential through his library of audios, videos, and articles in the areas of big thinking, sales achievement, wealth building, publishing success, and personal and professional development. He is also the founder of the MEGA Seminar Series.

Mark has received numerous awards that honor his entrepreneurial spirit, philanthropic heart, and business acumen. He is a lifetime member of the Horatio Alger Association of Distinguished Americans.

You can reach Mark at www.markvictorhansen.com.

Amy Newmark is the bestselling author, editor-in-chief, and publisher of the *Chicken Soup for the Soul* book series. Since 2008, she has published 191 new books, most of them national bestsellers in the U.S. and Canada, more than doubling the number of Chicken Soup for the Soul titles in print today. She is also the author of *Simply Happy*, a crash course in Chicken Soup for the Soul advice and wisdom that is filled with easy-to-implement, practical tips for enjoying a better life.

Amy is credited with revitalizing the Chicken Soup for the Soul brand, which has been a publishing industry phenomenon since the first book came out in 1993. By compiling inspirational and aspirational true stories curated from ordinary people who have had extraordinary experiences, Amy has kept the thirty-year-old Chicken Soup for the Soul brand fresh and relevant.

Amy graduated *magna cum laude* from Harvard University where she majored in Portuguese and minored in French. She then embarked on a three-decade career as a Wall Street analyst, a hedge fund manager, and a corporate executive in the technology field. She is a Chartered Financial Analyst.

Her return to literary pursuits was inevitable, as her honors thesis in college involved traveling throughout Brazil's impoverished northeast region, collecting stories from regular people. She is delighted to have come full circle in her writing career — from collecting stories "from the people" in Brazil as a twenty-year-old to, three decades later, collecting stories "from the people" for Chicken Soup for the Soul.

When Amy and her husband Bill, the CEO of Chicken Soup for

the Soul, are not working, they are visiting their four grown children and their spouses, and their five grandchildren.

Follow Amy on Twitter @amynewmark. Listen to her free podcast — "Chicken Soup for the Soul with Amy Newmark" — on Apple, Google, or by using your favorite podcast app on your phone.

Sharing Happiness, Inspiration, and Hope

Real people sharing real stories, every day, all over the world. In 2007, *USA Today* named *Chicken Soup for the Soul* one of the five most memorable books in the last quarter-century. With over 110 million books sold to date in the U.S. and Canada alone, more than 300 titles in print, and translations into nearly fifty languages, "chicken soup for the soul®" is one of the world's best-known phrases.

Today, thirty years after we first began sharing happiness, inspiration and hope through our books, we continue to delight our readers with new titles, but have also evolved beyond the bookshelves with super premium pet food, television shows, a podcast, licensed products, and free movies and TV shows on our Crackle, Redbox, Popcornflix and Chicken Soup for the Soul streaming apps. We are busy "changing your life one story at a time®." Thanks for reading!

Share with Us

We all have had Chicken Soup for the Soul moments in our lives. If you would like to share your story or poem with millions of people around the world, go to chickensoup.com and click on Submit Your Story. You may be able to help another reader and become a published author at the same time. Some of our past contributors have launched writing and speaking careers from the publication of their stories in our books!

We only accept story submissions via our website. They are no longer accepted via mail or fax. Visit our website, www.chickensoup. com, and click on Submit Your Story for our writing guidelines and a list of topics we are working on.

To contact us regarding other matters, please send us an e-mail through webmaster@chickensoupforthesoul.com, or write us at:

Chicken Soup for the Soul
P.O. Box 700
Cos Cob, CT 06807-0700

One more note from your friends at Chicken Soup for the Soul: Occasionally, we receive an unsolicited book manuscript from one of our readers, and we would like to respectfully inform you that we do not accept unsolicited manuscripts, and we must discard the ones that appear.

Original Permissions

We would like to acknowledge the following publishers and individuals for permission to reprint the following material. (Note: The stories that were penned anonymously, that are public domain or were written by Jack Canfield or Mark Victor Hansen are not included in this listing.)

Hugging Is from *Let's Hug!* Reprinted by permission of Charles Faraone. ©1981, 1995 Once Upon A Planet.

On Courage and *Sachi* from *Sacred Journey of the Peaceful Warrior* by Dan Millman ©1991 Dan Millman — Reprinted by permission of the author and H.J. Kramer, Inc., P.O. Box 1082, Tiburon, CA 94920. All rights reserved.

The Gentlest Need. Reprinted by Fred T. Wihelms. Reprinted by permission of the author and *Educational Leadership*, 48, 1:51. ©ASCD.

My Declaration of Self-Esteem and *Everybody Has a Dream* reprinted with the express written permission of the AVANTA Network which was founded by Virginia Satir and has inherited rights to all of her intellectual property. For information about copyright materials of Virginia Satir and/or the AVANTA Network contact: Avanta Network, 310 Third Avenue N.E., Ste. 126, Issaquah, WA 98027 or call (206) 391-7310.

Why I Chose My Father To Be My Dad from *The Six Ingredients of Self-Esteem and How They are Developed in Your Children* by Bettie B. Youngs. ©1992 Rawson Assoc.

Willing To Pay The Price from *Self Made in America* by John McCormack. Reprinted by permission of Addison-Wesley Publishing Co., Inc., and the author. ©1990 by The Visible Changes Educational Foundation and David R. Legge.

Love: The One Creative Force. Reprinted by permission of Eric Butterworth. ©1992 Eric Butterworth.

All I Remember. Reprinted by permission of Bobbie Probstein. ©1992 Bobbie Probstein.

Heart Songs. Reprinted by permission of Patricia Jean Hansen. ©1992 Patricia Jean Hansen.

True Love. Reprinted by permission of Barry Vissell. ©1992 Barry Vissell.

It Can't Happen Here. Reprinted by permission of Pamela Rogers. ©1992 Pamela Rogers.

Who You Are Makes a Difference. Reprinted by permission of Helice Bridges. ©1992 Helice Bridges.

A Brother Like That. Reprinted by permission of Dan Clark. ©1992 Dan Clark.

Big Ed. Reprinted by permission of Joe Batten. ©1989 by AMACOM Books.

Love And The Cabbie. Reprinted by permission of Art Buchwald. ©1992 Art Buchwald.

A Simple Gesture and *I Am a Teacher.* Reprinted with permission of John Wayne Schlatter. ©1992 John Schlatter.

The Smile, Did The Earth Move For You and *Just One More Time.* Reprinted by permission of Dr. Hanoch McCarty. ©1991 Hanoch McCarty and Associates.

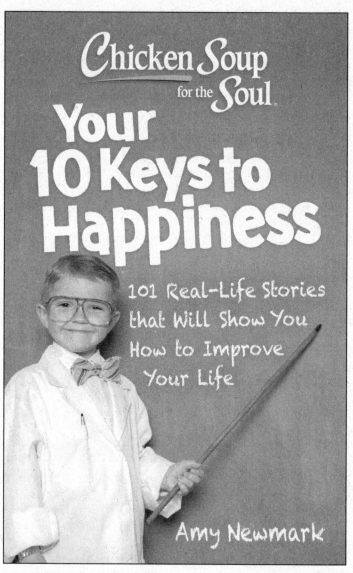

Chicken Soup for the Soul

Your 10 Keys to Happiness

101 Real-Life Stories that Will Show You How to Improve Your Life

Amy Newmark

Paperback: 978-1-61159-091-3

eBook: 978-1-61159-330-3

More Inspiration

Chicken Soup for the Soul®

GET OUT OF YOUR COMFORT ZONE

101 Stories about Trying New Things, Overcoming Fear and Broadening Your World

Amy Newmark

Paperback: 978-1-61159-103-3
eBook: 978-1-61159-340-2

for your better life

Changing the World One Story at a Time®
www.chickensoup.com